SHAKESPEAREAN POLITICS

SHAKESPEAREAN POLITICS

Government and Misgovernment
in the
Great Histories

C. G. THAYER

OHIO UNIVERSITY PRESS
ATHENS, OHIO
LONDON

Library of Congress Cataloging in Publication Data

Thayer, C. G. (Calvin Graham)
  Shakespearean politics.

  Includes bibliographical references.
  1. Shakespeare, William, 1564-1616—Histories.
  2. Shakespeare, William, 1564-1616—Political and social views. I. Title.
  PR2982.T4 1983 822.3'3 83-2450
  ISBN 0-8214-0726-0

For Bernie Fieler

in loving memory

Table of Contents

Preface

Books on governors and governing poured from the pens and presses of Renaissance Europe and Tudor England, and it is not surprising that Shakespeare made his contribution to the deluge or that his contribution is among the most interesting and the most lively. I suspect that the subject had a special urgency for him at the end of the Tudor era. For the first time in *his* life, England was going to have a new monarch, soon, and of necessity that monarch was going to be *chosen*, as there was no unquestioned successor; the succession was among the most pressing issues of the last decade of the sixteenth century. It was a good, if risky, time to take a long reflective look at a brief and striking period of English history, at the reigns of a king deposed, the problems of the ruler who deposed him, and the stirring triumphs of that ruler's son and successor. They were all the subjects of much contemporary attention, and the Queen herself was occasionally compared with the first of the three, Richard II, while the third, Henry V, was still a model of English heroism against fearful odds.

It was likely enough that Richard II, Henry IV, and Henry V would, among them, supply objects to avoid and to emulate and that their mixed reigns would provide instructive and delightful matter for the stage. It was also likely that so sensible a man and so original an artist as Shakespeare would, discreetly, offer reasonable objections and suggest alternatives to some of the more or less institutionalized political doctrines, dogmas, and practices of his age, a few of which would have to be described as objectionable by any standards held by reasonable people. The one dogma important in shaping this study is that Shakespeare was no spokesman for Tudor orthodoxy.

He was certainly no revolutionary, no Marlowe or Milton, but neither was he a narrow-eyed apostle of passive obedience or political mysticism, phenomena at the heart of *Richard II*, a play that deals concretely with some of the chief abstractions of contemporary political thinking.

To deal with a complex subject, I have tried to describe the internal political structures and attitudes—the "arguments"—of *Richard II, 1* and *2 Henry IV*, and *Henry V* and, more or less in tandem, to describe and define the relationship between the political argument of each play and some important political ideas, events, and figures of late sixteenth-century England, without confining myself in any way simply to a gloss of political topicalities—these are, after all, plays, not pamphlets. I agree, though, with Sigurd Burckhardt that "Shakespeare's plays have messages [meanings anyhow] and that these messages are discoverable, in fact statable."[1] One cannot, and should not, always state the "messages" of literary works with absolute certainty; I have aimed for "superior probability as based on the available evidence,"[2] the available evidence in this case consisting of the plays themselves, sixteenth-century treatment of the same material, the practices of a few other playwrights dealing with the same or similar material or problems, and the general political-religious-social context of England at the end of the Tudor period. And I have tried to follow the texts where they lead, without recourse to the efficient but destructive procedures roughed out by Procrustes, only insisting on the integrity of the four plays as a tetralogy.

* * * * *

To record all my obligations for assistance, counsel, and encouragement would be nearly impossible; special debts of gratitude are due (and payable) to Dean Norman S. Cohn, the Faculty Research Committee, and the Research Institute of Ohio University, for strong, unambiguous, and concrete encouragement; Mr. and Mrs. Edwin Kennedy, for their extraordinarily generous support of scholarly and creative work; the Ohio Conference for Renaissance-Reformation Studies, for listening to my discussion of Shakespeare and Dante and discussing it extensively; and the Rockefeller Foundation and the Aspen Institute for Humanistic Studies and its president, J. E. Slater, for making possible a period of reflection and enduring a lecture. My debts to colleagues are enormous, for indispensable assistance and encouragement. Professors John Desmond, B. A. Park, and D. C. Peck have over the years exerted a salutary restraining influence. Professors Phillip N. Bebb, Samuel R. Crowl, Wayne Dodd, C. G. Masinton, John L. Murphy, R. Vance Ramsey, and P. A. Yuckman have read the manuscript at various stages, in whole or in part, and have suggested many improvements. Professor Helen Mackenzie has lent a patient and durable ear and has repaid its abuse with wisdom and kindness. Most important, the late F. B. Fieler was goad and (almost) *éminence grise*, reading the entire manuscript, some of it more than once, listening at weary length, helping, correcting, encouraging; my admiration and gratitude are immense. My wife Mary has steadfastly and wisely avoided Shakespearean entanglements; her commitment to other entanglements has made the completion of this study possible and elicits another order of gratitude and admiration. Affection, too.

I

The Death of Divine Kingship
Richard II

The Dilemma

Act i, scene ii of Richard ii is critical to an understanding of these plays. Thomas of Woodstock, Duke of Gloucester, has been murdered at the order of the King. His widow is urging his brother-in-law, "old John of Gaunt, time-honoured Lancaster," to do something about it, and he can't.

> *Gaunt.* God's is the quarrel—for God's substitute,
> His deputy anointed in His sight,
> Hath caus'd his [Gloucester's] death; the which
>   if wrongfully,
> Let heaven revenge, for I may never lift
> An angry arm against His minister.
> *Duchess.* Where then, alas, may I complain myself?
> *Gaunt.* To God, the widow's champion and defence.
> *Duchess.* Why then, I will. Farewell, old Gaunt.
>   (*RII*, I.ii.37–44)[1]

Gaunt's words suggest a bleak temporal outlook for noble widows and a fairly good one for royal murderers, and they add a specifically Tudor dimension to the play's late-medieval historical setting. The historical Richard would have approved of the sentiments expressed here by Gaunt, but the historical Gaunt, a great feudal baron with designs on a good part of the real estate of southern Europe, would have found them bizarre, if comprehensible at all.[2] Shakespeare's

1

Gaunt is a loyal, patriotic, politically impotent subject who, early in the play, offers Tudor-style passive obedience as the unsatisfactory answer to a widow's prayer. If there is no obvious reason why Shakespeare should have made such a striking alteration in the character of Gaunt, or why he should have chosen to introduce so curious a political anachronism, a *politic* reason is that the subject of this play was a dangerous one in the 1590s, potentially an explosive one.[3] A forthright statement of the virtues of passive obedience, a fundamental of Tudor orthodoxy, early in the play has its political uses, as does Carlisle's defense of Richard, and attack on Bolingbroke, in act IV, scene i: it may allay suspicions of seditious intent on the part of the players, who were liable to such suspicions, and it has other uses as well.

Gaunt's words do not reveal Shakespeare's commitments; they are part of a dramatic process whereby contemporary official notions of passive obedience, regal infallibility, and divine kingship are systematically undermined by being followed out to their logical conclusions. The widowed duchess wants Gaunt to forestall a possible murderous attack on himself by avenging her husband's, and Gaunt's brother's, death at the King's orders.[4]

> Call it not patience, Gaunt, it is despair;
> In suff'ring thus thy brother to be slaught'red,
> Thou showest the naked pathway to thy life,
> Teaching stern murder how to butcher thee.
> That which in mean men we intitle patience
> Is pale cold cowardice in noble breasts.
> What shall I say? to safeguard thine own life,
> The best way is to venge my Gloucester's death.
>
> (I.ii.29–36)

Gaunt's view that he can never lift an angry arm against God's minister the King and that the only source of redress for the widow is "God, the widow's champion and defence," is not helpful, but it is orthodox, and Gaunt's orthodoxy is a way of rationalizing political impotence. It does not go quite so far as to assert regal infallibility, but it does argue the sanctified invulnerability of kingship to temporal chastisement: no matter how grossly fallible a king might be, correction lies in the hands of God, not of men.[5] The King is not infallible, but in effect and by law he can do no wrong—a rather one-sided arrangement bound to be more agreeable to a king than to his subjects; agreeable to a queen, too, as we shall see later. It follows from what Gaunt tells his sister-in-law that there is no conceivable crime of which a king might be guilty, no possible royal criminality, not even murder, that would justify his punishment at the hands of his subjects. An easy inference from Gaunt's argument is that the subject must not only passively endure all royal crimes already committed but must also be prepared to endure all royal crimes that might be perpetrated in the future—a monstrous notion, but there it is, not of Shakespeare's devising but of the government under which he lived.[6] Gaunt does not live to see the crime that cuts the moral heart out of his argument, but it is his death that makes the crime possible.

Shakespeare has introduced a staple of Tudor political dogma into a late-medieval historical context, but if his doing so suggests a mirror of Tudor policy, it is a cautionary mirror, a mirror for kings and queens and magistrates. The cautionary aspect is suggested by the immediate context, by the way the scene glosses Bolingbroke's accusations against Mowbray in act I, scene i, by the way Gaunt states the case, and by Richard's elaborate deposition. Gaunt's weary impotence is not designed to teach the virtues of passive obedience but to demonstrate its potential viciousness.

The dramatic situation is vivid enough: a distraught widow is seeking vengeance for her husband's death and a way to prevent more deaths of the same kind. Where the real guilt lies, a question raised ambiguously in act I, scene i, is made clear. The very orthodoxy of Gaunt's response is jarring since it invokes an abstract principle as the answer to a concrete grievance: "God requires that we obey our rulers." An obvious and not necessarily anachronistic rejoinder would be, "Yes, but even if they murder us?" Perhaps Gaunt's orthodoxy is a little *too* orthodox: could the authorities have appreciated such a bald statement of one of their favorite and most repugnant devices of repression? Gaunt responds to a specific grievance with an abstract argument, but what the audience and the reader must assimilate is the combined effect; we understand the grievance and we hear the argument: "The King caused your husband's death, with no form of justice, but we can do nothing about it because the King is God's deputy and may therefore kill your husband and my brother with impunity." This sort of rationale is implicit in the situation; the scene states a doctrine in such a way as to establish its indecency while demolishing its credibility. Gaunt's exalted station ("Old John of Gaunt, time-honoured Lancaster" [I.i.l]) gives strong moral force to his speeches condemning Richard in act II, scene i; but in act I, scene ii, he has already fallen into an ideological trap: the doctrine of passive obedience is likely to retain plausibility only to the extent that it is abstractly stated—with reference when possible to cosmic unity. In the play's second scene the plausibility of an abstract theory is ruined when it is used as a comment on something that has actually happened and as a reason for not doing something about it.

Lily B. Campbell noted that this scene "does not further the action, and . . . can have been introduced only to restate the Tudor theory of kingship."[7] It was her view that the theory was one that Shakespeare accepted. It is true that the scene does not "further the action," and it is certainly part of the *dianoia*, the play's intellectual content. I do not know that it was introduced to restate a theory of kingship, but it does invoke a false and immoral premise. The notion of kingship and obedience that Gaunt specifies with such sad fervor is there not to be swallowed but regurgitated. As Shakespeare presents the matter, it has more to do with the history of tyranny and repression than with any reasonable idea of order and justice.

Gaunt upholds a doctrine of total obedience and unlimited, God-given regal authority thoroughly familiar to a contemporary audience but undercut by the play's action. Passive obedience (and by implication the whole idea of divine right) is shown to be a dangerous and destructive doctrine. By the time King Richard comes to give eloquent expression to ideas of subjects' obedience and monarchs' divinely ordained impunity, the plain facts of the situation make the whole idea of unlimited regal authority seem dubious, abstract, almost absurd. Richard cheers himself up, in act III, scenes ii and iii, with statements of a cherished but insubstantial conviction, its wrongness, both factually and morally, demonstrated again and again throughout the play until its eloquent and almost endless repetition becomes an empty ritual, a series of symbolic incantations divorced from the terrible reality that confronts him.

Both Richard and Gaunt are caught in ideological traps from which there is for them no escape. On the basis of what become, through the strategy of the playwright, wrong notions about kings and subjects, both Gaunt and Richard refuse, or fail, or are unable, to take necessary actions. And they both seem unaware of a controlling implication of their abstract theories: they both maintain that a king is subject only to divine discipline (Richard may not make even this concession), but neither considers the ways in which divine displeasure might display itself. Shakespeare had useful precedents at hand: the suggestion by both Hall and Holinshed that Bolingbroke's rise and Richard's fall seemed providentially ordained (Hosley, p. 81), and perhaps more potent in its implications, Richard's lament in the *Mirror for Magistrates* that Fortune had brought about his deposition and death in payment for his sins as king. The title of Richard's lament is edifying; "Howe kyng Richarde the seconde/was for his euyll gouernaunce/deposed from his seat, and/miserably murdred in prison."[8]

Gaunt's statement that when the time seems ripe, the heavens "Will rain hot vengeance on offenders' heads" (I.ii.8) is worth considering. How *do* the heavens proceed in such matters?—a salutary abcess, or boils, or a timely shower of fire and brimstone? For the author of Richard's lament in the *Mirror*, the answer was deposition and miserable murder, and perhaps that is Shakespeare's implicit answer too, although in a more sophisticated form. In the scene following Gaunt's observation about offenders and the heavens, Mowbray, who appears to have offended by supervising a murder and covering for his king, is sent into exile for life. And by the beginning of the third act, Richard, who has more than one major offense to his discredit, has for all practical purposes ceased to be king. In fact, by the end of act II, scene i the survival of his kingship is already in doubt, since his disinheriting of Bolingbroke has destroyed one of the principles by which he was a legitimate ruler. The sixteenth century (e.g., Edward Hall, Raphael Holinshed, Samuel Daniel in *The Civil Wars*, the *Mirror*)

seems to have taken a fairly extensive view of divine vengeance
with only the most tacit assumptions about earthly causes: the
writers and works mentioned tended to see the historical
Richard's fall as something almost ordained by fate; and then, un-
hampered by pedantic consistency, Tudor historians (for the most
part, semiofficial propagandists) invented the "Wars of the
Roses" as an instance of divine retribution against England for
permitting the deposition.[9] It seems likely that Shakespeare, in
his very complex way, partly shares the first of these views (a
point to be discussed later), but it is very unlikely that he
shares the second. It is certain that Richard, assuming divine
sanction, commits a series of actions that ensure his destruction. Two of those actions, the murder of Gloucester and the
disinheriting of Bolingbroke, are crucially important, and
yet it seems impossible for him to perceive or to acknowl-
edge his culpability in either of them. These actions are particularly important not only because they assume divine
sanction but also because they arrogate divine prerogative. It
is not necessarily true, as is sometimes claimed, that the murderer says in effect, "I am God, disposing of human life as I
will." Most murders are crimes of passion (starting anyhow
with the killing of Abel), seldom carefully rationalized. It is
very different when someone who regards himself as the
deputy elected by the Lord *orders* a murder. Bolingbroke, ordering the executions of Bushy and Greene, at least goes through the
elaborate formality of reading off an extensive list of charges
against them. But Richard, playing out the role of God's lieutenant, unconsciously and disastrously plays God, taking one
man's life and disinheriting another, with no pretext of formal
justice. His assumptions about the status, prerogatives, and tenure
of the deputy elected by the Lord blind him to issues that are not
obscure. It is only after his unkinging, his own "disanointing,"
and not long before his death, that he is able to make an easy and
accurate *political* prediction about Northumberland. His prediction that Northumberland will be as treacherous to his new master as
he has been to his old one (V.i.55-69) provides a timely secular note

amidst the godly discourse of the King, who is, in respect to his talents, if not his position, the most unpolitical character in the play.

Gaunt's upholding of passive obedience is an ideological defense of the indefensible and a confession of political impotence from a man of unassailable rectitude and integrity. And while we meditate, if we wish, on Gaunt's dilemma, Shakespeare allows us to see Richard's personal disaster as a public necessity. Gaunt's political principles make it impossible for him to take steps to prevent the ruin of the commonwealth, while Richard's actions make Gaunt's principles simply untenable, potentially disastrous. In this connection it should be noted that if Richard's fall is an instance of divine displeasure as well as a result of political—and national—necessity, King Henry IV's political troubles are the results of political conspiracies that we can see being developed and carried out, not at all an obvious instance of divine retribution. It should also be noted that if divine displeasure is visited upon King Richard, it is through the agency of Bolingbroke, who made a decision to return from exile, a decision to which we are, interestingly, not privy.

We are often reminded that the crown almost falls into Bolingbroke's hands; his good luck is astonishing. But once Richard is deposed, once Bolingbroke has become King Henry IV, and not merely a de facto, or acting, king, the providential hand, if it had been proffered, seems to be much less in evidence, unless it is inconsistently taking back what it had given. The new king is supposed to exercise his stewardship, to be a king in fact as well as in name, to establish his government, to pass on his crown to a legitimate heir; he is expected to work at his job. King Henry IV is confronted with political problems of a familiar and predictable kind, and he finally deals with them effectively. Richard's problems are represented as being of his own making. And since, as Gaunt recognized, his actions threaten the very existence of the body politic, he must go. If one can imagine a deputy elected by the Lord, one can imagine such a deputy mismanaging his duties and being replaced. A deputy called Angelo had roughly similar difficulties.[10] But for the erring King Richard, heaven's hot vengeance is also a fact of political life—assuming the existence of someone who can *make* it a fact.

I have put much emphasis on act I, scene ii and its implications because it displays, in Gaunt's words on passive obedience, a political-theological point of view held by establishment dogmatists, but not by them alone, in England from around the middle of the sixteenth century until well into the seventeenth,[11] a point of view that seems systematically undercut by the total dramatic action of the great histories from *Richard II* to *Henry V*. Shakespeare reduces it from dogma to dangerous theory and then shows, by implication and by action, how destructive such a theory can be when put into practice.

It would have been easy enough for Shakespeare to give Richard all the speeches in support of passive obedience and divine kingship, and he does give him most of them. But someone other than the King must also enunciate doctrines whose limitations the play's action displays, particularly if those doctrines were accepted and, so far as possible, enforced during the time Shakespeare was writing. To give all the arguments to Richard would have been indiscreet, and the play's subject, the deposition of a rightful king, was indiscreet enough anyhow. And the King's arguments, or his ritual incantations, would have been reduced to mere special pleading. But to have the doctrines articulated by a character of unquestioned standing, who has a genuine grievance against the King, is to give them a time-honored respectability and to suggest the urgent need to reexamine them; and it may even suggest reexamination of political doctrines and assumptions by responsible men in the 1590s. The fact that a political doctrine is time honored does not necessarily demonstrate its justice, a point that might have occurred to a judicious spectator listening to Gaunt's words in act I, scene ii and reflecting on the context in which he speaks them. In that context, what Gaunt says isn't much to the point.

There is nothing accidental, or incidental, about what Shakespeare does with passive obedience or about the way he has Bolingbroke's successes come about. Hall and Holinshed both suggest strongly that Bolingbroke had something like a popular mandate, with elaborate conspiracies afoot to bring him home and make him king. The country at large, Parliament, the Church, and most of the great nobility seem to have supported him and, more important, persuaded him. In the play there is no such massive political effort; there is hardly any political effort at all. But if Gaunt's dilemma arises from his acceptance of passive obedience, it is also true that no playwright of Shakespeare's age, except possibly Marlowe, is going to offer a very concrete, clearly rationalized argument against official dogmas. It can be done, though, through a complex dramatic action, one that, in this case, occupies four splendid plays. Instead of rationalizing a conspiracy, Shakespeare shows something like the effect of God decommissioning his lieutenant and appointing a new one who has more talent, if not more outright enthusiasm, for his work. Something like that; it is possible, but not demonstrable by proof, that Bolingbroke has a stronger claim than Richard to the title "The Deputy Elected by the Lord," elected to rectify the disasters of Richard's nonreign. But it is possible only if one thinks of such a title metaphorically. Richard does not. The England of King Henry IV is neither a theocracy nor a utopia—far from either—but it is a country whose king is trying, finally with some success, to establish justice, and nothing could have been further than justice from King Richard's thoughts. If God delegates authority, Henry IV knows how to use it. His kingdom is characterized by decency and duty at the top, and that decency and duty emerge as justice when King Harry the fifth is crowned. It is a long way from Richard's notion that God has in pay an angel for every Lancastrian soldier to Henry IV's courageous willingness to face necessities as necessities, rather than as fated and overwhelming disasters (2HIV, III.i.92–93). As Carlisle had tried to explain, the Lord helps those who help themselves, and if they do so with enough skill, the Lord's help may not even be necessary. It is appropriate to say, "God gave me the strength to do this," absurd to say, "He has an army of angels to protect me from the results of my own follies."

Act I, scene ii suggests strongly that King Richard's England is characterized by rank injustice, and injustices perpetrated by the

King run through the play's first two acts; Shakespeare makes that point clearly enough. Although he is not writing a formal indictment, an historical study, or a political tract, one can discern elements of all three. Gloucester has been murdered, and the rules of the game permit his kinsmen no legal recourse except the potentially dangerous trial by combat, dangerous to the King since the rationale for such a trial was that God would give victory to the right; and Richard prevents recourse even to that kind of justice. Richard "farms" his realm, roughly analogous to an American president selling the functions of the Internal Revenue Service to General Motors or Chase Manhattan; and he issues blank charters for extortion, apparently a version of "Morton's Fork," allegedly invented by that pious, lovable, yet playful ecclesiastic during the reign of Henry VII: "We note that you made a rather small donation last year; surely you can do better this time," or "You made a handsome donation last year; it would be splendid if you could manage to do even better this year." Most dangerous to Richard himself and most indicative of his moral and political fatuity, he disinherits Bolingbroke, thus, as York carefully explains, violating the principle of correspondence and primogeniture by which he is himself a king. Richard displays no understanding of the significance of his actions since they are all legitimate according to his own far-from-unique conception of regal prerogative. What is missing from Richard's notions of kingship, but not from other well-known sixteenth-century justifications of tyranny, like James VI's *The Trew Law of Free Monarchies* (1598),[12] is any understanding that while he may not be answerable to his subjects, he will assuredly be answerable to God. A realization of that might have led him to some consideration of the possibility of trying to institute good government. But it seems to be his constant assumption, until the evidence on the other side is over-whelming, that God will protect His lieutenant, under all circumstances, against turbulent and discontented subjects—and will punish *them* for their unruliness. And in fact his repeated references to himself as Christ and his enemies as Pilates suggest that unconsciously he does not think of himself as God's *lieutenant* at all—his unthinking pride takes him one large step beyond even that exalted position.

Not only does Richard make some foolishly comfortable assumptions about God's duty to preserve His deputy but he also, it would seem, attempts some sharp practices against his nominal superior by halting the trial by combat in act I, scene iii, thus in effect averting the Supreme Judge's decision—by a kind of regal obstruction of justice. According to Gaunt's notion of a subject's duty, Richard's transgressions are not to be punished on earth; and according to Richard's notion of a king's prerogatives, he will not only not be punished on earth but it is also highly unlikely that he will be called to account in the next world. With people in high places holding views like those of Richard and Gaunt, the prospects for justice in this world are not promising.

The formal representation of injustice is emphasized most strongly in three scenes, act I, scenes ii and iii and act II, scene i, although it is endemic in other parts of the play as well. In the first, Gaunt declares himself powerless to chastise the murderer of his brother; in the second, the King halts the trial by combat that he had already authorized and sends the combatants into exile (not a notably just act itself, although seemingly prudent); in the third, Richard disinherits Bolingbroke, an action the legal and moral implications of which York clearly explains to an astonishingly heedless King. It is fair to say that some of the most eloquent language in the play, particularly that of the King, is in unconscious defense of injustice. But York in act II, scene i and Bolingbroke in act II, scene iii clearly speak for order, law, and justice; and specifying those principles, and acting on them, represents the beginning of the process of restoring, or achieving, a just polity. York and Bolingbroke specify points of law (to be discussed below) that Richard has violated or ignored. They are points that any reasonable person might accept, but King Richard is not a reasonable person.

Shakespeare emphasizes not only the irresponsibility of Richard's rule but also something that emerges, at least by inference, as its illegality. The lawful king behaves unlawfully, and he commits various acts that, not necessarily illegal in themselves, are nevertheless prejudicial to that general welfare that Richard never swore to defend but which he was surely obligated, as part of his stewardship, not to destroy. The whole movement of the great tetralogy is from injustice to justice. England is not punished for allowing Bolingbroke to depose Richard, not in this group of plays and not in the first tetralogy; it is rewarded, with strong efforts toward good government under King Henry IV and the final restoration of justice and a great national triumph under Henry V. The movement and the reward are rendered concrete in the wholly opposed figures of Richard II and Henry V.

* * * * *

To turn the two tetralogies upside-down, to read them in reverse order, a procedure much less frequently recommended now than it once was, to accept one of the most regressive and outrageous sections of the "Tudor myth" and assume that the French disasters and the so-called Wars of the Roses—not to mention Richard III—all represent divine displeasure at the deposition of God's lieutenant Richard and that the coming of Henry Earl of Richmond indicates an end of divine wrath—to do all of these things and accept all of these pronouncements is not sensible. It reduces the entire dramatic action of the second tetralogy to futility. Fortunately, Shakespeare does not ask us to execute these bizarre intellectual arabesques; Tudor historians asked their readers to; some modern scholars ask us to; but Shakespeare doesn't. In the Epilogue to *Henry V* he tells us clearly enough that too many men—ambitious and ruthless men, as we know from the *Henry VI* plays—"had the managing" of the young king's state and ruined it. In fact, in the process of trying to reach an accurate understanding of the second tetralogy, we might take Sigurd Burckhardt's excellent advice and put the first out of our minds altogether. Intellectual and artistic light years intervene between the two tetralogies, and the first gives us little help in understanding the second.

Unthinking the first tetralogy is, of course, not easy to do, particularly in view of Tillyard's illuminating pioneer study. His most serious error, the suggestion that understanding comes with reading the tetralogies in reverse order, *Richard II* through *Richard III*, rather than in the order of their composition, *Henry VI* through *Henry V*, is seductive for obvious reasons. But it produces a spurious chronology, one that Shakespeare clearly did not intend his audiences to follow. And it tends to linger in our minds not quite as error but as something like old truth. It is almost programmed into our thinking, and inevitably it causes short circuits and wrong answers. The four plays of the second tetralogy are closely linked, to one another, not to their predecessors.

In the preceding pages I have described what appear to me to be some central issues, particularly as they arise from Gaunt's defense of passive obedience. But we are concerned with plays, not pamphlets, plays populated not merely by issues but by human characters whose words and actions are of absorbing interest in themselves as well as in the way they illuminate the condition of the body politic. Nevertheless, Gaunt's conversation with his widowed sister-in-law in act I, scene ii is an index to the condition of the body politic under Richard. It is not healthy. If the hand of God seems to lie heavy on this play, that is partly because passive obedience is an effect, so to speak, of divine kingship; and one of Shakespeare's great undertakings in these four plays is to demonstrate, through action, structure, conversation, and character, the desirability, the necessity, of human, man-centered kingship. It remained for later generations of his countrymen to develop institutions that made it possible to remove an inept head of government from office without the necessity of forcing him through a formal deposition or of murdering him. The point is almost too obvious to mention, but not, perhaps, to remember.

* * * * *

Much has been made of Shakespeare's alleged adherence to a specifically Tudor doctrine of order, with its political-theological overtones, and the doctrine itself has been elevated into a kind of philosophy. It would be absurd to deny that Shakespeare saw the necessity for orders and hierarchies and believed in them. But political and social order and hierarchies need not be mystical to be effective. Ulysses' famous speech on degree (*Troilus*, I.iii.73–137) has been adduced as conclusive evidence of the playwright's doctrinal commitments. But Ulysses addresses himself to a single question: "The war has been dragging on for seven years; why haven't we won it yet?" And his answer is that "the specialty of rule hath been neglected" (I.iii.79). He does not talk about passive obedience, divine kingship, or even lineal descent. He says nothing about a king as God's deputy, nor does he allude to raising angry arms against God's minister (and Shakespeare was quite capable of giving him at least a few such anachronisms). He talks about military, social, and political order and compares it with the natural order; but he does not predict that God will ultimately punish those who, like Achilles and Patroclus, violate the principle of order in the Greek camp. It is a matter of political and military order and discipline.

As it is necessary to make a clear distinction between a philosophical idea of order and whatever political principles may be adduced from it, it is also necessary to distinguish between Ulysses on order, and Gaunt, a Tudor homilist, or King Richard on the same subject. Tudor apologists based their political doctrine of order on philosophical and theological ideas; but the fact that they could find scriptural support for their ideas represents for the most part a happy accident rather than any genuine commitment to piety (many of them were no doubt pious, some in the typically bloody-minded way of the sixteenth and seventeenth centuries). One can find scriptural authority for almost anything, and Tudor homilists and political propagandists were scarcely the only people to have done so.

It is worth reiterating that Gaunt's and Richard's political views are presented in terms more Tudor than medieval. The religious underpinning of Tudor absolutism, the use of religion to justify tyranny, was no doubt in Marlowe's mind if he actually said what was attributed to him in the Baines note: "That religion was first invented only to keep men in awe." They were probably in Marlowe's mind whether he made the statement or not. Shakespeare would have had it somewhat differently: religion was not, properly speaking, invented, certainly not invented to keep men in awe (not in Marlowe's sense, anyhow); but it had often been systematically perverted to that end. The Tudor doctrine of passive obedience, defined in the powerful rhetoric of Gaunt, decked out in the equally powerful rhetoric of Richard, invoked religion in support of the insupportable. Some very specific words in *Richard II* express Tudor views on divine kingship, obedience, and the almost unthinkable evil of rebellion. But the *action* of the play and of the entire tetralogy mitigates these words and undercuts their credibility. As Shakespeare presents it, a fundamental difference between King Richard and the first two of his Lancastrian successors is that they are *worthy* of obedience and he is not. A king is not automatically entitled to obedience; he earns it. And a king's main responsibility is to provide good government, not to impose bad government, or not to govern at all, and then invoke uninterested angels to do battle with rebellious subjects. Richard's Tudor doctrine of kingship and obedience provides no effective secular redress for even the most severe grievances, and it should not be surprising that in all ages some men at least have found such a situation intolerable. Shakespeare draws the issue with great clarity: blind passive obedience is wholly inconsistent with good government and human dignity, and Shakespeare believed in both.

FIRST MOVE

Bolingbroke makes the play's first move, against Mowbray, but the immediate response probably tells us more about the King than it does about either of the peers. The play begins with an apparently clear-cut issue: Bolingbroke's omnibus charges of treason against Mowbray, including withholding "for lewd employments" eight thousand nobles intended for soldiers' pay, contriving every treason in England over a period of eighteen years, and plotting and carrying out the murder of Gloucester. The only charge that remains significant after the first scene is that concerning the murder of Gloucester. It is the subject of the conversation between Gaunt and the Duchess of Gloucester in act I, scene ii, and Bolingbroke is still interested in the matter, in somewhat different terms, at the beginning of act IV. If we take Bolingbroke's accusation literally, we are forced to credit the incredible—that he is actually ignorant of Richard's responsibility.

When he raises the subject again in act IV, scene i, he takes Richard's guilt as a matter of course, asking Bagot, "What thou doest know of noble Gloucester's death,/Who wrought it with the king, and who perform'd/The bloody office of his timeless end" (IV.i.3-5).

At the outset one clearly gets the impression that Bolingbroke believes that Mowbray "plotted" the death of Gloucester as he had once conspired unsuccessfully to murder Gaunt; and Mowbray's answer is, as everyone knows, weak, ambiguous, and unsatisfactory (in Holinshed he does not respond to the charge at all): "I slew him not, but to my own disgrace/Neglected my sworn duty in that case" (I.i.133-134). Perhaps the ambiguity is increased by the stiff formality of the couplet and the semilegalistic effect of "in that case." Any member of the audience who had read his Holinshed would have known what Mowbray meant by his own disgrace and could probably deduce what he meant by "my sworn duty." "Disgrace": the King's anger because Mowbray had delayed having Gloucester murdered; "that case": his order, from God's anointed, to have a murder committed under his auspices; his "sworn duty": to obey any command of God's lieutenant, the King. But the popularity of Holinshed gives us only rough evidence of what an audience knew or could deduce. My assumption is that some members would have understood what Mowbray was talking about and some would not, not necessarily an unusual situation in Shakespeare but rather puzzling here.

In act I, scene ii, however, there is no question that Richard's responsibility for Gloucester's murder is well known, not even an open secret, but simply a fact; Gaunt and the Duchess are not gossiping. Bolingbroke's question to Bagot in act IV again indicates that Richard's guilt was widely known—as does the way in which half the peers of the realm step in with their own charges and countercharges. The peers, of course, are being tested here, not Richard or Mowbray, and the peers do not do well. The question is not did Richard commit a crime but who urged him to, "Who wrought it with the king?" Most students of the play assume that the real target of Bolingbroke's accusation in act I is Richard, that he is charging Mowbray with the King's crime as a kind of beginning of a campaign to force Richard out of office. This may well be true; something is going on. We shall return later to other possible explanations for Bolingbroke's behavior in the first scene.

Richard's guilt, in any case, is assumed without question by Gaunt and the Duchess in act I, scene ii, by both Gaunt and York in act II, scene i (by York in the King's presence with, as in act I, scene i, no response whatever from Richard), and again by Bolingbroke and the peers in act IV, scene i. And it is independently established by Holinshed, who gives two different accounts, in both of which the King is guilty. Richard's silence on this subject in act I, scene i, in act II, scene i, and particularly in his long soliloquy in act V, scene v, can hardly be explained in terms flattering to the King. It would be unreasonable to expect him to chat about it in public, but not in private, especially in a passage in which he is assessing the state of his soul. No "O, my offense is rank, it smells to heaven." In view of the King's deep involvement in Gloucester's death and his total silence about that death or his involvement, it would seem that he counts on Mowbray to cover for him or that he regards the matter as a trifle or that he tries to "unthink" the whole business, banishing it even from his private meditations in prison. The deputy elected by the Lord has an enviable freedom of action—and freedom from conscience.

"You Broke The Rules!"

Richard is the play's chief spokesman for the idea of divine kingship and passive obedience, with unwitting help from Gaunt early on. I suggest that King Richard suffers from the psychopathology of divine kingship. He has been described as actor, poet, homosexual, and game player (categories not mutually exclusive). And he is certainly eloquent: in his anguish he *talks* so well that one may forget what he has been *doing*—the things that made the anguish inevitable. His faults have not been venial: murdering an uncle, disinheriting a cousin, robbing and ruining a kingdom. To add the accusation of committing poetry seems excessive, and the suggestion of homosexuality seems not relevant, unless it figures in Bolingbroke's charges against Bushy and Greene in act III, scene i. To describe him as an actor or a game player is more to the point. An actor, however, as a rule, consciously plays his roles. He knows, or should know, that he is acting in a play, that when he is on stage he is one person, another when he is off. Game playing can be conscious or unconscious or something in between. The deliberate game players are confidence men or the sort of tricksters entertainingly invented by Stephen Potter or people who play war games in "think-tanks" or those who write or read books on how to succeed at everything. It doesn't seem quite right to describe what they do as game playing. But there are also the unconscious game players described by Eric Berne in *Games People Play*, people who have developed neurotic ways to manipulate others to get what they want. Sometimes they seem partly to understand what they are doing, sometimes not; if they do partly understand, they seem unable to do much about it.

Winston Weathers has suggested that King Richard is a game player of the sort described by Berne, and I would like to develop further some of Professor Weathers's points here.[13] As game player, Richard is faced with an adversary who either consciously plays a game or is no game player at all. When things are going reasonably well, Richard can, consciously, play his game well enough. He plays a game with Bolingbroke and Mowbray in act I, scene i; he is every inch a king, if not exceptionally forceful or brilliant, as he listens to their accusations, and again, temporarily, in act I, scene iii, when he sends them both into exile; and he manages the business of the preparations for the trial by combat, then halting it at the last moment, well enough. But the rules of his game do not require him to be resourceful or adaptable. Perhaps they do not even permit him to be, because his game is Divine Kingship, or King Body Politic (see below). The idea of divine kingship carries always the possibility of the kind of neurotic behavior displayed by Richard since it requires the observance of certain rules without necessarily requiring any particular talent for governing, or even any real effort to govern. The rules are simple: all of his subjects, including the very greatest, are to obey without question all of his commands, and God is to punish anyone who doesn't. If his opponents in the game—his subjects—commit slight infractions of the rules, he can still carry on the game by seeming to relent (the Compassionate Judge variant), by pretending not to hear, by remaining silent, by devising appropriate ploys, with the body politic as prize or victim. Sending Mowbray and Bolingbroke into exile is a kingly move but not a way of dealing politically with the problems raised by Bolingbroke's accusations.

But already at, or before, the beginning of the play, there has been an infraction of the rules: Mowbray had delayed in carrying out the King's order to have Gloucester killed. He had neglected his "sworn duty," and that had somehow brought about his own disgrace, although the play does not tell us what form the disgrace actually took. Sometimes the rules of the game contain built-in provisions for handling a polite refusal to obey the King. Thus the King can accept with relatively good grace Bolingbroke's and Mowbray's refusals to resolve their differences without violence because the trial by combat is written into the official rules; God will have proven the winner right, in theory, at least. But assume that Mowbray kills Bolingbroke in combat: the King is then rid of a dangerous subject, but he is left with one, too—the one who knows more than anyone else about the King's guilt in relation to Gloucester's murder. Assume that Bolingbroke wins: the King is rid of Mowbray, but he is left with the murdered man's loyal nephew, who knows about the King's guilt. Banishing both men, with the stipulation that they never see each other in exile, may have seemed politic and wise to the King, but only because he naturally assumed that his orders would be obeyed. That's what a king's orders are for. In the event, one has to admire Mowbray's fidelity, to the King or to the King's rules.

But Richard's game playing is dangerous; he assumes certain rules without really thinking about them, and although he considers himself to be "the deputy elected by the Lord," he doesn't think much about a deputy's place and, no doubt unthinkingly, usurps from time to time his Superior's office and prerogatives, like Angelo in *Measure for Measure*, even though Angelo's game is very different from Richard's and deadlier to the spirit. However, Richard is intelligent enough to know—games or no games—that the trial by combat is a potential threat to himself, no matter what his status vis-à-vis his subjects or the Lord. He resolves the problem in his own way, sending both men into exile, thus circumventing an expression of higher providential justice. Mowbray, for good reasons, feels himself badly used, and his lament evokes a characteristically kingly response from Richard: "It boots thee not to be compassionate;/After our sentence plaining comes too late" (I.iii.174-175). Mowbray has forgotten one of the rules. The weakness of the rhyme in Richard's arrogantly insensitive remark may reflect the weakness of his own position—because any "plaining" *before* the sentence would almost necessarily have revealed Richard's implication in the murder. One must be impressed by Mowbray and more than just a little put off by the terms and moves of Richard's game. At best, Mowbray has been an accomplice in a murder, but he seems genuinely to have regarded it as his "sworn duty," however distasteful. His loyalty now is impressive, if morally misplaced; in response to the sentence of exile for life he might have been expected (but not by his king) to say more in remonstrance than he does: "A dearer merit, not so deep a maim/As to be cast forth in the common air,/Have I deserved at your Highness' hands" (I.iii.156-158). The rest of his speech (twenty lines in all) is devoted to the sorrows of exile, of being a lonely foreigner in lands where the English tongue is unknown. It is that sad speech that evokes Richard's terse unfeeling couplet, with its heartless "It boots thee not to be compassionate." Richard's treatment of Mowbray is abominable, however appropriate to his notions of his prerogatives as the deputy elected by the Lord. A better man, and king, than Richard might have said to Mowbray,

> The guilt of conscience take thou for thy labor,
> But neither my good word nor princely favor;
> With Cain go wander thorough shades of night,
> And never show thy head by day nor light.
>
> (*RII*, V.vi.41-44)

But Mowbray was no Exton, seeking royal favor by committing a murder; and Henry IV was no Richard II, maintaining utter silence about his own responsibility—no matter how tenuous in fact King Henry's guilt was. Mowbray has much to answer for, and he does. He accepts the guilt of conscience, and he does wander, although not like Cain, through something like shades of night; he makes his atonement, literally, as Henry IV does figuratively, by going on pilgrimages and crusades. Henry IV's crusade was at home, but he did die in Jerusalem, which vainly he had supposed the Holy Land, whereas it was in fact Gaunt's "other Eden, demi-paradise."

The rules of Richard's game permit but do not require generosity: Gaunt's grief at his son's ten-year banishment leads the King to shorten the term to six years. Bolingbroke's response to this generosity suggests, in its tone, that before long perhaps the wrong player will be breaking the rules, or inventing new ones: "How long a time lies in one little word!/Four lagging winters and four wanton springs/ End in a word: such is the breath of kings" (I.iii.213–215). Perhaps Richard does not perceive the irony of "such is the breath of kings"; perhaps he exercises his option of choosing not to hear it; or perhaps he takes it as a mere statement of fact, too obvious to require comment. He is certainly capable of not perceiving the irony and of taking the remark as a compliment; it is consistent with his idea of kingship. He can't stop time, but he can easily change it.

Taken literally, Bolingbroke's words do not break the official rules. However, a literal and overt breaking of rules does occur when the dying Gaunt, who had earlier argued official doctrine in his conversation with Gloucester's widow, bitterly rebukes the young king for his gross mismanagement of national affairs (II.i.93–115). Gaunt speaks out of concern for the country he loves, but Richard, whose concern for his country is essentially proprietary, is enraged. He is not a child, playing a children's game, but his response to Gaunt's rebukes is certainly childish. We are familiar with the indignation and sense of outrage of which young children are capable when they are convinced that someone, particularly an adult, has broken the rules of a game, violated some sort of important and accepted ritual. A distressing sign of growing up is the young person's developing acceptance of the idea that cheating (and not always at games) is a fact of adult life and that games become increasingly complex, sophisticated, and sometimes deadly. Adults sense the anguish: children who habitually lie, cheat, steal, and the like not only require attention, they are also, somehow, *precocious*— hence the familiar argument that juvenile criminals should not be dealt with by juvenile courts—they should be treated as adults because they are acting like adults (certain kinds of adults, to be sure).

Obviously a cardinal rule of Richard's game, fundamental to his idea of kingship, is that the king can do no wrong, no matter how absurd or abominable his actions may appear to mere mortals. Shakespeare has most certainly loaded the deck against his Richard, but, as I have suggested, he does so by following some contemporary doctrines out to their logical conclusions. Francis Bacon had occasion to observe, in 1600, "that by the common law of England, a Prince can do no wrong" (see note 5, above). But Gaunt accuses *this* prince of doing wrong, and on at least two counts this is bad: first, the subject, no matter who he is, has no business accusing the King of anything (one reason, perhaps, why the politic Bolingbroke accused Mowbray—but only one reason); second, since the King can do no wrong (no matter *what* he does), Gaunt's accusations constitute a gross violation of Richard's automatically assumed rules. It might be argued that Gaunt's offense is even more serious: he is not just breaking the rules, he is not playing a game at all (not even Elder Statesman). Richard's outraged and petulant response is based on a deadly implied assumption: "I was having fun playing games, but you're ruining it by talking about life and other things that *you* can't find in *my* rule-book." Game playing is a part of "real life," but that does not make it immune to disaster.

When Gaunt told his brother's widow that he could not lift an angry arm against God's minister, he was not playing a game in Richard's sense at all. He was defining an idea of order, a mistaken and disastrous idea but one based at the outset on a reasoned view of a civil polity: the excesses of an irresponsible king, however serious, are not so bad as the excesses of rebellion or regicide. In stating his

own view, he is also defining one of Richard's rules of disorder. Both
are disastrous; they won't work as a game, they won't work as political theory—not when translated into action. An obvious flaw in the
notion of passive obedience is in the unlikelihood of everyone's remaining passively obedient, nor would the general welfare of society
be advanced, necessarily, if everyone did; it isn't sensible; it would
merely introduce the lemming principle into the body politic.
Shakespeare took a pragmatic view of such things. He surely believed in obedience as a general rule, but not in socially suicidal obedience, the Tudor version, which he attributes to the unfortunate
Richard II and turns into a kind of pseudo-theocracy. As we have
seen, passive obedience, with all its cosmic overtones, loses credibility as soon as it is applied to certain concrete problems. It may be that
Gaunt, in his impassioned lament for the end of English greatness and
again in his direct attack on Richard, has come to some sense that his
original attitude toward his brother's murderer as God's minister
was wrong.

Richard's supporters are not game players and are increasingly
frustrated by his refusal, or inability, to stop playing. Carlisle and
Aumerle, understanding something of the psychological problem
without quite defining it, try to bring him to face it firmly and intelligently. Having arrived in Wales and having heard of the presence
of rebels in his country, Richard seems to think that the earth itself
will protect him and his kingship:

> This earth shall have a feeling, and these stones
> Prove armed soldiers ere her native king
> Shall falter under foul rebellion's arms.
>
> (III.ii.24-26)

It's not a long way from armed stones to miraculous dragon's teeth
or warlike anti-Lancastrian angels. Perhaps Richard is reassuring
himself, cheering himself up, with an agreeable invented fantasy,
daydreaming out loud; more likely, he is working on one of his fundamental assumptions: God will protect His Richard against rebels.
Carlisle sees something wrong but agrees with the King up to the
point where political reality becomes disconnected symbol and

where an orthodox Christian idea verges toward an impotent combination of pride and despair; he can distinguish symbol from reality,
particularly when the two are so tenuously connected:

> Fear not, my lord. That Power that made you king
> Hath power to keep you king in spite of all.
> The means that heaven yields must be imbrac'd
> And not neglected; else, if heaven would,
> And we will not, heaven's offer we refuse,
> The proffered means of succour and redress.
>
> (III.ii.27-32)

It seems unlikely that Richard would have comprehended even if
Carlisle had been a bit less tactful and said, "The Lord helps those
who help themselves." Aumerle is more direct: "He means, my lord,
that we are too remiss:/Whilst Bolingbroke, through our security,/
Grows strong and great in substance and in power" (III.ii.33-35).
The problem is that they are not speaking Richard's language.

For him, the rules say that if he is threatened, God will look out for
him. For them, God is surely on Richard's side, but He requires His
lieutenant to take some responsibility. The King hears the words, all
right, but they seem to mean nothing to him; their perfectly reasonable meaning doesn't apply to his game. When he rebukes his "dis-
comfortable cousin," he does so on the grounds that his cousin
doesn't understand the rules: if Bolingbroke makes a move, Richard
does not have to make a countermove, because Bolingbroke's move
was in violation of the rules. (Banishing Bolingbroke was perhaps a
countermove of sorts, but in that case Bolingbroke's move was
overtly against Mowbray, or so the King could pretend to think, and
between those two disputants he could, consciously, play Impartial
Magistrate.) There is an elegant fecklessness about Richard's reply
to Carlisle's and Aumerle's efforts to rouse him from his regal fatuity, and its elegance has led some critics to assume that Richard's
words express Shakespeare's feelings (confusing skilled rhetoric
with truth has always been a cardinal humanist fallacy; we are all
guilty of it and a pair of instances would multiply like rabbits):

> Not all the waters in the rough rude sea
> Can wash the balm off from an anointed king;

The breath of worldly men cannot depose
The deputy elected by the Lord;
For every man that Bolingbroke hath press'd
To lift shrewd steel against our golden crown,
God for his Richard hath in heavenly pay
A glorious angel: then, if angels fight,
Weak men must fall, for heaven still guards the right.

(III.ii.54–62)

The language of the first four lines rolls on with such relentless majesty that it seems almost bad taste to note that they represent an opinion of the King, not anything like a demonstrable fact: "the waters in the rough rude sea" are already doing the work that Richard says they can't. And of course the last five lines definitively cancel out the first four. Shakespeare knew well enough that those five lines embody a proposition that could have been shared only with some misgivings by his audience—not just Hamlet's judicious spectator; and his audience knew well enough that it was not going to see armed angels (led by St. Michael, with scales and sword?) descending to the stage like Jupiter on his eagle in *Cymbeline*. That is to say, the audience knew that the King was wrong, and it knew that his wrongness existed in a verifiable historical context; and that left the audience free (or tempted it) to assume that if it could happen once, it could, as they say, happen again, that the official line was not necessarily so.

Shakespeare juxtaposes contemporary political dogma with hyperbolic fantasy, embellishing orthodoxy with absurdity, with results that ought to be predictable. Richard's resounding piece of self-deception is immediately followed both by Salisbury's news that the Welsh have dispersed and fled to Bolingbroke and by the beginning of what has been called Richard's "passion," a term suitable enough if stripped of its specifically Christian connotations. Richard speaks of his cross, of *the* Passion, of Pilates, without having given much thought (as far as I can tell) to the Synoptic Gospels: the Son *always* knew what was going to happen and why. And as Richard oscillates desperately between self-pity and defiance, between dreams of glory and dreams of death, Carlisle tries to take him in hand, amid news of mounting disaster:

My lord, wise men ne'er sit and wail their woes,
But presently prevent the ways to wail.
To fear the foe, since fear oppresseth strength,
Gives in your weakness strength unto your foe,
And so your follies fight against yourself.
Fear and be slain—no worse can come to fight;
And fight and die is death destroying death,
Where fearing dying pays death servile breath.

                                        (III.ii.178–185)

Carlisle's advice may not be politically sound and for the King it can't be encouraging (its constricted, gnomic syntax doesn't help, either), but if Richard had taken it when it was given, instead of just before his murder, he would at least have left a better impression. His follies, as Carlisle boldly labels them, have been almost incalculable (although Carlisle seems not to be referring to the follies that got his master into this fix), and they have been the result, first, of his pathological game playing and, second, of his shocking realization that he is, after all, a mortal, human deputy elected by the Lord and that the election has been reversed and that he is a man, something like other men—a discovery that neither of his successors had to make: they knew it all along. It had apparently not occurred to him that God's deputy must "live with bread like you, feel want,/Taste grief, need friends" (III.ii.175–176). Compare King Harry the fifth, alone, the night before Agincourt. The realization that he is merely mortal leads Richard to the absurd but touching conclusion that he is *therefore*, because mortal, not a king (III.ii.177). The two Harrys know all about mortality and kingship.

Richard's symbols, the symbols that give meaning to his game, are nonreferential—they don't refer to anything that is real in the world that everyone has to live in. In act III, scene ii, Carlisle and Aumerle try to bring him into touch with reality, with the facts of his situation, with a world in which an anointed king has some responsibilities, at least to God and to himself. And it is interesting and important, and usually overlooked, that neither of them has much to say about a king's duties to his country. They are enthusiastic spokesmen for a Point of View, and the health of the body politic is of no obvious concern to them at all. The most shocking thing in this scene is the contrast between Richard's confidence in his special status as God's deputy and his abject acceptance of the fact of his mortality, his misunderstanding of what that fact means, and his realization that a king can be destroyed. When he wants to "sit upon the ground/And tell sad stories of the death of kings" (155–156), he concludes that they were all murdered: "some have been depos'd,/Some poisoned by their wives, some sleeping killed,/All murthered" (157–160). No matter that the insistent generalization cannot include the speaker's predecessor, let alone his first two successors. If they were all murdered by death "with a little pin," that pin seems only to be a symbol for murderers in general. For God's anointed, death, any death, seems to be a kind of murder, and that does shock.

Now we see a terrible struggle on Richard's part to emerge from his private and illusory world of symbols and safety into a world where even kings may die. That his struggle is unsuccessful is indicated by the ubiquity of *murdered* kings in his fantastic catalogue. A dead king is a murdered king, not the other way round. Richard struggles from unreality to unreality, with anything concrete contributing to further disconnection: expecting Northumberland to kneel, for example. And he struggles from game playing to an understanding that the game is up without quite realizing that it had been a game. The intensity of his (partial) realization takes it beyond reality and into a new world of exaggerated horror. Carlisle observes that "wise men ne'er sit and wail their woes." But Richard is not a wise man. The advice of Carlisle and Aumerle would probably not have saved the King, even if he could have acted on it. If he had been able to, that action would have trebled Bolingbroke's guilt; he would have had to take, or kill in battle, an anointed king. Richard, not altogether intentionally, spares Bolingbroke that particular guilt.

Richard's hopelessly neurotic situation is perhaps best indicated by his words to Aumerle when he learns that his uncle York has gone over to Bolingbroke: "Beshrew thee, cousin, which didst lead me forth/Of that sweet way I was in to despair!" (III.ii.204–205). Setting aside the question of mortal sin (sweet way to despair, half in love with easeful death), he displays at the very least a self-destructive state of mind from which he is scarcely to emerge until his kingship is gone and he is reduced (if that's the word) to Richard

Plantagenet the man, reflecting on mortality and fighting for his life; the sight of eight murderers wonderfully fixes the concentration. But in fact, long before his collapse in act III, scene ii, Richard had behaved with nearly incredible obtuseness, in his responses to York's outrage over the confiscation of Gaunt's property and the disinheriting of Bolingbroke and to York's monitory comparison between the King and his father, the Black Prince:

> His face thou hast, for even so look'd he,
> Accomplish'd with the number of thy hours;
> But when he frown'd, it was against the French,
> And not against his friends; his noble hand
> Did win what he did spend, and spent not that
> Which his triumphant father's hand had won;
> His hands were guilty of no kindred blood,
> But bloody with the enemies of his kin.
> O Richard! York is too far gone with grief,
> Or else he never would compare between—
>
> (II.i.176–185)

There is no ambiguity about what York is saying. Only Richard could miss the point. But he manages to do so, in a question of stunning obtuseness: "Why, uncle, what's the matter? (II.i.186).

The chronicles agree that Richard was not actually vicious, but foolish and inept and too young for his work (he and Bolingbroke were actually the same age), easily swayed by his unscrupulous, fun-loving friends. (Without wishing to seem in any way prudish or eccentric, I must say that murder does *seem* vicious, particularly the kind that starts all the trouble here.) Most of the chroniclers were not writers of distinction: Holinshed is a notorious example. Hall is perhaps an exception; he is seldom dull and his gift for vituperation is impressive. But, as a playwright, how does one put his expertise to work to demonstrate beyond question King Richard's mind-boggling incompetence? Have him do something stupid (confiscate Gaunt's estates, disinherit Gaunt's tough son) and then hear an impassioned and wholly explicit remonstrance from his uncle and ask, when it seems to be over, "Why, uncle, what's the matter?"

Dover Wilson, with that Machiavellian ingenuity that has put us forever in his debt, makes Richard as inattentive to York as he made

Claudius to the dumb show, with one of his favorite and most bane-
ful devices, the noncanonical stage direction (in this case, two). In
Wilson's edition, Richard hears nothing that York tells him, because
he is busy: "He goes about the room, rating the costly objects there-
in" (S. D., II.i.163), the archaic diction no doubt designed to simulate
an authentic Shakespearean stage direction. And at line 185 he is suddenly brought to attention because York "sobs aloud."[14] Well,
naturally, if you hear your old uncle sobbing aloud, you are going to
ask him what's the matter.

In the passage immediately following, York propounds what
ought to be one of the immutable principles of the game—at least to
anyone conscious of game playing; it is a principle that no one could
possibly overlook in late-sixteenth-century England:

> Take Herford's rights away, and take from time
> His charters and his customary rights:
> Let not tomorrow then ensue today:
> *Be not thyself.* For how art thou a king
> But by fair sequence and succession?
> (Emphasis added; II.i.195–199)

The principle of correspondence is familiar enough, as are the magic
words "fair sequence and succession." Richard's offense against
Bolingbroke anticipates, and in a sense precipitates, Bolingbroke's
against Richard. Regal infallibility doesn't make much sense if you
see a king clearly fallible; lineal succession retains no credibility
when a king violates it.

But Richard is not really violating a rule of *his* game because for
him divine kingship has nothing to do with lineal succession (except
perhaps his own succession as son of the Black Prince); it is not even a
purely secular political convenience. He scarcely mentions the subject, except perhaps obliquely in a reference to himself as "a rightful
king" (V.i.50). Shakespeare has his Richard ignore the succession in
this play, and that is to be taken as a measure of Richard's regal
irresponsibility—and some measure of Shakespeare's political sophistication. In a political world that has no provision for periodic
democratic elections, lineal succession is sensible enough, provided
there is some way to prevent a criminal or a mental defective from

inheriting the throne. Divine kingship is another matter, and when one tries to attach it inseparably to the principle of lineal succession, one has a potentially poisonous combination, a sort of political theology that sanctions any kind of regal malfeasance.[15] Shakespeare was hardly the only Englishman of his time to be aware of the problem. Shakespeare's Henry V, it might be noted, makes his claim to the French throne on the basis of lineal succession (heavily rigged by the playwright), but certainly not as God's lieutenant, a claim that he would have thought not only distasteful but blasphemous. He takes the responsibility and gives the credit to God, and that is not Richard's way at all.

The issue of the Mortimer succession does not arise in this play, and it is raised in *1 Henry IV* only to be discredited: in that play, Henry is the legitimate king. For Richard, then, York's outburst is simply the emotionally stated opinion of a nice but exasperating and befuddled old uncle, as his reply suggests: "Think what you will [it's only a matter of opinion], we seize into our hands/His plate, his goods, his money and his lands" (II.i.208-209). The childish petulance of the words is reflected in the rhyme. Nothing in Richard's rule book forbids his killing one uncle and stealing the estates of another, although one might have thought that some ethical sense, some decent regard for the opinion of mankind, might have deterred him. However, by disinheriting his cousin Bolingbroke, Gaunt's legitimate heir, Richard, although he may not be violating his own rules, is throwing everybody else's rule book out the window. And he does it in a way that makes it possible for Bolingbroke to introduce a principle of law into the constitutional chaos created by King Richard:[16] "If that my cousin king be King in England,/It must be granted I am Duke of Lancaster" (II.iii.122-123). As might be expected, principles of law do not have much meaning for King Richard, but in an odd way they finally prevail in the play.

Richard never sees the point, never recognizes it as a point, and Shakespeare chooses not to have Bolingbroke push it again as a legal issue; the restoration of his dukedom is simply part of the ultimatum he sends to Richard in act III, scene iii. The doctrines of passive obedience and divine kingship forbade Gaunt to lift an angry arm against God's minister, but God's minister had violated his ministry—

governing. Richard is not interested in government except insofar as he might arbitrarily decide to govern or not to govern. Bolingbroke, on the other hand, intends to govern, and he does.

It has not been my purpose, in describing Richard as a game player, to use a loose metaphor, although such a term naturally assumes metaphorical value, particularly when applied to a character in a work of art. His personality operates for the most part in a world of symbols and is typically unable to relate the symbols to the realities for which they should rationally be expected to stand. His assumption that for every Lancastrian soldier "God for his Richard hath in heavenly pay/A glorious angel" is as good an example as any of his state of mind: it has nothing to do with the facts. Also symptomatic is his response to Carlisle's and Aumerle's efforts to persuade him to defend himself and his prerogatives as king. (And we should recall, not quite in passing, that their loyalties are specifically to King Richard and not to any conception of good government, about which neither has anything at all to say.) Even Richard's one serious effort to rouse himself to action comes essentially in terms of game playing: urged by Aumerle to take comfort and "remember who you are" (III.ii.82), he replies in the language of fantasy:

> I had forgot myself, am I not king?
> Awake, thou coward majesty! thou sleepest.
> Is not the king's name twenty thousand names?
> Arm, arm, my name! a puny subject strikes
> At thy great glory. Look not to the ground,
> Ye favorites of a king, are we not high?
> High be our thoughts.
>
> (III.ii.83–89)

Twenty thousand unarmed names may be momentarily reassuring to the King, but only momentarily; for his adversary, the King's name is one, unarmed, and the actual transfer of kingship is as bloodless as that alleged in 1688 and, except for Northumberland's part, a good deal less bloody-minded. As Richard finishes the speech just quoted he seems to be coming to some sense of reality, but in pathetic, almost childish terms: "I know my uncle York/Hath power enough to serve our turn" (III.ii.89–90); Uncle York, who had reprimanded him (that is one thing uncles are for), will also save him (another thing uncles are for). But this is an emphatic comedown from "Not all the waters in the rough rude sea/Can wash the balm off from an anointed king." If God won't help me—and the rules say He should—my uncle York will. *Somebody* will.

Richard, by Bolingbroke's very presence in England, is forced from unreality to unreality; he is not, as they say, crisis oriented. If one game won't work, maybe another will. There is no need to point out that the struggle is dreadful, as he compares himself, again and again, to the sun, to Christ betrayed by "Judases" into the hands of "Pilates"; deprived of his kingdom, he will be a hermit, his realm an obscure grave: he will become a *memento mori*. And in act IV, scene i, as he unkings and "disanoints" himself, he will be a renegade priest, a traitor to himself. He will play a series of roles; he will become an emblem. But his roles and his emblems are all chosen on the basis of his controlling assumption, that he is "God's substitute,/His deputy anointed in His sight," and that he is therefore not answerable to mortals for any of his actions—one reason why he refuses to read Northumberland's list of allegations against him, a psychological point that Bolingbroke seems to understand.

It is clear enough that Richard thinks much of God's duties to him; it is not at all clear that he regards himself as accountable to God for his own actions. He implicitly denies responsibility to his subjects, to his country, even to himself (God or "my uncle York" will rescue him); and he never defines, specifies, or mentions his responsibility to God. When he sees himself about to be delivered to his "sour cross," he makes a painfully unconvincing analogy because he had never really thought much about anyone but himself. It was Gaunt who said:

> But since correction lieth in those hands
> Which made the fault that we cannot correct,
> Put we our quarrel to the will of heaven,
> Who, when they see the hours ripe on earth,
> Will rain hot vengeance on offenders' heads.
>
> (I.ii.4–8)

Richard must be beaten at games—many games—before he can gain something like a command of reality, and Gaunt's words just quoted, taken in the context of Richard's infatuated game playing, will suggest something of the irony and subtlety of the play's political-theological content. Like Carlisle and, apparently, Aumerle, Gaunt and York believe in divine kingship, but they believe in it in very different ways. Carlisle, to be sure, reprimands Richard for not taking measures to defend himself against Bolingbroke and the rebels, and he implies strongly that God will not help Richard unless Richard tries to help himself. But he never suggests that Richard is in any way responsible for what is happening except insofar as his "follies" are self-destructive. His attitude is, by implication, another version of Gaunt's, but he cares a good deal less than Gaunt does about the health of the civil polity. He never alludes to Richard's guilt in the death of Gloucester or the disinheriting of Bolingbroke—any more than Richard himself does. In his eloquent defense of the royal prerogative and divine kingship in act IV, scene i, lines 114-149, he may well echo official Tudor doctrine, but he never so much as drops a hint that Richard had been anything less than a model king: that would have been irrelevant. Gaunt also upholds the royal prerogative, believes, apparently, in divine kingship, and regards the king as God's (perhaps inscrutable) minister. But he absolutely cannot overlook the fact that this king can misbehave, that he can nearly ruin the kingdom. Carlisle is more consistent, but he is consistent at the expense of good sense. Gaunt's inconsistency is more interesting and more revealing; he is hopelessly trapped between loyalty to an idea of kingship and loyalty to his country, and the two loyalties are irreconcilable. But perhaps he was right when he said that the heavens "Will rain hot vengeance on offenders' heads." Certainly, Bolingbroke's luck seems almost providential, and he was certainly not alone in raining hot vengeance on this offender's head.

THE KING'S TWO BODIES

Whether Bolingbroke is God's instrument or his own (it would be easy to say he is both), his function in the psychological drama is to force Richard out of games and into the objective facts of life, out of symbols and into reality. He is almost successful, but not quite (I don't mean to suggest that he is consciously Richard's therapist—

England's, maybe): down to the very end, Richard the King, Richard of Bordeaux the man, never alludes to the murder of Gloucester even though that murder is a fact as well established as any in the play, and he never refers to the disinheriting of Bolingbroke, a fact equally well established. Perhaps the transition from divine king to mortal man is enough because one great intellectual achievement of these plays—the intellect and the art are here inseparable—is to undercut and finally to annihilate the doctrine of the King's Two Bodies. It is no exaggeration to say that Shakespeare takes aim at the heart of Tudor political-theological-legal theory, and he doesn't miss.[17]

It is no accident that when Shakespeare uses the phrase "the divinity that doth hedge a king," the reference is to Hamlet's murderous, incestuous, usurping uncle, one of the great villains in all drama. If *Richard II* is, as Ernst Kantorowicz says, "the tragedy of the King's Two Bodies," it is so in the specific sense that it is the tragedy of a king who is infatuated, in love, with the myth of the sun-king, the King Body Politic. Richard's notion of kingship reflects several contemporary dogmas, one of which is based on the elaborate sixteenth-century legal fiction that subsumes and "legalizes," renders constitutional, divine kingship and passive obedience. Whether the work of lawyers, politicians, or theologians is most dangerous when they are all bent on mischief I cannot presume to say; but on the doctrine of the King's Two Bodies they seem to have combined some formidable talents.

Although the idea that kings are appointed by God has biblical origins and the idea that kings are at least semidivine beings can be found in the Middle Ages (usually worked out by learned monks who had quarrels with the Papacy), the legal fiction of the King's Two Bodies was mainly the work of English crown jurists of the sixteenth century. The *Commentaries or Reports* of Edmund Plowden provide a series of elaborations on this mystical-legal idea, one of the most notable instances arising, interestingly in the present context, in connection with the Duchy of Lancaster, "which the Lancastrian Kings had owned as private property and not as property of the Crown" (Kantorowicz, p. 7). Edward VI, who died before reaching his majority, had made a lease of certain lands of the Duchy, and a famous trial (4 Queen Elizabeth) concerned the legality of such leases when made by a minor. The crown lawyers, Plowden reports, agreed

> that by the Common Law no Act which the King does as King, shall be defeated by his Nonage. For the King has in him two Bodies,*viz.*, a Body natural and a Body politic. His Body natural (if it be considered in itself) is a body mortal, subject to all the Infirmities that come by Nature or Accident, to the Imbecility of Infancy or old Age, and to the like Defects that happen to the natural Bodies of other People. But his Body politic is a Body that cannot be seen or handled, consisting of Policy and Government, and constituted for the Direction of the People, and the Management of the public weal, and this Body is utterly void of Infancy, and old Age, and other natural Defects and Imbecilities, which the Body natural is subject to, and for this Cause, what the King does in his Body politic, cannot be invalidated or frustrated by any Disability in his natural Body. [Kantorowicz, p. 7]

The extravagance of a mystical doctrine that says that the king has a body "utterly devoid of Infancy, and old Age, and other natural Defects and Imbecilities" (no matter how delightful its language) is slightly—very slightly—mitigated by the fact that a secularized version of it is implicit in the acts and attitudes of many elected and appointed public officials, some of whom (not all) are occasionally sent to prison for it, briefly. Very few, unless they are writing books on the subject, will admit that they have any "natural defects and Imbecilities," in spite of the plain evidence.

Even more important than the baldly stated doctrine of two bodies, one incapable of imperfection, is the idea that the perfect body, the Body Politic, contains "certain truly mysterious forces which reduce, or even remove, the imperfections of the fragile human nature" (Kantorowicz, p. 9). Thus one way to document the view that the king could do no wrong was to state the basic doctrine of the King's Two Bodies and adduce the legal maxim, "*quia magis dignum trahit ad se minus dignum.*" For Shakespeare's Richard, the "worthier" (*magis*), i.e., the King Body Politic, draws to itself the "lesser," the King Body Natural, and any defects or imbecilities of the latter are obliterated by the former. It is of passing interest that this particular notion grew out of the Duchy of Lancaster case, for there the judges

argued that the Lancastrian kings held the Duchy in their Body
Natural, Henry IV having inherited it from his father before making
himself king, whereas Edward IV and his successors held it in their
Body Politic, "which is more ample and large than the Body natural" (Kantorowicz, p. 9). I find no explanation of why, in 1399, with
the consent of Parliament, Henry IV ordained that the Duchy of
Lancaster was to remain the *private* property of the king, "as though
we would never have achieved the height of royal Dignity" (Kantorowicz, p. 403). It could have been a source of tremendous revenue
(as it apparently is now, with its chancellor and its imposing office
building on the Thames); and it could have been something im-
mensely useful to fall back on in the event of serious rebellion. When
Edward IV seized power in 1461, he seized also the Duchy of Lancaster, it being forfeit to the crown on the attainting and conviction
of Henry VI of high treason. The new king, a gifted businessman and
financier, specified that the Duchy was to have the legal status of a
corporation, separate from all his other inheritances, administered
separately, with the proceeds of the corporation accruing to him as
private owner by right of the crown (Kantorowicz, p. 404). Thus the
properties once seized by Richard II and reclaimed by Bolingbroke
("I come for Lancaster," literally) became, in effect, the Duchy of
Lancaster, Inc. (Kantorowicz, p. 404), and the question of its legal
status under the Tudors was immediately responsible for giving rise
to the elaborate fiction of the King's Two Bodies, although the re-
finements which that doctrine underwent during the sixteenth,
seventeenth, and eighteenth centuries suggest that it might well have
developed in any case as a natural result of medieval theorizing about
divine kingship. It should be emphasized that the medieval theories
were usually antipapal, and notions of divine kingship were designed
to place king above pope. Wycliffe developed some interesting but
inconsistent ideas along these lines (Figgis, pp. 66-80); Tyndale pur-
sued the subject of divine kingship more carefully and elaborately
(Prior, pp. 139-140); and Foxe, as might be expected, got into the act
in his *Acts and Monuments* (Aston, pp. 294-300), a book with which
Shakespeare must have been familiar as he seems to have been familiar with parts of Plowden's *Reports*, a book widely quoted in an
age that adored litigation.

The relevance of Tyndale and Foxe, particularly, to this study of Shakespeare, *Richard II*, and divine kingship and the King's Two Bodies is that Tyndale and Foxe saw, or claimed to see, Richard as a divinely ordained king who allowed simple Christians to pursue the dictates of conscience independently of ecclesiastical authority, and they saw Henry IV and Henry V as regressive and bigoted hunters (and burners) of simple and pious Christian folk. Shakespeare's Catholicism was at all times tempered with the greatest prudence,[18] and King Richard's (and Gaunt's) attitudes toward Lollards have nothing to do with this play. Instead, he centers it in the vastly capacious figure of Falstaff and raises it again, with almost diabolical ingenuity, at the beginning of *Henry V* in such a way that it could hardly give offense—even to those who perceived what he was doing.

It is idle to speculate on the extent to which Shakespeare would have been familiar with the constitutional details of the doctrine of the King's Two Bodies as a specifically legal fiction. But although he does not have his Richard explicitly (and anachronistically) use the term, the King seems clearly obsessed with the idea of the King Body Politic and unwilling to consider the implications of the other half, the King Body Natural, until he is forced to face it when he looks in a mirror. It is in the context of King Body Politic, that is, a king not subject to defects and imbecilities, that Richard's troubles become particularly painful and dangerous. Yet his imbecilities seem readily apparent to almost everyone but the King himself: even Carlisle and Aumerle are distressed by his refusal or inability to exploit his kingship in order to save it. If the play is "the tragedy of the King's Two Bodies," it is, more specifically, the tragedy of a man infatuated with that doctrine, a man who, when he finds that he lives with bread, feels want, tastes grief, and needs friends—when he finds, that is, that he is mortal—can ask, "How can you say to me, I am a king?" (III.ii.177). The terrible dichotomy between divine king and mortal man—terrible especially in Richard's mind—may be partly attributable to Shakespeare's thorough understanding of the issues and to his obvious reservations about divine kingship; it may be the result of his sense of the tragic values of the *De casibus* tradition and the falls of kings, a tradition that takes on a new poignancy when combined with the idea of the King's Two Bodies; and it may be the result of his skepticism about the validity of the whole idea of the King's Two Bodies. Most likely it is all of these, brought together and shaped in the psychological matrix of Shakespeare's recognition of the significance of game playing. Some Tudor political dogmas could fairly be described as pathogenic, if not downright pathological.

In the context of divine kingship, the King's Two Bodies, and game playing, Richard's worst folly (as opposed to crime, ordering Gloucester's murder) was "stealing Lancaster"; Bolingbroke's most plausible action was "coming for Lancaster." Shakespeare's sources provided him with some evidence that Bolingbroke returned from exile only to claim his dukedom, stolen by Richard, even though Shakespeare, quite deliberately, as we will see later, does not show him making the so-called Doncaster oath. (He swore that he had returned from exile only to claim his own inheritance—and to cause the payment of taxes and to bring the king to "good government." [See Hosley, pp. 77.] The same sources, of course, also make it clear that he was returning from exile to depose Richard and to make himself king.) But in view of the testimony of Plowden's *Reports* regarding the importance of the Duchy of Lancaster in the formulation of the doctrine of the King's Two Bodies, it is possible that the familiar historical sources may not have been much more important for a fundamental theme of this and the following plays than were the dazzling legal acrobatics of crown lawyers in the sixteenth century.

I can find almost nothing in Tudor ideas of divine kingship and passive obedience and nothing in the Tudor legal fiction of the King's Two Bodies which specifies or implies that to be a good king one must first be a good man—and very little that suggests that a king ought to be good in order to rule well, although regal virtue was always to be commended. The nearly universal insistence is that once someone becomes a king or a queen, he or she is by definition infallible, or, as Bacon put it, "by the common law of England, a Prince can do no wrong." Positive laws have no necessary connection with abstract ideas of right and wrong (hence the common annoyance and outrage at the spectacle of people doing things widely regarded as wrong but not known to be illegal—"there ought to be a law!"). But although Shakespeare brings into these plays some explicitly legal concepts, he seems to write about positive laws and constitutions like the author of an exceptionally elegant and brilliant dramatized courtesy book or like the author of a book on the education of the prince and the qualities to be exhibited by a virtuous and able ruler. He *does* make a connection between positive laws and constitutions on the one hand and ideas of good and evil, right and wrong, on the other. He is working toward the image of an Ideal King.

Only a very mad, or astonishingly candid, ruler would bluntly say, "I am a sorry specimen, considered merely as a human being, but as a divine corporation I am by definition excellent." But evil or inept or venal men in positions of authority have always publicly proclaimed or privately assumed certain virtues residing in their offices. Richard M. Nixon was a perhaps extreme example. What makes Shakespeare's Richard a kind of tragically absurd figure is that although he claims for himself no positive virtues, his actions and proclamations as king imply either that he *needs* no virtues or that they are his automatically, an effect of kingship—thus his remarkable "Why uncle, what's the matter?" After all, he has only been stealing his cousin's patrimony and undermining the principle of hereditary right.

"JUST BETWEEN OURSELVES. . . ."

It is a familiar observation that almost all of Richard's proclamations, decisions, and actions through act IV, scene i are made on more or less public or ceremonial occasions; and it might be argued that we are simply not expected to ask what kind of *private* man he is. Such a nonexpectation would be consistent with the doctrine of the King's Two Bodies. Shakespeare seems to have considered his strategy with exceptional care, even for him, in this connection. Official doctrine, not including books on the ideal prince, was relatively silent on the subject of monarchs simply as fallible mortals, and the doctrine of the King's Two Bodies implies that that issue is in any case irrelevant: the "ample and large" and mysterious Body Politic negated, canceled out, or subsumed the inevitable defects of the natural and mortal man. Thus Richard in public, and often in private, is the King Body Politic, the divine king, the sun-king, about whose mere personal moral qualities it is pointless to inquire. It is obvious enough that he does not execute his stewardship with intelligence or probity, but then, although he uses the word once (III.iii.78), he doesn't think of kingship as stewardship. York and Gaunt do, and they direct their excoriations specifically against their nephew's corrupt stewardship. From what they say and from Richard's responses, one may make easy inferences about Richard the man.

But in two very telling scenes we see Richard talking business, as it were, in private: in act II, scene i, with his uncles Gaunt and York, a scene we have already considered; and in act I, scene iv, in private with his friends Bagot, Greene, and Aumerle. The quality of the discourse is not high. And even though his remarks here relate directly to some of his affairs as King, they are not made on anything resembling a public occasion; they are cynical, irresponsible, unfeeling, dishonest, and outrageous. Unbraced among his friends (but perhaps not with a masseur, as in the BBC television production), he is an informal, private version of the king we have already seen and will see again, to even less advantage, in the scene following (II.i.). The identity of the King Body Politic, the ceremonial identity, the authoritative identity, is briefly dropped, and we see in its place the king body bloody natural—cynical, corrupt, and self-indulgent, with a very full share of defects and imbecilities. The effect of this scene is highly unpleasant. Richard and Aumerle speak ironically of "high Herford," and Aumerle notes that

> . . . would the word "farewell" have length'ned hours
> And added years to his short banishment,
> He should have had a volume of farewells;
> But since it would not, he had none of me.
>
> (I.iv.16–19)

Richard replies pleasantly if somewhat ambiguously:

> He is our cousin's cousin, but 'tis doubt,
> When time shall call him home from banishment,
> Whether our kinsman come to see his friends.
>
> (I.iv.20–22)

It is not quite clear whether Richard means that he intends to extend the period of banishment, that Bolingbroke will return as an enemy, or that it is to be feared that when he comes home it will be to see his friends, people, that is, hostile to the King. Mowbray had already implicitly predicted Bolingbroke's future role in response to the latter's urging him to confess his "treasons":

> No, Bolingbroke, if ever I were traitor,
> My name be blotted from the book of life,
> And I from heaven banish'd as from hence!
> But what thou art, God, thou, and I do know,
> And all too soon, I fear, the king shall rue.
>
> (I.iii.201–205)

The last two lines are perhaps not quite so straightforward as they seem because of Mowbray's peculiar notions of treason and loyalty: he was loyal to his king, and therefore no traitor, when he finally ordered the murder of Gloucester. Presumably Mowbray had (or imagined he had) a clearer notion than the audience could have in act I about Bolingbroke's motives in accusing him of treason in the death of Gloucester; and the King apparently sensed something of the same thing, giving us an ambiguous clue as to his motives for stopping the trial by combat and banishing Bolingbroke:

> Ourself and Bushy
> Observ'd his courtship to the common people,
> How he did seem to dive into their hearts
> With humble and familiar courtesy;
> What reverence he did throw away on slaves,
> Wooing poor craftsmen with the craft of smiles
> And patient underbearing of his fortune,
> As 'twere to banish their affects with him.
> Off goes his bonnet to an oyster-wench;
> A brace of draymen bid God speed him well,
> And had the tribute of his supple knee,
> With "Thanks, my countrymen, my loving friends"—
> As were our England in reversion his,
> And he our subjects' next degree in hope.
>
> (I.iv.23–36)

If Bushy and Richard were reliable witnesses, we might get the impression that Bolingbroke was almost as popular in 1399 as, say, Essex was in 1595. Greene's reply is relevant if not quite prophetic: "Well, he is gone; and with him go these thoughts" (I.iv.37)— almost as though the banishment had been prearranged between the King and his friends, rather than with his council, specifically to get what they regard as a very dangerous man out of the country, as though they could somehow unthink "high Herford." The peace-loving statesman-king of act I, scene iii, whose "eyes do hate the dire aspect/Of civil wounds plough'd up with neighbours' sword" (127-128), who did not want "fair peace" frighted "from our quiet confines" (137), now reveals himself as a cynical and not very talented schemer. His game (maybe "King-in-the-Clouds Unbrac'd") is shoddy and his technique atrocious. He is not like Prince Hal at the Boar's Head; he is not witty, clever, or engaging, even in a small way. And it gets worse. He will go in person to the Irish war,

> And for our coffers, with too great a court
> And liberal largess, are grown somewhat light,
> We are inforc'd to farm our royal realm,
> The revenue whereof shall furnish us
> For our affairs in hand.
>
> (I.iv.43-47)

One occasionally reads that we do not see Richard doing the things he is accused of doing in this play, and Shakespeare's version of show and/or tell is certainly problematical; but in this passage we see and hear Richard doing something. He is selling, for cash on the line, the right to collect taxes; but perhaps farming the realm will not bring in enough cash:

> . . . if that come short,
> Our substitutes at home shall have blank charters,
> Whereto, when they shall know what men are rich,
> They shall subscribe them for large sums of gold,
> And send them after to supply our wants;
> For we will make for Ireland presently.
>
> (I.iv.47-52)

If one form of corruption and extortion won't work, another will. On the other hand, maybe these extreme measures won't be necessary after all, for, as Bushy reports, "Old John of Gaunt is grievous sick." The little prayer that ends the scene is not edifying:

> Now put it, God, in the physician's mind
> To help him to his grave immediately!
> The lining of his coffers shall make coats
> To deck our soldiers for these Irish wars.
> Come, gentlemen, let's all go visit him,
> Pray God we may make haste and come too late!
> *All*. Amen.

(I.iv.59–65)

What is remarkable here, aside from the cynicism and folly, is that the King seems to have no sense that there might be something *wrong* about farming his realm, extorting money, and appropriating the linings of Gaunt's coffers—and in the process disinheriting the exiled Bolingbroke. Richard's performance here is about as insensitive and feckless as "Why uncle, what's the matter?" We don't really learn anything new about King Richard in this scene, but we do see him from a new perspective, in a new context, alone with his friends, the people he really likes, talking the way he sometimes likes to talk. The scene is not designed to elevate the King in the audience's eyes.

Furthermore, the King Body Politic does not and cannot erase the faults of the King Body Natural. Here is Richard the man telling his chums about some things that are going to be done by Richard the King, and the man's imbecilities, translated into action by the King, are going to cause him some trouble. We may infer from this scene that Shakespeare is perhaps suggesting that in order to be a reasonably good king, one must also be a reasonably good man, and that Richard is neither. Morally, the King Body Natural renders the King Body Politic irrelevant and inoperative in this scene. The formal destruction of the King Body Politic occurs in act IV when the King himself begins to learn, definitively, what can happen to a king, when he looks in the mirror, sees that a king's face and a man's are the same, and smashes the mirror and the mocking face of the King Body Natural. Perhaps this fatal gesture can be called the suicide of the King Body Politic.

THE MIRROR AND THE TENURE OF KINGS

Bolingbroke seems to have no interest in the idea of the King Body Politic, divine kingship, or game playing (at least in the sense in which the last term is used here); but he must find something strange in Richard's attitudes and behavior, and he sees some of Richard's actions as clearly illegal. The climax of King Richard's game playing, in act IV, as far as one can tell, seems to Bolingbroke like mere posturing; and if he perceives something more than posturing, he doesn't say so. Thus when Richard asks for a mirror, "That it may show me what a face I have/Since it is bankrupt of his majesty" (IV.i.266–267), Bolingbroke's laconic reply is, "Go some of you, and fetch a looking-glass" (288). The distinction between a mirror and a looking glass is not great, but the mirror, generally speaking, was more likely to have metaphorical connotations than was the looking glass, or connotations of a slightly different sort. The mirror provided a special and instructive view of the world; so did the looking glass, but the looking glass was also, specifically, an aid or adjunct to vanity. Literally, they are the same thing, and Bolingbroke has a way of taking things literally. The mirror is an instrument of instruction, and Richard is instructed by what he sees. Adopting Bolingbroke's usage, he asks for "that glass" (276), and in the glass he sees that Richard Plantagenet looks like King Richard II. The mirror tells him the truth, and he destroys it. Who needs a mirror if it merely shows us who we are? (I do not intend to make any absolute distinction between mirrors and looking glasses; there was a *Steel Glass* and a *Looking-Glass for London* as well as a *Mirror for Magistrates*. But I think the generalization made above is reasonable.)

To those who approach this play in the spirit, say, of Dover Wilson's description of it as "this gorgeous essay on the Divine Right of kings" (whether or not they care to think of a play as an essay), many of the foregoing comments on King Richard will no doubt have seemed one-sided and unfair. But the fact is that in the early parts of the play he behaves with a bizarre ineptitude and a cold indifference to human values which clearly threaten the life of the kingdom, a point made most emphatically by Gaunt in act II, scene i. And it is in the context of preserving the kingdom, the body politic but not the King Body Politic, that some of Wilson's views seem most plausible. Thus, says Wilson, Shakespeare

takes sides neither with Richard nor with Bolingbroke; he exhibits without concealment [surely the best way to exhibit] the weakness of the King's character, but he spares no pains to evoke our wholehearted pity for him in his fall. Indeed, it is partly because it succeeds in holding the balance so even that *Richard II* is a favorite play with historians. It develops the political issue in all its complexity, and leaves judgment upon it to the spectator. Shakespeare's only prejudices [sic] are a patriotic assertion of the paramount interests of England above those of king or subject, an assertion which, following a hint in Froissart, he places upon the lips of the dying John of Gaunt, and a quasi-religious belief in the sanctity of an anointed monarch; and it is part of his dramatic setting that these two prejudices or ideals are irreconcilable under the historical circumstances with which the play deals. . . . Bolingbroke is not rightly understood, until he is regarded as in part at least the puppet of fortune. [But the] . . .break in the lineal succession of God's deputies-elect meant the beginning of political chaos. [Wilson, pp. xxxv,xxxvi]

Certainly Shakespeare displays "a belief in the paramount interests of England," and it is in the context of that belief that the play's action tells us that Richard must go and that Bolingbroke must succeed him. He may or may not have had "a quasi-religious belief in the sanctity of an anointed monarch" (I don't think he did; see below), but we can hardly accept Richard or Carlisle, or even Gaunt, as spokesman for the playwright, not consistently, anyhow. As for the break in lineal succession—well, historically there was such a break, but in the play that Shakespeare wrote there is only one extant possible successor to King Richard, and that is Bolingbroke, a lineal successor because of their common descent from Edward III, not the historical Bolingbroke's argument. As we shall see in more detail later, Shakespeare does not so much as hint at an established line of succession in this play—or perhaps it would be more accurate to say he *only* hints at such a line: Richard is a rightful king as the son of the eldest son of Edward III. The only specific references to the idea of lawful succession come when York reproves Richard for having violated "fair sequence and succession" by disinheriting Bolingbroke and when Bolingbroke himself, having returned from exile, says, "As I was banish'd, I was banish'd Herford;/But as I come, I come for Lancaster" (II.iii.112–113). As far as King Richard is concerned, the succession is an object of benign neglect. He sees himself specifically as the deputy elected by the Lord, not as the grandson of Edward III and therefore his successor.

If Shakespeare had wished to show that there was already a lineal succession beyond Richard—that Richard, that is, had named a successor, having no children of his own—he could easily have done so.

He could have had Richard name Mortimer his heir, as Holinshed tells us the historical Richard did. If Shakespeare had wished to demonstrate that Bolingbroke's usurpation actually violated the principle of lineal succession, there is no obvious reason why he should not have done so in this play. Instead, we have one of those strange Shakespearean silences, a silence that allows us to infer Richard's irresponsibility about the succession and Bolingbroke's legitimacy as successor. And if Bolingbroke is to be seen "as in part at least the puppet of fortune," then it is fortune (or providence) who is in part at least responsible for the decommissioning of God's lieutenant, the "disanointing" of His deputy, and promoting another in his place. Bolingbroke is certainly responsible for his actions, as Richard was for his, but providence and free will have always been bound in an uneasy and ambiguous alliance.

The evidence of the play and of the whole tetralogy suggests that for Shakespeare lineal succession was important, but that it was violated fundamentlly and fatally by King Richard and restored by Bolingbroke, who, as King Henry IV, spends a good deal of time and endures a good deal of anguish lecturing his heir on responsibility and trying, sometimes desperately, to prepare him for kingship. Lineal succession was not, as Shakespeare saw it, a kind of divine mandate, but a reasonably satisfactory way of preserving the continuity of order and justice (see discussion of "Fair Sequence and Succession" below). The paramount interests of the country are decidedly an issue in this play; lineal succession is not, except insofar as it is most striking by its absence from the thinking of King Richard. The play in fact shows how fragile a thing is the sanctity of an anointed monarch, how utterly dependent it is on kingship and on the King's public life, how certain kinds of "defects and imbecilities" render impossible any automatically sanctified condition of the King Body Politic, or of the King. Richard is a human being with serious defects that make him unfit and unable to rule; and I find no evidence that he is *interested* in ruling, or willing to rule, except on a scale altogether inappropriate to his office. He likes to be king, and he wants to remain king, but Shakespeare neatly and elegantly suggests that a king who cannot or will not govern is no king at all. And he shows Bolingbroke governing effectively, if a trifle heavy-handedly, as early as act III, scene i, some time before he ascends the regal throne. The executions of Bushy and Greene may be summary justice, but at least the charges are read to them, and they do not deny those charges. Bolingbroke is interested in governing, and that, I think, is one important reason why, in act IV, he seems much more interested in Gloucester's murder, "who wrought it with the king," than he is in Richard's own unkinging, which has to do with ceremonies and rituals, matters of little concern to Bolingbroke, who has been acting like a king (he has also been Acting King) and who has been thinking of himself as a king—king specifically as chief magistrate.

Richard has been, simply, a destructively incompetent king, feckless and irresponsible, not a great villain like Shakespeare's other Richard, for example, but villainous enough to order Gloucester's murder, which can easily be seen also as part of the King's general unthinking, unkingly irresponsibility. My uncle Gloucester is troublesome: I wish he were dead. Richard's sanctity, as he conceived it, protected him from his conscience, or killed it, or made it irrelevant. He is most attractive and appealing, as everyone knows, when his sanctity is gone forever, when he is, beyond recall, Richard the man, not Richard the king, alone and waiting for death in a spirit very different from that in which he made himself a pathetically absurd *memento mori* in act III, scene ii. But even now, waiting for death, he does not reflect on Gloucester.

Competent or wholly inept, however, Richard is a legitimate king by the criteria of Shakespeare's time, by Shakespeare's own criteria, I should think; and one of the trickiest problems in the play is to try to answer the theoretically unasked question, How far does a king's legitimacy make him invulnerable to rebellion and deposition? At what point, if any, may a legitimate king be deposed? The political orthodoxy of Shakespeare's time had the answer: a king is *always* invulnerable to rebellion; he may *never* be deposed (having arrived at such a reassuring answer, late-Tudor orthodoxy was quite predictably capable of dealing with apparent exceptions—Richard III, for example, and his successor). But the dramatic action of *Richard II* and of the tetralogy that it begins, suggests a very different answer: a legitimate ruler is subject to deposition when he fails to govern or when he misgoverns so seriously as to threaten the destruction of the commonwealth, when he presents a clear and present danger. In taking sides in regard to the destruction or the salvation of the commonwealth, Shakespeare does in fact take sides between Richard and Bolingbroke since destruction lies in King Richard's mis- or non-government and recovery lies in King Henry's. Deposing Richard was, under the circumstances, almost a public duty, a point established in the first two acts; deposition because Bolingbroke was not a Member of Parliament from, say, Wolverhampton East and the leader of his party, calling for an election. After the first two acts, something else is established: as Shakespeare arranges matters, no one but Bolingbroke is qualified to succeed Richard, who has made no provision for the succession and does not do so until he is forced to. In connection with the questions of rebellion, succession, and deposition, I do not find it surprising that Elizabeth said *she* was Richard II, with particular reference to this play. She might even have been thinking of Shakespeare's attack on the King's Two Bodies. In addition to attempted rebellions and depositions, for example, the rising of the northern earls in 1569 and the thoroughly scouted Babington Plot of 1586, there was, at the time the play was written, no more immediately pressing issue than that of the succession. Richard is not the only monarch to be put to some discomfort by this play.

TRAGICAL-PASTORAL-HISTORICAL

The "garden scene" (III.iv), almost purely allegorical, defines the tension between the play's private, human themes and its political themes. It establishes, through the grief of the Queen, the pathos of Richard's situation and hers but in such a way that we are bound to have more sympathy for her than for him. And it establishes, through the allegorical language of the gardeners, both the fact and the necessity of Richard's fall. It is strategically placed, following the King's debasement in the base court and preceding the official un-kinging, the surrendering of the crown to Bolingbroke; it is planted at the center of the play's political action.

The first twenty-three lines deal, in formal and figured language, with the Queen's grief at the absence of her husband. In a brief transitional passage the gardeners appear and the Queen and her ladies "step into the shadow of these trees" to listen to the gardeners "talk of state, for everyone doth so/Against a change" (III.iv.27–28). And they do talk of state, of the garden as a state, in a curiously formal way, developing a short allegory and explicating it, although the allegory is so extraordinarily specific that it is hard to see why an explanation should be required (to pound the lesson in?). The head gardener is, indeed, guilty of poetry in the first degree, but it is not the sort that taxes the interpretive powers (although it has done so); and then he is guilty of something like pedantry for explaining the obvious (if not quite clearly enough for every reader). The scene does not give us information in any ordinary way, and it does not "advance the plot" (merely defining the point at which it has arrived). But, coming between the great confrontation and the deposition, it gives us our bearings in an atmosphere of pastoral calm and in terms of pastoral allegory. It enforces a perspective on our responses to Richard's anguished rhetoric in act III, scenes ii and iii, and act IV, scene i, and it is appropriate that the important thematic material of this scene should be presented in the second language of the sixteenth century, that of clearly defined allegory. It might be argued that the scene has a "realistic" function: to show us how the "common man" responds to the deposition of the King, a point Professor Tillyard seems to have had in mind when he wrote that "the gardener was against the deposition of Richard,"[19] a point not quite accurate and wholly irrelevant. The gardener does find it a pity that the deposition was necessary. Perhaps the Queen's words as she retires to listen give some faint support to Tillyard's view:

> Let's step into the shadows of these trees.
> My wretchedness unto a row of pins,
> They'll talk of state, for everyone doth so
> Against a change: woe is forerun with woe.
>
> (III.iv.25–28)

But these gardeners speak in verse and use elaborately formal similes, and the head gardener can be described as a common man only with reference to his trade or in the framework implied by the Queen's later reference to him as "old Adam's likeness set to dress this garden" (III.iv.73). It is wonderfully appropriate to have "old

Adam's likeness" discussing the failures and the fall of someone who has seen himself, and will continue to see himself, as resembling the new Adam. The gardener is something more than the common man: he is the garden's king and conscience, and the garden, of course, is England. The idea of the first Adam is strongly reinforced by the recollection of Gaunt's reference to England as "this other Eden, demi-paradise." The gardener speaks for the best values of a commonwealth as well as the best human values; and he is a spokesman, or reflector, for the values that Shakespeare intends, or hopes, the audience will hold as .t watches the play and listens to it.

> Go, bind you up young dangling apricocks,
> Which like unruly children make their sire
> Stoop with oppression of their prodigal weight,
> Give some supportance to the bending twigs.
> Go thou, and like an executioner
> Cut off the heads of too fast growing sprays,
> That look too lofty in our commonwealth:
> All must be even in our government.
> You thus employed, I will go root away
> The noisome weeds which without profit suck
> The soil's fertility from wholesome flowers.

(III.iv.29–39)

Almost, the impression is more that of a statesman talking about gardening than of a gardener talking about either gardening or statecraft. The second gardener, not quite in the humble language of his calling, echoes Gaunt's speech in act II, scene i and uses one of the magic phrases of the period in such a way as to call attention to Richard as instigator of the first and fundamental disorder:

> Why should we, in the compass of a pale,
> Keep law and form and due proportion,
> Showing, as in a model, our firm estate,
> When our sea-walled garden, the whole land,
> Is full of weeds, her fairest flowers chok'd up,
> Her fruit-trees all unprun'd, her hedges ruin'd,
> Her knots disordered, and her wholesome herbs
> Swarming with caterpillars?

(III.iv.40–47)

The second gardener, who presumably also bears old Adam's likeness, sees the destruction of "law and form and due proportion" in
Richard's mismanagement of his realm. We have seen it too, from
other vantage points, but the gardeners have a very special perspective. They labor in their vocation; Richard did not labor in his,
hence, the second gardener's somewhat petulant question. His superior answers him: the bad gardener destroys himself as well as his
garden. "He that hath suffered this disordered spring/Hath now
himself met with the fall of leaf" (III.iv.48-49), as nature and the
seasons march irresistibly on. The figure is not easy to miss, and it is
important. Before and after this scene, Richard refers to himself as
the sun and, more often, Christ. But here he is a bad husbandman
who has allowed ("suffered") this disordered spring and met with
the fall of leaf. This is the appropriate comparison, not with the second Adam, but the first, not the God who became man, but the man
who disobeyed God, who failed in his stewardship of the garden,
"this other Eden, demi-paradise." The gardener takes no pleasure in
recording the King's deficiencies as a husbandman:

> O, what pity is it
> That he had not so trimm'd and dress'd his land
> As we this garden! We at time of year
> Do wound the bark, the skin of our fruit-trees,
> Lest, being over-proud in sap and blood,
> With too much riches it confound itself;
> Had he done so to great and growing men,
> They might have liv'd to bear, and he to taste
> Their fruits of duty. Superfluous branches
> We lop away, that bearing boughs may live;
> Had he done so, himself had borne the crown,
> Which waste of idle hours hath quite thrown down.
>
> (III.iv.55–66)

The "great and growing men" are often taken to be Bolingbroke and
Northumberland. They could also be Bushy and Greene, proper
enough subjects for a gardener's remarks.

The Queen in her grief, seeing in him Old Adam's likeness, develops the figure in accordance with the formal pattern of this scene and
asks, "What Eve, what serpent" has tempted him "To make a sec-

ond fall of cursed man?" (III.iv.75-76). The biblical figure continues
in the gardener's well-chosen reply:

> Pardon me, madam, little joy have I
> To breathe this news, yet what I say is true.
> King Richard he is in the mighty hold
> Of Bolingbroke. Their fortunes both are weigh'd;
> In your lord's scale is nothing but himself,
> And some few vanities that make him light.
> But in the balance of great Bolingbroke,
> Besides himself, are all the English peers,
> And with that odds he weighs King Richard down.
>
> (III.iv.81-89)

This is not your common garden-variety gardener. It seems likely
enough that the assessment of Richard ("And some few vanities that
make him light") and of "great Bolingbroke" is intended by the
playwright to be taken as accurate. In the speeches of the Queen and
the gardener we have echoes of Genesis, Psalms, Daniel, and Job—
more than enough evidence, one would think that in this gorgeous
dramatic essay on the divine right of kings, biblical allusions and authority can cut both ways. I see no reason to doubt that the gardener,
who appears nowhere else in the play, speaks essentially what is on
Shakespeare's mind or that he, and the scene in which he appears,
were designed to do anything else. In Richard's scale is nothing but
himself and some few vanities that make him light, a pity: "O, what
pity is it/That he had not so trimm'd and dress'd his land/As we this
garden!" This unusual gardener sees clearly the political consequences of Richard's folly, but he also sees its human implications, its
effect on another human being:

> Here did she fall a tear; here in this place
> I'll set a bank of rue, sour herb of grace.
> Rue, even for ruth, here shortly shall be seen,
> In the remembrance of a weeping queen.
>
> (III.iv.104-107)

The most moving account of the Queen's sorrow comes not from her
but from this eloquent gardener. He presides over this garden; he is
its *genius loci*, the genius of the garden, and his garden is the entire

realm, this other Eden; and he speaks for it. Speaking for it, he makes a judgment about King Richard: "And some few vanities that make him light." That is a very charitable judgment, but the scale will perhaps prompt us to recall St. Michael. His last speech makes of the Queen an emblem, like pity on a monument. The technique enforces the pity of it while insisting on an emotional distance sufficient to prevent our wanting to see Richard restored. The Queen's sorrow and the Queen's tears remind us that someone loves Richard, that his fall is lamented by a weeping Queen. He has another life, of which we here catch the barest glimpse, not much like the life we see elsewhere, but much better. The Queen weeps for the fall of her husband, not for the destruction of the King Body Politic.

If act I, scene ii gives us a paradigm of the play's central dilemma, act III, scene iv, in the archetypal garden, gives us the pity of its resolution. "Down, down I come, like glist'ring Phaeton" (III.iii.78) becomes pitiful and absurd in comparison with the gardener's account of the reenactment of the Fall in the Garden. The figure of the garden as kingdom will reappear in Burgundy's great speech on peace in *Henry V*, and again it will be the prescribed duty of a king to restore the garden, a garden even more profuse and meaningful than the sea-walled garden of *Richard II*.

The Mortal Remains of the King's Body

No matter how light Richard's vanities, no matter how obsessional his idea of the deputy elected by the Lord, something sensible remains of the King Body Politic even after the King is reduced to mere mortality. The King Body Politic lives in the office of kingship. Plowden's report on the Duchy of Lancaster case indicates that the jurists were saying in effect that the king can do no wrong, that the fact of kingship gives a rightness to decisions and actions that might otherwise be doubtful or worse. The idea that the worthier draws to itself the less worthy is particularly relevant here because it says, or seems to say, that the idea of kingship is more important than the mortal king and that this importance gives a special sanctity to the king's actions. Kantorowicz argues that Richard as King Body Politic is appalled at his recognition of the fact that he is also a mortal who can make mistakes and who can die. Carlisle and Aumerle do not see Richard specifically and legally as King Body Politic but, nevertheless, as a divinely appointed monarch who makes the disastrous mistake of refusing God's proffered aid (although it does not seem to be proffered in an especially usable form: the loyalty and good will of Aumerle and Carlisle are only as useful as Richard is able to make them). And Shakespeare shows us Richard as a mortal king full of natural defects and infirmities the seriousness of which is intensified by the fact that he is a king. Someone called Sir Richard Plantagenet, for example, could hardly have seized John of Gaunt's estates and titles and disinherited Gaunt's son. For Shakespeare, the "greater worthiness" of kingship does not subsume or cancel out the lesser qualities of the man who is king; the fact of being a king does not negate defects of mind and character. Richard does almost everything wrong, and the hot vengeance rained upon him is all the more shocking to him because of his conception of himself and his office. Nothing bad can happen to God's lieutenant, but in fact everything happens, and it is all bad.

Shakespeare's King Henry IV is at least a relatively good man in the sense that he tries to do the right thing, tries to rule well, tries to heal his kingdom, and is concerned for its welfare, both for his own lifetime and for the future. He wants to establish good government, and he is thoroughly committed to the principle of lineal descent. His almost constant worry about his eldest son is an effect of his concern for England as well as a more personal sorrow. And Henry V is a good deal more successful, as man and as king: the Chorus alone is almost decisive, but throughout his play, except for one episode, he is represented as a much-loved ruler and an exceptionally gifted one. He loves his work and he is very good at it. It must be easy to dislike Henry V, judging from the number of readers who do; but I would suggest that such dislike must result from disagreement with Shakespeare's idea of a great national hero. If some of us don't like him (I do), the dislike was not shared by the playwright. The sense of responsibility, the joy, the chivalry, the gallantry, the humor, and the humility—all illustrate the point. Clearly, there has been a steady progression from Richard II to Henry V: from Richard, the King, who thinks of God's and his subjects' duties to him, to Henry IV, who thinks of his duties to his country, to Henry V, who thinks of his duties to his country and to God.

In *Richard II*, the state is badly wounded by the follies of the King; in *Henry IV*, the wounds are for the most part healed, part of them by radical treatment; in *Henry V*, the state becomes once more a healthy organism, as close to a perfect one as we are going to get in a history play. The reign of Richard is characterized by rampant and shameless injustice—the murder of Gloucester, gross extravagance, exorbitant taxation, extortion, the disinheriting of a great lord; in *Henry IV* justice slowly reasserts itself under the guiding hand of the King and through the actions of Prince Hal and others (but not Prince John of Lancaster or Westmoreland), with the allegorical figure of Justice appearing early in *2 Henry IV* and emerging triumphant at the end; in *Henry V*, a system of justice is in operation, with only enough defects to remind us that we are seeing an at least theoretically possible world, not an unqualified utopia. Everything that happens in *1* and *2 Henry IV* and *Henry V* negates the idea of a kingship that does away, by definition, with natural defects and imbecilities on the part of the king. The world gets better as the men who run it get better. We may object to the war with France. On historical grounds alone we ought to object to it, even on the purely practical grounds that its consequences were predictably disastrous. But it produced a stunning (and exciting) English victory, and King Harry's notion was that victory should be followed by marriages, his marriage to Kate, England's to France. The England of Henry V is shown by the playwright to be immeasurably better than the England dishonored, described with such anguish by Gaunt in act II, scene i of *Richard II*.

And a new aspect of the doctrine of the King's Two Bodies, very different from that represented by King Richard, has been brought into play. The king is dead; long live the King. That familiar paradox sums up the special sense in which, according to the doctrine, the King never dies. In fact if not in law, by act III, scene i, when Bushy and Greene are sent off to execution for corrupting the King, one king has already died figuratively, and another has taken his place. By act III, scene i, England has once more an effective king, Bolingbroke, whereas Richard has scarcely functioned as a king at all, having in effect vacated his office when he disinherited Bolingbroke. According to the jurists who decided that the boy Edward VI could lease lands of the Duchy of Lancaster, the King Body Politic was an infallible divine corporation whose actions could not be defeated by any mortal technicalities. But as the doctrine developed, the infallible king, the King Body Politic, became the Idea of kingship, and the metaphor of the immortal king became the idea of the continuity of government, which, in any rational system, must be the idea of the continuity of order and justice. It would seem that for Shakespeare, at least, this continuity did not depend nearly so much on a strictly observed line of succession—although that is certainly important—as it did on the competence of the ruler, his desire to provide good government, and his ability to earn loyalty and/or enlightened acquiescence from his subjects.

As we descend from the speciously dazzling heights of Richard the sun-king to the flawed but impressive humanity of Henry IV and Henry V, we ascend from the injustice of King Richard's time to the settled order and justice of King Henry V's time. This twofold reverse parallels the reverses in the fortunes of Richard and Bolingbroke in *Richard II* and the decreasing strength of King Henry IV and the growing strength of Prince Hal in the *Henry IV* plays.

At the same time, we move from a notion of God-centered kingship, shown to have been false, to an idea of man-centered kingship; and from a concern with divine retribution to political cause and effect, including the "necessities" that King Henry IV grimly perceives and is finally prepared to meet in act III, scene i of *2 Henry IV*. Carlisle's eloquently horrendous predictions of disaster in act IV of *Richard II*, just before Richard's somewhat extended surrender of his crown, were no doubt politic on Shakespeare's part, perhaps even necessary: if you are going to show on the stage the justifiable deposition of a rightful if not very righteous king, you had better have someone on hand to say that it is a bad business and to make the orthodox prophecies. But as prophecies they are wrong, even if one takes them to refer to the struggle between York and Lancaster usually called, with quaint exaggeration, the Wars of the Roses, a Tudor invention. There was a struggle, and from time to time it was serious enough, as was the Percy rebellion; but England did not become a field of Golgotha and dead men's skulls, not in the plays and not in historical fact. Carlisle is an expert spokesman for Tudor political and historiographical orthodoxy, and like real-life Tudor apologists, he speaks with considerably more skill than truth.

For a Christian writer like Shakespeare, man-centered kingship was clearly preferable to any notion of God-centered kingship, particularly Richard's conception of it, and it is consistent with orthodox and familiar Christian doctrine. It gives man, or king, freedom of will and of choice (Richard is merely willful), and the exercise of that freedom is man's, or king's, test and challenge. One is free to make right choices or wrong ones. Richard, acting out his regal charade, made some notoriously bad choices and committed some notable crimes. Thinking of himself as God's deputy, he tended, unconsciously and not at all surprisingly, to get the roles reversed. If you really imagine yourself to be the deputy elected by the Lord, you are likely to fall into a kind of human parody of the Lord's behavior—particularly if you preside over a political system that encourages your belief. The deputy Angelo in *Measure for Measure* finds himself in an analogous situation and falls into roughly analogous criminal behavior; unlike King Richard, however, he knows what he is doing.

The dichotomy between mortal king and immortal kingship appears in the climax of the deposition scene, particularly in act IV, scene i, lines 244–320. Richard has undecked "the pompous body of a king" (250). Quite coherent with grief, he sees himself as no man's lord, having no name, no title. In a passage of almost embarrassing self-pity, he wishes that he "were a mockery king of snow,/Standing before the sun of Bolingbroke./To melt myself away in water-drops!" (IV.i.260–262). He hasn't precisely changed places with Bolingbroke, but now Bolingbroke is the sun, and Richard, if not dazzled, would like to melt. He calls for a mirror, sees in it the reflection of a man, and smashes the mirror: "A brittle glory shineth in this face;/As brittle as the glory is the face,/For there it is, crack'd in an hundred shivers" (IV.i.287–289). "As brittle as the glory is the face." The glory is that of the king, the face is that of the man. Both converge in the mirror and turn out to be the same. Hence Richard destroys the mirror, the brittle reflector of his brittle glory. The face of the man Richard remains. "Mark, silent king, the moral of this sport—/How soon my sorrow hath destroy'd my face" (IV.i.290-291). The sorrow of the undecked, mortal Richard has destroyed the glory of the immortal king, the King Body Politic. Bolingbroke, whose interest in theories of kingship is minimal, is moved only to a laconic pun: "The shadow [darkness] of your sorrow hath destroy'd/The shadow [image] of your face" (IV.i.292-293)—unless Bolingbroke, irritated by Richard's elaborate performance, thinks of him now as simply a player-king and by "shadow" means "image" both times. Richard, in any case, picks up the shadows and dwells in, and on, them for a while longer:

> 'Tis very true, my grief lies all within,
> And these external manners of lament
> Are merely shadows to the unseen grief
> That swells with silence in the tortur'd soul.
> There lies the substance. And I thank thee, king,
> For thy great bounty, that not only giv'st
> Me cause to wail, but teachest me the way
> How to lament the cause.
>
> (IV.i.295-302)

The very silence of the "silent king" has its own eloquence. And no doubt Bolingbroke understands well enough what Richard is talking about; but by now it doesn't matter—not to him. Richard's show of grief is in every sense a formality. The substance of the unseen grief lies in the tortured soul, not in the clamorous shadows of his public displays. He is through with talking about Pilates delivering him to his sour cross, and in his next allusion to Scripture, he is setting the word against the word and having difficulty reconciling them: " 'Come, little ones'; and then again,/It is as hard to come as for a camel/To thread the postern of a small needle's eye" (V.v.11-17). In his newly found mortality—his humanity—he has undergone a great change. To his Queen:

> Join not with grief, fair woman, do not so,
> To make my end too sudden. Learn, good soul,
> To think our former state a happy dream;
> From which awak'd, the truth of what we are

Shows us but this. I am sworn brother, sweet,
To grim Necessity, and he and I
Will keep a league till death.

(V.i.16–22)

"Our former state" included being the deputy elected by the Lord—"a happy dream," no more. "The truth of what we are" is very different: there is no deputy elected by the Lord, not in Richard's sense. And then there is the human sorrow and the enforced separation, not of king and queen, but of man and wife. It is different from that "divorce" that Bushy and Greene are alleged to have made between the King and the Queen (III.i.11–15). That allegation, if true, represented a part of Richard's self-indulgence. Here, he understands very well the nature of the "grim necessity" that requires their separation.

He is far more attractive as a man than as a king, and Richard the unkinged man is a better man than King Richard had been. Shakespeare implies all through the tetralogy that in order to be a good king one must first be a good man, but he must also be something more; and it remains for King Henry V to be the good man, the good king, the soldier, the lawgiver, the learned theologian, and the amusing lover. Henry V is so persuasively and agreeably drawn that he becomes almost believable. The sad sun-king recedes into a sad and cautionary tale told to "good old folks" (V.i.41); "And some will mourn in ashes, some coal-black,/For the deposing of a rightful king" (V.i.49–50). Shakespeare is very insistent here that, in our relatively new-found sympathy for Richard the man, we do not forget his former pretensions, of which he has not quite been able to rid himself—assuming that the allusion above is to Ash Wednesday. At the time he parts from his queen, he still has much to learn, and he is still rather like pity's emblem. He is still obsessed with the pathos of his situation, and down to the moment of his death he does not refer specifically to any of these actions that made his deposition necessary, that made a rightful king unrighteous. As a human figure, he is a lot more impressive than the hollow image of a king. At the hands of Exton's thugs, he meets something like Gloucester's fate, but there is no indication that Gloucester's death has yet touched his conscience. Something is still missing.

Richard has learned some political lessons, of course, and can accurately predict Northumberland's future treachery (V.i.55–68); but that prediction was an easy one to make, and Warwick uses it again, as a kind of explanation of Northumberland's actions, in *2 Henry IV* (III.i.80–92). And his education has proceeded in other areas as well. His resourceful imagination leads him, in his solitude, to play many people, none contented:

> But whate'er I be,
> Nor I, nor any man that but man is,
> With nothing shall be pleas'd, till he be eas'd
> With being nothing.
>
> (V.v.38–41)

Never quite having understood what he had been, he knows what he will be. The tragedy of the King's Two Bodies is about over. Richard cannot call on his name to arm itself and fight for the King. He is unkinged, "and straight am nothing," unaccommodated man. It is hard to be pleased by that, better to be eased by being nothing. The sign of his conversion is the sound of music, but the music doesn't keep time:

> . . . how sour sweet music is
> When time is broke and no proportion kept!
> So is it in the music of men's lives.
> And here have I the daintiness of ear
> To check time broke in a disordered string;
> But for the concord of my state and time,
> Had not an ear to hear my true time broke:
> I wasted time, and now doth time waste me.
>
> (V.v.42–49)

It will remain for Prince Hal to imitate the sun, not Richard's way, and redeem the time when men least think he will.

Earlier, in a reflective moment, Richard might have asked himself, "Why so large cost, having so short a lease,/Dost thou upon thy fading mansion spend?" He doesn't need to now: it is too late, and he has the answer. The sweet music signifies the new order of Richard's soul; the broken time reminds him of the past. He wasted time, but for a king to waste time is not to be merely idle and trivial: it is to neglect his duties—all of them—to himself, to his country, to God. Now, as a man, he can do what Carlisle and Aumerle had urged him to do as a king. According to Holinshed, when the murderers rushed in (there were eight, enough to do the job), Richard seized the weapon of one of them and killed four before being poleaxed by Exton (Hosley, pp. 96–97). And in the play, after the murder, Exton says, "Take hence the rest, and give them burial here" (V.v.118). This is not the Son of God, or the sun-king, delivered to his sour cross, but a man fighting for his life and losing, resisting this kind of death but not defeating it. His follies as a king caught up with him, and his discovery that they had done so gave him strength as a man.

Richard is not reduced to humanity, he is elevated to it. His game-playing days, if not his genius for self-deception, were over when he smashed the mirror, and so was the idea of infallible kingship. But the King is not dead: "On Wednesday next we solemnly set down/ Our coronation. Lords, prepare yourselves" (IV.i.319–320). And in fact Bolingbroke had been king since act III, scene i. Time wastes Bolingbroke very quickly; in the opening scene of *1 Henry IV*, he has already aged perceptibly. But he did not waste time. He did think that his kingship had been for the most part a failure, but it wasn't. He never claimed divinity, but at his death the King is still alive, to redeem his father and to redeem the time.

II

The Silent King; Providential Intervention Fair Sequence and Succession

ONE OF THE MOST STRIKING FACTS ABOUT THE BOLINGBROKE OF RICHARD II is that at critical points he does not tell us what he is thinking about or what he plans to do. He takes important actions that must certainly have been based on hard decisions—or so it would seem; but the decisions we hear him utter are almost redundant: "In God's name I'll ascend the regal throne" (IV.i.113); "On Wednesday next we solemnly set down/Our coronation" (IV.i.249-250). But he has been acting king since act III, scene i at least (the sentencing of Bushy and Greene). He has no soliloquies and no confidants in *Richard II* (and only one real soliloquy and two confidants in *Henry IV*, Warwick and Westmoreland, with whom he mainly discusses his son, not affairs of state). Unique among the great Shakespearean, Jonsonian, and Marlovian conspirators, tragic or comic, he keeps his motives and decisions to himself, so much so that we might be justified in asking to what extent he is actively engaged in a conspiracy at all. It would be unreasonable to require stage conspirators to confide in their victims, but they all confide in audiences in soliloquies or inform them through talk with their fellow conspirators or, like Claudius in *Hamlet*, reflect on their crimes and on what they have gained or lost by them. Shakespeare obviously found political conspiracy of more than routine interest, and he represented some fascinating ones on the stage; but Bolingbroke seems almost to be engaged in a private conspiracy of silence.

We assume that Bolingbroke has something definite in mind

when, in the first scene of *Richard II*, he accuses Mowbray of a staggering array of treasons, the murder of Gloucester being the most important. No doubt we can safely assume that he is somehow getting at Richard, who bears the major guilt in Gloucester's death; and we naturally assume that Bolingbroke knows about Richard's guilt, since everyone else seems to. But these are merely assumptions based on hindsight: Bolingbroke himself says nothing about Richard's responsibility until act IV. To most of us it is simply inconceivable that Bolingbroke's charges are directed solely against Mowbray, but nothing in the play's opening scene tells us anything else. We are, perhaps, invited to guess at what he actually has in mind when he makes his accusation; but he doesn't talk about it, not even with his father, before going into exile, even though, in view of what has been happening, Gaunt might have expressed some curiosity about what his son has been up to. Gaunt was conspicuously present when the charges were made ("Old John of Gaunt, time-honoured Lancaster"—I.i.1), yet when father and son part for the last time (at the end of I.iii), the talk is about the sorrows of exile and how to lighten them. These facts are particularly striking in view of the substance of act I, scene ii—the absolute necessity of passive obedience. Presumably, Gaunt has not perceived what his son has been up to, and we should therefore be cautious in making our own assumptions.

It is important to remember that the King's responsibility for Gloucester's death was so clearly established in the chronicles and in *Woodstock* (an understandably anonymous play much more openly emphatic than Shakespeare's play in its condemnation of Richard) that it can hardly have been a mystery to many people watching the play.

Again, and even more important, at the end of act II, scene i when we learn from Northumberland that the just-disinherited Bolingbroke is returning from exile equipped for an invasion ("eight tall ships, three thousand men of war" [II.i.286]), it does not require great sublety of mind to see that he must have decided to do what in fact he does. Both Hall and Holinshed describe widespread hatred of Richard and a movement to recall Bolingbroke, a movement so vast as to suggest something more like a popular mandate than a plot. Yet in the play, all, or almost all, is silence. We don't know when Bolingbroke decided to return or the details of his decision, in spite of that decision's overwhelming importance. Shakespeare maintains silence on the subject when anyone who could read might well have known the story and might well have been puzzled by the omissions. The conditions of Bolingbroke's decision should be of consuming interest, and that interest is systematically frustrated. One may argue that actions speak louder than words, but on this subject some words would clarify something that we must assume Shakespeare did not want to clarify. A major part of the action of four plays arises from a decision, made in Brittany, by a principal character; and about the circumstances of that decision, as opposed to its outcome, we really know nothing—hence all the guesswork, some of it demonstrably bad.

In fact, we don't know when he made his decision—before or after his father's death and his own disinheriting—although it is possible that on this matter we can make something like a passable assumption. The problem is familiar: we learn that Bolingbroke is on his way home at the end of the same scene (II.i.277 f.) that contains the death of Gaunt and the disinheriting of the man who was his rightful heir "by fair sequence and succession." We are shown a good reason for Bolingbroke to return, and then we learn that he has embarked before (presumably) that reason existed. At least that's the way it looks to most readers, and perhaps that is the way it sounded to contemporary audiences. But Shakespeare's chronological games are notorious, like those of most of his fellow playwrights, and I do not think it is self-evident that Shakespeare intends his audience to see Bolingbroke jumping the gun: at this point, it is almost a relief to know that he is on his way. Perhaps this is why Shakespeare has Northumberland specify "eight tall ships, three thousand men of war." Holinshed, in his amiable way, repeats conflicting reports: "fifteen lances" or "not past threescore persons" or the force specified by Northumberland (Hosley, pp. 76–77). In view of the outrage just perpetrated by Richard, eight tall ships and three thousand men of war seem appropriate. Bolingbroke's return with fifteen or thirty chums would be less likely to raise the spirits. It is certainly possible that "Shakespeare's strategy makes Bolingbroke's return morally ambiguous,"[1] but I suspect that an audience is less likely going to be troubled by the chronology and what it implies than is the curious reader. One other odd detail: when Bolingbroke arrives, the text does not give us the impression that he has an army with him; he *appears* to have arrived more or less alone, although we must no doubt assume that he didn't. Then, as in Holinshed, his friends begin to gather—not all of them the sort of friends one would choose if the choice were wider. The information that he is coming with an army indicates that Richard will have his work cut out for him; if we then get the impression that Bolingbroke arrives alone, there will be a clear contrast with Richard on his return from Ireland, with Richard's friends forsaking him as rapidly as Bolingbroke's assemble. (The most specific statement about a popular uprising comes, briefly, from Scroope, III.ii.104–120. It's interesting to hear about, but we don't see it—one of many instances of Shakespeare's version of show-and-tell, not-show-and-tell, show-and-not-tell.)

Even if we assume, however, that Bolingbroke has embarked for England before hearing of his father's death and his own disinheriting, there is on the face of it nothing particularly surprising about his return (unless surprise must spring from violations of Tudor notions of obedience), just as there was nothing notably just about his banishment—Richard's alternative to a duel that would have actually settled something. The banishment was no doubt legal enough, but in King Richard's England, under the circumstances associated with his notions of kingship, legality and justice aren't necessarily the same, just as positive laws generally have no necessary and automatic connection with considerations of right and wrong. At worst, Richard's grand larceny provides a *post hoc* justification for Bolingbroke's decision to return home (just as the Dauphin's providential tennis balls provided King Harry the fifth with a legitimate reason to go to war with France—they are a challenge to a duel and as such are a good deal more convincing a motive than is Canterbury's exposition of the Salic Law, which may justify a claim on the French throne but not a war to make the claim good). Everyone has seen that Bolingbroke has extraordinary luck at key points on his way to the crown (e.g., Richard's proximity, in Flint Castle). Whatever his original intentions in returning from exile with a small army and navy, Richard or God or providence provided a nearly unanswerable argument. If he intended to return as a rebel with ambitions for the crown, Richard, by his unadvised violation of fair sequence and succession, has made him a rebel with a cause, a cause with which almost anyone else can easily sympathize.

It is precisely when Richard casually, and with some lack of sensitivity, disinherits his cousin and ignores York's instructive protests that one is likely to run definitively out of patience with him. And it is in that scene that we learn just how serious his situation is likely to become, just how swift and condign the retribution is likely to be. Shakespeare has made it easy for any member of an audience to regard Northumberland's good news as providential—just as both Hall and Holinshed thought they saw the hand of providence at work in the rise of Bolingbroke and the fall of Richard (Hosley, p. 81). However we interpret the timing of events in act II, scene i, it is clear enough that Richard has misbehaved prodigiously and that hot vengeance is on the way, and that point, I think, is underscored by Bolingbroke's silence. We can guess all we want about his specific reasons for returning, but Shakespeare makes such guessing more or less irrelevant. It would have been another matter if he had shown the Archbishop of Canterbury negotiating a coup with Bolingbroke (as historically he did) or Bolingbroke sitting down to discuss strategy with the Duke of Brittany or Sir Thomas Erpingham, but that is exactly what he does not show us. Bolingbroke does not even discuss strategy with Northumberland; when the time comes, he simply sends him to Richard with an unanswerable ultimatum.

We may ask why Shakespeare is so reticent about specifying the idea of providential intervention since Hall and Holinshed have already led the way. But they were not writing a tendentious play about the justifiable deposition of a rightful king. And after giving us an almost interminable list of Richard's shortcomings as king, Holinshed can say, with his characteristic lovable idiocy, that Richard "was a prince the most unthankfully used of his subjects of any one of whom ye shall lightly read" (Hosley, p.89). Perhaps Holinshed thought such a *pro forma* protestation was necessary, although it certainly doesn't amount to much; but in any case, he was writing an enormous and not wholly exciting chronicle in rather soporific prose, not a play for the public stage, about a king who was compared with Elizabeth during the later years of her reign. Some of Bolingbroke's silences are probably Shakespeare's as well (and, as we know, the deposition scene was omitted from the first two quartos of the play), understandable and discreet silences. If people are comparing Elizabeth with Richard, one had better not specify that Richard's fall was providential.

There is another possible reason for considerable caution on this subject. As we have seen, Robert Persons paid his negative compliments to the idea of the King's Two Bodies in *A Conference about the Next Succession to the Crown of England* (1594). In the same work, he describes how providence manifests itself through rebellion against tyrannical or incompetent rulers and then often provides better rulers than those deposed. In all Christian realms, princes have been deposed

> for just causes, and . . . God hath concurred and assisted wonderfully the same, sending them commonly very good kings after those that were deprived, and in no country more than in England it selfe, yea in the very lyne and familye of this king Richard, whose noble grandfather king Edward the third was exalted to the crowne by a most solemne deposition of his predecessor king Edward the second, wherefore in this point there can be little controversie. [p. 62]

And

> I know not whether every man here have considered the same, to wit that God hath wonderfully concurred for the most part, with such judicial acts of the commonwealth agaynst their cruel Princes, not only in prospering the same, but by giving them also commonly some notable successor in place of the deposed, thereby to justify the fact, and to remedy the faulte of him that went before. . . . God disposeth of kingdomes and worketh his wil in Princes affayres as he pleaseth. [pp. 33–34]

It seems to me that Shakespeare takes the same view, differing perhaps on a very minor point: God sent a king as good as a king could be under the circumstances, and that king was succeeded by one of Persons's and Shakespeare's "very good kings," a wonderful concurrence and assistance in a judicial act of the commonwealth. I assume that Shakespeare was familiar with some of Persons's work (it certainly caused a sensation when it appeared in England), but he needn't have gone to Persons for the view that the first two Lancastrian kings were superior to Richard II.

But Shakespeare is not wholly silent on the subject of providential intervention: he does raise it once, in York's familiar account of Bolingbroke's and Richard's riding into London. The crowd received Bolingbroke with cheers, but not Richard:

> No man cried "God save him!"
> No joyful tongue gave him his welcome home,
> But dust was thrown upon his sacred head;
> Which with such gentle sorrow he shook off,
> His face still combating with tears and smiles,
> The badges of his grief and patience,
> That had not God for some strong purpose steel'd
> The hearts of men, they must perforce have melted,
> And barbarism itself have pitied him.
> But heaven hath a hand in these events,
> To whose high will we bound our calm contents.
> To Bolingbroke are we sworn subjects now,
> Whose state and honor I for aye allow.
>
> (V.ii.28–40)

This passage, with its seemingly perfunctory concluding couplet, is often attributed simply to York's weakness, but since he has been established throughout the play as a kind of reflector for audience responses to both Richard and Bolingbroke, I see no reason why he should be deprived of that function now, even though he is shortly to be involved in a spectacle of low comedy. Richard is an object of pity, but God had "some strong purpose," and "heaven hath a hand in these events." If we can believe York here, we can easily enough believe that the same agencies, under the general rubric of providence, had also been at work earlier, all along, since all those other events prepared the way for this sad but necessary sight. To pity Richard is not to wish him to resume his throne.

Another silence is rather different from the ones just discussed. The so-called Doncaster oath was to be of some importance historically. Holinshed tells us, in his engaging way, that when

Bolingbroke returned from exile he swore (at Doncaster) to Northumberland, Sir Henry Percy (Hotspur), and Westmoreland "that he would demand no more but the lands that were to him descended by inheritance from his father and in right of his wife" (Hosley, p. 77). "Moreover, he undertook to cause the payment of taxes and tallages to be laid down, and to bring the King to good government" (p. 77). One detects a certain inconsistency here. More important, this account follows one in which the same historian describes how "divers of the nobility, as well prelates as other, and likewise many of the magistrates and rulers of the cities, towns, and commonalty . . . devised, with great deliberation and considerate advice, to send and signify unto Duke Henry [Bolingbroke], . . . requiring him with all convenient speed to convey himself into England; promising him all their aid, power, and assistance if he, expelling King Richard as a man not meet for the office he bore, would take upon him the scepter, rule, and diadem of his native land and region" (Hosley, p. 76). After *that*, the Doncaster oath doesn't amount to much, and in *1 Henry IV* it is used against the King only by men who might be described as having interested motives.

Maybe it was politically discreet for the historical Bolingbroke to swear his oath in public to the magnates who were to help him to the throne. It was even more discreet for Shakespeare's Bolingbroke to do nothing of the sort. His only comment on that subject is to York: "As I was banish'd, I was banish'd Herford;/But as I come, I come for Lancaster" (II.iii.112–113)—an ambiguous statement, perhaps, but no oath; and since the founder of the Tudor dynasty claimed, not with total candor, to be of Lancastrian (as well as Arthurian) descent, and therefore to be restoring the house of Lancaster to the throne, a statement like "I come for Lancaster" could have its own peculiar and complex resonances. The Doncaster oath put the historical Bolingbroke in the wrong since it is well known that all politicians must and do keep their promises. For Shakespeare's Bolingbroke, such an oath would be not only untrue but also superfluous: you don't invade your native country without some notion of putting yourself in charge. Shakespeare, therefore, has Northumberland allude to the oath, with no great precision of language, at II.iii.147–150 and III.iii.103–120, and Northumberland is a notable liar, here and in the two plays that follow. (For Bolingbroke he is a useful liar but a liar anyhow.) Shifting the blame to Northumberland is another way in which Shakespeare cleans up the historical Bolingbroke. In *Richard II* and *1 Henry IV* the Doncaster oath becomes a fiction of Northumberland's, not a lie of Bolingbroke's. The whole business is worth some reflection: Shakespeare cleans up Bolingbroke, but he is to be seen, obviously enough, in the context of human political standards, not of impossible moral absolutes. As with his son, the measure by which he is to be judged is human, nothing else. There are, of course, different kinds of politicians—Richard and Bolingbroke, for example.

* * * * *

"His Very Words"

As the king dies in the chamber called *Jerusalem*, rather than in the Holy Land toward which his eyes have for so long been turned, the second of the worries that have beset him has already ceased, for he dies reassured as to the worthiness of his son to rule his kingdom. But he has not washed away the blood of Richard that sprinkled him to make him grow. The rebel has conquered rebellion. The usurper has not been parted from his crown till death. But the primal sin of murder has not been expiated. It is necessary to recite these facts again and again if the moral significance of the plot [of *Henry IV*] is to be understood. [Campbell, p. 240]

Repetition is naturally an aid to understanding, but the facts recited again and again need much consideration. The King dies "in the chamber called *Jerusalem*." The dying King's words about Jerusalem are specific, and he speaks them in gratitude:

Laud be to God! Even here my life must end.
It hath been prophesied to me, many years,
I should not die but in Jerusalem,
Which vainly I suppos'd the Holy Land.
But bear me to that chamber; there I'll lie;
In that Jerusalem shall Harry die.

(Emphasis added; IV.v.235-240)

I take it that the key words are "Laud be to God!" and "Which vainly I suppos'd the Holy Land.'' He would hardly offer praise to God if he thought that the purpose of his intended pilgrimage had been thwarted. He gives thanks because he senses that he has succeeded, not that he has failed. This may be, as most critics have argued, an irony or an anti-climax, but I strongly doubt that it is. King Henry now realizes that the Jerusalem which he had erroneously supposed to be the Holy Land is, instead, England's green and pleasant land. The rebellions are finally over, he has been reconciled with a beloved son, and he believes that that son will do well enough. He himself has done all that he could, with resolution and fortitude and self-sacrifice. Laud be to God indeed. Why not?

On yet another matter Shakespeare seems to have imposed a remarkable silence. Hardly anyone doubts that King Henry IV was responsible for the murder of Richard, that he hinted so strongly at his wish for Richard's death that the discreditable Exton couldn't resist. This is what we learn from Exton himself in one of the play's shortest scenes (V.iv—eleven lines). The consensus on this matter is so strong that it is not unusual to find the flat statement that Henry "ordered" Richard's murder, as Richard ordered Gloucester's. Naturally, the historical Richard's fate was sealed by Henry's coronation. The continued existence of a deposed monarch is bound to be a constant threat to his successor (in history, on the stage), and Henry IV would have been uncharacteristically naive if he thought his own kingship safe while Richard was alive. And when the time comes, when Exton, not with the most exquisite tact, appears with the body, King Henry assumes the blame for having wished Richard dead and vows a pilgrimage in expiation for that fatal wish.

Although I do not wish to seem serpentlike in legalistic subtlety, I must say that King Henry is guilty of precisely what he takes the blame for. That there is moral guilt is beyond question, but Shakespeare has done everything possible to minimize Henry's direct involvement with the crime, giving a partial falsification of history in the process, just as, in *3 Henry VI*, he had gone along with a popular falsification of history by having Richard Duke of Gloucester murder the deposed Henry. The fact is, we don't see or hear King Henry breathing his pathetic sigh: "Have I no friend will rid me of this living fear?" (V.iv.2). We hear it repeated by a (presumably) total stranger, so to speak, toward the end of the play, in a very brief scene, the stranger's recollection of the king's words corroborated only by his own servant, who was perhaps in no position to disagree: "These were his very words, . . . he did" (V.iv.3,6). Exton is apparently the kind of political opportunist who can be counted on to turn up to perform useful services—without being asked. He knows well enough that the deposed Richard is a threat to his successor, and he knows very well what to do about it.

Shakespeare shows us Richard III and Macbeth looking for murderers and giving them their commissions; he shows us Claudius conniving with Laertes for the murder of Hamlet and sending the order for Hamlet's death to England; he has Oliver commission Charles the wrestler to do a job on Orlando and Frederick order Oliver to do another. In *Richard II* he shows us no such thing. In Holinshed there is no question. Immediately after putting down the rebellions that followed his coronation, the new king caused "King Richard to die of a violent death" (Hosley, p. 96). Dramatically, there seems to be no good reason why Shakespeare could not have followed his usual practice when dealing with murders, suborned or otherwise, if he wished to be unequivocal on the subject; it is, after all, an important point.

It may be argued that "everyone knew the story" from Holinshed and that Shakespeare was merely writing a kind of dramatic shorthand; but the murder of Richard is very different from the murder of Gloucester. Everyone knew about *that* from Holinshed too, and from *Woodstock*, but it is also discussed at some length in the play, and in such a way as to leave no doubt whatever about Richard's guilt. Furthermore, King Henry admits to having wished Richard dead (on that subject he is not silent), but Richard never, not even in his last soliloquy, assessing his spiritual state, mentions his guilt in his uncle's death. King Henry's confession of guilt is precise—that is like King Henry; King Richard's is nonexistent—even though silence was not his specialty. Another problem is that the words of the new king as repeated by Exton sound nothing at all like the Bolingbroke we have come to know in this play, nor, so far as I can discern, is he much given to looking "wishtly" at people (V.iv.7). He ensured Richard's death by deposing him, but Shakespeare seems intent on keeping as much distance as possible between the King and the crime.

Having gone this far—more than far enough, no doubt—I am of course bound to concede that at the end of *Richard II*, King Henry IV vows to make a pilgrimage of expiation, "To wash this blood off from my guilty hand." He has conceded that he "wished" Richard dead. If the wish was voiced, particularly within earshot of Exton, that wish caused Richard's death, and King Henry is guilty to the (considerable) extent that anyone in his position would be. But Exton, not Henry, is the murderer; Henry did not hire a murderer; and he did not "order" a murder. The direct cause of King Richard's death was Exton and his murderous ambition, suitably rewarded.

The question, then, is not whether "the primal sin of murder" has been expiated, but whether another sin has, and if so, how. Professor Campbell argued that the primal sin has not been expiated: King Henry never made his pilgrimage. She does not specify that making the pilgrimage would have done the job, but she does seem to suggest that the failure to make it indicates that the sin has not been expiated. Wishing for someone's death, even under circmstances that may well encourage someone else to bring it about, does not quite constitute the primal sin of murder; the wish and the act are two very different things. Particularly, it does not constitute that sin as the term is generally understood. *That* primal sin, as we know, occurred when God rejected one form of sacrifice and accepted another. The murder that followed was an archetypal crime, and it was a brother's murder (this is not quite a mere technicality). Cain wished Abel dead and he killed him. That is the primal sin, or at least the sin that hath the primal eldest curse upon it. Shakespeare understood fully the significance of that, as he abundantly demonstrates in *Hamlet* and clearly enough in *Richard II*. It is Exton who commits the sin of murder, and he is rewarded with words appropriate to the primal sin: "With Cain go wander thorough shades of night,/And never show thy head by day nor light" (V.vi.43-44).

Henry IV vows a pilgrimage "To wash this blood off from my guilty hand." He was not guilty of the primal sin of murder, Exton was; but he has finally expiated the lesser but still very serious sin of having wished Richard dead, and he has done so by making an appropriate pilgrimage. A kind of pilgrimage begins as he goes into exile in *Richard II*, and a crusade ends with his death in Jerusalem in *2 Henry IV*. It is worth recalling that Mowbray, too, dedicated his life to crusading (*RII*, IV.i.91–100) and, as Carlisle's language suggests, to expiating his sin, which bears some resemblance to King Henry's: he had been, reluctantly, and after long delay, responsible for having Gloucester murdered on King Richard's orders. (It requires a far more gifted casuist than I to determine whether the greater guilt is to be attached to first resisting and then carrying out the command of the deputy elected by the Lord, or wishing the ex-deputy dead in the presence of someone capable of making the wish come true.) It is also worth recalling that Bolingbroke, before the interrupted trial by combat, had described himself and Mowbray as resembling "two men/That vow a long and weary pilgrimage" (*RII*, I.iii.48–49). One pilgrimage, one crusade, is more conventional than the other, but both are important: both men expiate their sins. Mowbray's "black Pagans, Turks, and Saracens" (*RII*, IV.i.95) are Henry's rebels; Mowbray's Holy Land is Henry's England, Gaunt's "other Eden, demi-paradise."

The pilgrimage ends, I suppose, and the crusade begins, when the fighting starts—the fighting in which the King is directly involved—almost at the beginning of *1 Henry IV*. The idea of the crusade, as Shakespeare presents it, is an extension of the idea of the pilgrimage; it symbolizes a desire for expiation, and it represents a commitment to Christianity. There is nothing new about the idea of life as a pilgrimage, and the pilgrimage of an embattled king committed to the restoration of justice can certainly pass for a crusade. (In the present discussion pilgrimage and crusade are closely linked and more or less interchangeable.) The idea of the crusade first appears at the very beginning of *1 Henry IV*, a crusade that must be deferred because of the military reverses in Wales. Holinshed mentions neither pilgrimage nor crusade until late in his account of Henry IV (Hosley, p. 115). Shakespeare makes the crusade a continuing if somewhat muted aspiration of the King's, from the beginning of his reign to the end, perhaps taking his cue from Holinshed's account of the prophecy about death in Jerusalem (Hosley, p. 117).

Holinshed reports the facts, and Shakespeare, as usual, gives them special meaning.

That Shakespeare intends the pilgrimage-crusade theme to be taken seriously is indicated by several details: the references to pilgrimage and crusade early and late in *Richard II*, the obvious seriousness, even passion, with which King Henry speaks of his projected crusade in act I, scene i of *1 Henry IV* and again, briefly, at the end of act III, scene i of *2 Henry IV*, and especially by the "Laud be to God!" passage of act IV, scene v of the same play. The crusade, as it turns out, is to bring Jerusalem to England, not to take Englishmen to Jerusalem. A later poet had a similar idea. The dying King's revelation may again suggest the idea of providential intervention: while King Harry was doing what had to be done, the heavens, far from raining hot vengeance on his head, had it in mind that he should be surprised by joy. His career can be seen as a continuing act of expiation, none of it pleasant, and a crusade to restore domestic peace and justice; it ends with reconciliation with his son and the much desired death in Jerusalem, that is, home, other Eden, demi-paradise.[2]

It is worth adding that, aside from his other topics of silence, Bolingbroke is silent on the joys of kingship and regal pomp and ceremony; kingship, ruling England, has no obvious attraction for him; it is a job, and the only possible satisfaction he derives from it is suggested by his dying speech. The other silences call attention to this one. He returned from exile to make himself king but said nothing about that, which means also that he said nothing about his expectations: would it be *agreeable* to be King Harry the fourth—perhaps like riding in triumph through Persepolis? It seems to be just barely conceivable that he thought so, but the only evidence is a weary confession that he had not realized how miserable it could be (*2HIV*, III.i.45-79). Like his predecessor, under different circumstances, he was sworn brother to grim necessity. He wanted Richard dead; presented with the fact, he dealt wisely and appropriately with a murderer he had not employed but whose action solved a problem for him, at a dreadful cost: *Richard II* ends with the moving words of a sorrowful monarch who had never expected to enjoy being king but who had not known how bitter it could be. He does, however, achieve his one firmly stated ambition, metaphorically: his pilgrimage to the Holy Land. It is part of the sadness surrounding this king that he did not realize until shortly before his death where his true Jerusalem lay.

Bolingbroke was never infatuated with the glories of kingship or the pleasures of power. Nothing he says or does in *Richard II* suggests for a moment that he *likes* the prospect of being king; nothing in *Henry IV* suggests that he enjoys it or had expected to. Everything in the three plays demonstrates a compelling sense of duty and responsibility. He is no Claudius or Macbeth, conscience stricken but unable to surrender his regal pleasures; for him there *are* no regal pleasures, and he had not expected any—except possibly the love of his eldest son. The hand that put Henry IV on the throne did not provide enjoyment or gratification, not in the anticipation nor in the far-from-glad possession.

It would be wrong to imagine that providential intervention in the affairs of men and states is necessarily both kind and pleasant. Providence was not kind to Richard or to his successor, but arguably (I believe this is Shakespeare's argument) it was kind to England. Providential intervention notoriously does not absolve its immediate recipients of responsibility for their actions, or even, perhaps, for their thoughts. Bolingbroke's return from exile was finally a good thing for England, but not for Bolingbroke. Exton's murder of Richard solved a serious problem for England and its new king, but it certainly gave no pleasure to anyone. This does not mean that Bolingbroke was a mere passive instrument—far from it—although in purely practical terms his luck was remarkable, if not pleasant. He made some decisions, and providence in effect bore him out. He came to the crown, as he says at the end, by "by-paths and indirect crook'd ways" (*2HIV*, IV.v.184), and he certainly paid for it. Until then, he had had little reason to praise God or bless providence. He had, however, done what he was supposed to do; he did pull a kingdom together for his heir.

*   *   *   *   *

That Shakespeare held "a quasi-religious belief in the sanctity of an anointed monarch" (Wilson, p. xxxv) seems to me just barely possible, but very unlikely; and in fact I doubt that he held a *quasi-*

religious belief in anything. If he believed in such sanctity while writing *Richard II*, he resolved the implicit dilemma by having Richard "desanctify" himself. Bolingbroke doesn't force Richard to do that; Richard does it himself, because Shakespeare wanted him to. With Richard's ritual of unkinging goes a good deal of the soil of his successor's achievement. Strictly speaking, Bolingbroke did not depose an anointed monarch (a technicality, but an important one), and it is important that we see King Richard "disanoint" himself. Furthermore, if Shakespeare believed in the sanctity of an anointed monarch while writing *Richard II*, he seems to have forgotten about it while writing the three histories that follow—and not because he thought that Henry IV and Henry V were not legitimate kings. And, having obliterated divine kingship and the most dangerous aspects of the doctrine of the King's Two Bodies in *Richard II*, he emphasizes their opposites, man-centered kingship and the King Body Natural, in the plays about Henry IV and Henry V. He represents these views of kingship as preferable to those held by Richard.

It is not at all certain that Shakespeare believed all rebellion against anointed monarchy on the face of it indefensible. Aside from the obvious examples, there is the special case of the great rebellion of 1399. But his ground rules for rebellion were stringent, whether he was dealing with English or with Roman history (or with fake Roman history, as in *Titus Andronicus*); and I assume that in questions of rebellion and deposition, the English ground rules apply also to Rome.[3]

Thus, to glance at a pretty piece of knavery: in *Titus Andronicus*, rebellion against Saturninus is justified because, although he has impeccable credentials (eldest son of the late emperor), he has the bad habit of condoning and committing particularly nasty atrocities under the tutelage of his "Gothic" queen, who seems to be a kind of preliminary study for Cymbeline's nameless second wife. *Titus* is of course a transparent political parallelograph, to use Professor De Luna's word. The Romans accept the aptly named Lucius (apt in both the Roman and the British contexts) as their savior when he enters the city leading a disciplined army of well-disposed "Goths," recent converts to the cause of Rome—that same Lucius who had treated the Gothic prince Alarbus to what appear to have been the cozier aspects of burning (of heretics) and of hanging, drawing, and quartering, part of "our Roman rites," the smoke of which ascends to heaven like incense. Another Lucius leads another successful Roman rebellion, all huddled up in the last stanza of *The Rape of Lucrece*, a strange, partly political poem that has much in common with *Titus* but is a good deal less offensive.

In a somewhat more satisfying play, *Julius Caesar*, the murder of Caesar is not justifiable (I include murder of a *de facto* head of state in the general category of rebellion), partly because murder seldom is, partly because the motives of the conspirators are inconsistent and self-interested; and Brutus's rationale (II.i.10–34) is suppositious in substance and conditional, so to speak, in mode: "may" and "would" are the chief operative verbs as Brutus speculates on what Caesar *might* do if he *were* to become emperor. It is even weaker than his defense, which can be distilled to "Caesar was ambitious; I am honorable; trust me." The conspirators are agreed on the desirability of murdering Caesar but not on the reason for doing so or on who else should be favored with assassination. Furthermore, they have no plans for a replacement for Caesar even though he is represented as being in effect the head of state. We do not always notice this conspiratorial omission, but it is likely to have seemed a glaring one to an audience in 1599. Scholars occasionally refer to Brutus's attitudes and actions once he is in power, but he is *never* in power. The conspirators succeed in murdering Caesar, but they have no notion whatever of what they should do next except leave Rome quickly. They are rounded up or wiped out with almost ridiculous ease. Except for the fact of Caesar's murder, there is an almost uncanny anticipation of the Essex rebellion, which lay over a year in the future. (I guess Shakespeare wrote *Julius Caesar* late in 1599, after Essex's return in disgrace from Ireland, during the first part of his time of despair, desperation, and depression; and after Henry V, with its reasonably graceful compliment to Essex. I suspect, but cannot prove, that the play contains a warning: this is no time for a rebellion; nature will soon run its course; you can't produce a successor; you would infuriate the populace; and you certainly would not be able to cope with the Queen's loyal followers and councilors, who are in any case much cleverer than you are and have their own political axes to grind—and who know how to grind them. I guess and suspect these things.)

Back at home, rebellion against Henry VI is wrong because it is carried out under the wrong auspices, for mainly self-interested reasons (no matter that historically Edward IV was a far better ruler than Henry VI and was in fact one of the best of kings), and because although Henry is an incompetent king, he is also a good and decent man. Cade's rebellion is of course simply awful, and for Shakespeare, proletarian rebellion would seem to be absolutely indefensible. There is an interesting variation in *Coriolanus*: the mutinous citizens in act I, scene i certainly have a case, although perhaps not an adequate one, for rebellion; Menenius's musty parable of the belly and the body does not answer it. But, most important, the unnamed First Citizen is no Jack Cade; he is a highly intelligent, shrewd, articulate, literate, professional proletarian revolutionary. He is a bad actor but a bright one, and he represents a danger that Shakespeare clearly perceived in the first decade of the seventeenth century.

Rebellion against Richard III and Macbeth is justified because they are represented (Richard mendaciously) as usurpers, murderers, and tyrants.[4] Rebellion against King John is not quite justified because, although he is deplorable, the rebel lords are even more deplorable for having done a deal with the French. (In *Richard II*, Shakespeare minimizes Bolingbroke's French connections, and in *Lear* the French king is suddenly called home on business so that the audience need feel no discomfort about Cordelia's expedition from France to rescue her father.) The rebel lords are not quite condoned, but hot vengeance is certainly rained on King John's head, or at least on his digestive system. Shakespeare had to be careful here, since, beginning with Bale, John was being rehabilitated as a Protestant martyr and was being favorably compared with Henry VIII for his sturdy independence from the Papacy. Finally, as far as I can discover, no one has ever found serious justification for the Percy rebellion in *1* and *2 Henry IV*, not even those scholars who love to savage Bolingbroke. The closest we can come to justification is to say that the King brought all his troubles on himself; but the rebels have no serious case, and they oppose themselves against a legitimate, rightful, although certainly not sacred, monarch.

Shakespeare took a pragmatic, almost professionally political, view of rebellion. It is not, on the whole, a good thing: it produces undesirable side effects; rebels are often worse than the rulers they depose; rebellion upsets the orderly transition of authority by fair sequence and succession; it tends to result in the murder of the deposed ruler; it usually does more harm than good. But it is not unthinkable, not always indefensible; it may under some circumstances be justified and not only against a jolly bogeyman like Richard III or a tormented tyrant like Macbeth or a Machiavellian murderer like Claudius but also against a thoughtless and dangerously irresponsible king like Richard II. But it must be managed carefully, by rebels and by playwrights, especially this playwright, who had firm but not obdurate convictions about the settled order of things and who was, in *Richard II*, dealing with a touchy, almost explosive subject.[5]

That settled order of things is pretty well summed up in York's famous and critical question to his feckless nephew just after the disinheriting of Bolingbroke: "For how art thou a king/But by fair sequence and succession?" (II.i.198-199). This is a constitutional question that Shakespeare takes seriously and with which he deals in constitutional and legal terms. Richard has no answer perhaps because he does not recognize a real question; but on this question hangs the legality of his kingship. There is really only one way to be King in England at least, and that is by fair sequence and succession.[6] When the principle is violated, there will be trouble, as every student of these plays knows—although not every student recognizes the precise nature of the trouble. Shakespeare has his own ways of defining the terms and establishing the claims. They are on the whole Tudor ways, applied in such a manner as to be not entirely pleasing during the later years of the last Tudor, who eventually knew, or thought, that she "was" Richard II.

When Bolingbroke first appears on stage after his return (II.iii), the game is already nearly up for Richard. He had appointed his uncle York Lord Governor during his absence in Ireland (II.i.219-220), and his uncle is in no position to hold the kingdom against Bolingbroke; furthermore, York knows very well the extent of Richard's injustice to Bolingbroke. To banish Bolingbroke, then disinherit him, farm the realm, issue blank charters for extortion, appoint York Lord Governor, and then leave for Ireland is not the best way to stay in control. And when Bolingbroke is confronted by his uncle York (II.iii.81 ff.) and scolded for breaking the terms of his exile, he responds with arguments that are answerable only by notions that will not bear examination: it was his duty to stay out of the country because the King had ordered him to do so; it was particularly bad to return in arms (although it would have been a little foolish to return unarmed). Richard's actions have already deprived that argument of credibility: it won't do to banish someone legally and then illegally disinherit him when he is out of the country. One might argue, I am not certain how convincingly, that Richard viewed banishment as a prelude to disinheriting the powerful son of a powerful but aged father.

We may assume (we usually do) that Bolingbroke's legal arguments are a smokescreen for his plan to make himself king, but, taken at face value, and in view of the circumstances surrounding his exile and disinheriting, they are more than credible—they are persuasive. The whole passage (II.iii.112-135) is important as a statement of his personal position and his position under the law. His motives may be questioned, but it would be hard to refute his arguments—and not merely the arguments that rationalize his return. The most important and least refutable is, "If that my cousin king be King in England,/It must be granted I am Duke of Lancaster" (122-123). It is a constitutional point and, though more concisely put, the point that York had made to Richard in act II, scene i. Its repetition, with Bolingbroke's characteristic, almost epigrammatic, conciseness, is not redundant. Richard has had expert and accurate advice, and he has ignored it. The repetition serves to remind York of something, and it may help keep a point fresh in the audience's mind. York can do his duty and scold his competent nephew for coming in "braving arms against thy sovereign" (II.iii.111), but in view of what he has already told, and asked, Richard, he is in no position to argue very seriously with Bolingbroke.

Bolingbroke is not only concise, he is also grammatically, legally, almost legalistically, precise: "If that my cousin king be King in England. . . ." The careful subjunctive implicitly repeats and glosses York's question, "For how art thou a king . . . ?" Perhaps the in-

definite article is merely metrical; it is certainly suggestive: "There
are lots of kings; you are one of them. How are you one of them except by the familiar, customary, orderly arrangement? That's how
people become kings. If you violate that principle by disinheriting
the son of the late Duke of Lancaster, your own kingship is in question." Bolingbroke's statement carries this same suggestion of kings
in general—"My cousin king . . . King in [not *of*] England"—
with the implication "There are lots of kings around; if my cousin is
the king here, the one *we* have, he had better not ignore our laws and
customs; if he does, he is not our king."⁷ There is nothing about
divine kingship or the King's Two Bodies here; Shakespeare is interested in a different kind of law, and he gives Bolingbroke a very
clear view of the legal bases of kingship; it is radically different from
King Richard's, and the action and argument of the whole tetralogy,
including the epilogue to *Henry V*, suggests that it is the view that
Shakespeare would like to see prevail. As a legal view it is generally
consistent with Tudor ideas about the succession, but it is radically
opposed to Tudor notions of regal infallibility.

Since Richard has not "granted" that his cousin duke is Duke of
Lancaster, since he has in fact deprived him of that title, what follows is obvious enough: "My cousin king" is not "King in England."
England now has an acting king called Henry, and as the scene ends,
Acting King Henry is on his way to weed and pluck away the cater-
pillars of the commonwealth, a procedure executed in act III, scene i
and discussed at length by the gardeners in act III, scene iv. He first
identifies them as "Bushy, Bagot, and their complices" (II.iii.165),
but in act III, scene i they are Bushy and Greene, a satisfying if unex-
plained change, Bushy the caterpillar and Greene the weed, weeded
and plucked. Weeding and plucking are what mainly occupy King
Henry IV until the end of his reign.

*   *   *   *   *

The weeding and plucking, and taking out some stings and teeth,
are necessitated by Henry IV's overriding preoccupation: the general welfare of his country and the problem of the Prince of Wales.
These concerns are inseparable; without a competent heir the future
would be bleak indeed. The historical Henry IV had a competent
heir and a very worrying one. The point here is his frequent and pas-

sionately expressed concern for the future welfare of England. His
paternal disappointment in his apparently erring son he subordinates
to the larger and more important problem of England's future. His
main efforts throughout his plays are devoted to ensuring, or trying
to ensure, at least the possibility of a tranquil civil polity; the whole
point of the dying King's extended conversations with his eldest son
is to see that England will not be populated, or misgoverned, by apes
of idleness. It is not that Shakespeare gives Henry IV any special
credit for begetting sons. Historically, he did and Richard did not,
and that is more or less that. But Shakespeare's King Henry is concerned about his country's future and Shakespeare's Richard was
not. King Henry tries to see to it that his heir abandons his wild ways
and prepares for kingship. Richard did not even name an heir whereas Henry has one and urges reform and responsibility on him; he
also urges one of his younger sons, Thomas, to "observe" his brother
carefully and mediate "Between his greatness and thy other breth-
ren" (*2HIV*,IV.iv.26). History, so to speak, provided the sons;
Shakespeare provided the King's profound care.

With regard to the whole question of fair sequence and succession, we may say (and often do) that the deposition of a rightful king
is in itself, by definition, a violation; but in *Richard II* Shakespeare dis-
arranges matters so that the burden of violation falls much more
strongly on Richard than on Henry: in *Richard II* the only heir in sight
is Bolingbroke. In this play, the childless Richard has no heir and
does not name a successor as the historical Richard did. This fact represents, I suppose, another rough similarity between Richard and
Queen Elizabeth. (Whether or not Elizabeth, on her deathbed,
actually named James VI as her successor is not an issue here. If she
named a successor, she did not do so until she lay dying in 1603. She
had excellent reasons for her silence, which she also enjoined from
her councilors and subjects; but the succession had been a serious
issue since 1558 and since 1567 a critical one.)

An understated, almost inaudible, aspect of Richard's general irresponsibility in the play is that he has not fathered an heir and does
not name one until he is forced to when the range of possible candidates is somewhat limited. When Richard ignores York's question
about the basis of his kingship, he ignores the basis itself. It is easy for

him to do this, as we have seen, because in disinheriting Bolingbroke, he has destroyed that basis; he has implicitly denied the principle of linear succession, a point driven home with utter clarity by York, to Richard, and again by Bolingbroke, to York, who understands the situation well enough but is not quite prepared to accept its implications: "If that my cousin king be King in England,/It must be granted I am Duke of Lancaster."

In effect, then, Shakespeare has his Richard violate lineal succession and his Henry IV restore it by passing on the crown to his son. One may argue that, having violated it himself, Henry simply sets out to legitimize his reign and establish a new succession: but if Shakespeare had intended that argument to prevail in those terms, he would, I should think, have shown Richard naming Mortimer his heir. Not only does Shakespeare *not* do that, but he also reserves the Mortimer claim until *1 Henry IV*, where it is raised only to be discredited and to discredit those who raise it. It becomes the pretext for a rebellion the aim of which is not to restore legitimacy but to depose the King and dismember the kingdom. The Percys had expected King Henry to remain their protégé. When he declared his independence of them, they reacted much as Warwick the King-maker was to do when his protégé Edward IV declared *his* independence.

Richard is as silent about the succession as he is about the murder of Gloucester, but Henry IV is utterly serious about it. He makes every effort to see that his heir will rule well, and the heir pretty well sums up the validity of the new succession and the provenance of the crown:

> My gracious liege,
> You won it, wore it, kept it, gave it me;
> Then plain and right must my possession be,
> Which I with more than with a common pain
> 'Gainst all the world will rightfully maintain.
>
> (*2HIV*, IV.v.220–224)

This nonnegotiable position is orthodox Tudor doctrine, almost super-orthodox, since Henry VII made himself king "by right of conquest" as well as by irregular Lancastrian descent. But it comes in the context of a dramatic action that includes also the justifiable deposition of a rightful king, and in the political context of an age in which unthinkable rebellion could be rationalized after the fact. What passed for Tudor political theory was as full of inconsistencies as anyone could reasonably expect, inconsistencies that Shakespeare knew how to exploit. As Lily B. Campbell put it: "The Tudors upheld the principle that 'the Crown once possessed, cleareth and purifies all manner of defaults or imperfections.' They had to. They also insisted that under no circumstances was a subject permitted to judge his king or to undertake to execute judgment upon him by rebelling" (Campbell, p. 156). It is unthinkable except when it succeeds. Or, "Until Bolingbroke succeeds, he is a rebel; once he is in power, England's citizens have no responsible alternative other than to submit" (Bevington, p. 245). This is Tudor doctrine, and one may apply it to these plays, as Professor Bevington and others have done. But it is a damned unpleasant way to do business. It may legitimize Henry IV; it may legitimize Henry VII. It could legitimize almost anyone, but I doubt that Shakespeare would have wished to go quite that far. It rationalizes and legitimizes rebellion after the fact; but Shakespeare had already, in *Richard II*, legitimized it *before* the fact. He not only justifies Henry IV as opposed to the Percys, he also justifies Bolingbroke as opposed to King Richard.

In Elizabeth's time, as we know, the deposition of Richard took on sinister implications, was subject to infamous analogies; and the performance of a play showing the justifiable deposition of King Richard (once, in February 1601, under extraordinary circumstances) could elicit from Elizabeth the famous and bitter observation, "I am Richard II, know ye not that? . . . He that will forget God, will also forget his benefactors; this tragedy [almost certainly Shakespeare's] was played 40tie times in open streets and houses" (quoted by Wilson, p. xxxii).[8] For Shakespeare, fair sequence and succession could result from deposition if the deposed presented a clear and present danger and the deposer had the proper credentials. The earlier Tudors "had to" see it this way too, but they could hardly have anticipated the particular construction that William Shakespeare was to put on the deposition of Richard II. The last Tudor didn't anticipate it, either, and she seems to have taken a hearty dislike to it when she saw it. No doubt she would have disliked it even more if the play had been printed with the deposition scene during her lifetime; but it wasn't. (There seems to be a consensus that the play was performed with the deposition scene although it was printed without it. The scene must certainly have been included in the special performance requested and partly commissioned by Essex's friends in February of 1601, who would have enjoyed seeing an anointed king disanoint himself. Guilty creatures, sitting at a play,...guilty players, too.)

*   *   *   *   *

Lineal succession to the throne of England is a relatively minor issue in *Henry V*, as is rebellion. Good kings have other things to do than putting down rebellions and begetting and trying to educate heirs. An incipient rebellion is snuffed out easily although it must cause the King some pain. And the familiar details of the reign of King Henry VI could not have encouraged much emphasis on the succession issue. After the reign of Henry V the succession became an increasingly important public issue, between York and Lancaster, brutally resolved by Tudor. Shakespeare has already dealt at length with that question and alludes to it only briefly, and poignantly, in the Epilogue to *Henry V*, where he asks us to look back and reflect on the reign of this star of England as an instance of how well a king could govern. In the next reign, he tells us, things went badly wrong, but that is no part of *Henry V*. The English succession is something of which we are briefly and entertainingly reminded: in the delightful persiflage attending the wooing and winning of fair Kate, the begetting of a son is part of the game, and part of the business, of kingship; but this king can combine business with pleasure, and in view of how badly things were destined to go in Henry VI's time, perhaps a brief, light-hearted allusion was the best kind.

But lineal succession is not exactly out of the picture; the legitimate King of England claims also to be the legitimate King of France, a claim more striking, even offensive, to some modern readers than to an audience in 1599. It is an important claim, because how we take it determines to some extent how we take King Harry and how much glory we can attach to his stunning victory at Agincourt. I assume that Shakespeare expected some members of his audience to penetrate the mass of crude indigest verbiage in which

Canterbury gives legal sanction to the claim and that he expected many more not to. For those who didn't follow Canterbury, there was the Dauphin's insult, the "Paris balls." The whole business is an excellent instance of the playwright's working his way up and down both sides of the political avenue, with something for almost everyone. Wars were not fought at the drop of a hint in Henry V's time, or in Shakespeare's, but a war against the French could easily be justified in the popular imagination, not, perhaps, by the King's claim, whatever its basis, but certainly by the Dauphin's frivolous response, which, whatever his original intention may have been, turns out to be a challenge to a duel. Shakespeare neatly exploits English feelings of superiority over the French, and perhaps he shared them—he certainly makes the French utterly trivial and the English gallantly serious. (Dr. Johnson, taking a similar view, happily confined it to the more peaceful realm of lexicography.)

As such claims go, King Harry's was probably good enough, but the question any modern reader with some knowledge of history is likely to raise (and it was raised in some quarters even in Shakespeare's time)[9] is, How can one use a dynastic claim, no matter how time-honored it had become, to justify an aggressive, expansionist war, a revival of the Hundred Years' War, a war that was finally to end so disastrously for England after Henry V's death? With characteristic brilliance, Shakespeare implies that the claim is a good one, but he justifies the war on other grounds—the war as a metaphorical duel—and, as we shall see later, it is victory in a war fought on those other grounds that gives supreme validity to the dynastic claim. The outcome of a duel reflects the will of the Supreme Judge.

The conquest of France and the stipulated joining of England and France are to be seen as desirable, a kind of wooing and a conquest that becomes metaphorical, a marriage, on the political level analogous to the wooing, winning, and wedding of Kate. This, in any case, is how the French King and the Queen finally see it:

Take her, fair son; and from her blood raise up
Issue to me; that the contending kingdoms
Of France and England, whose very shores look pale
With envy of each other's happiness,
May cease their hatred, and this dear conjunction

Plant neighbourhood and Christian-like accord
In their sweet bosoms, that never war advance
His bleeding sword 'twixt England and fair France.

And,

God, the best maker of all marriages,
Combine your hearts in one, your realms in one!
As man and wife, being two, are one in love,
So be there 'twixt your kingdoms such a spousal
That never may ill office, or fell jealousy,
Which troubles oft the bed of blessed marriage,
Thrust in between the paction of these kingdoms,
To make divorce of their incorporate league;
That English may as French, French Englishmen,
Receive each other! God speak this Amen!

(V.ii.366-386)

The point could hardly be made more emphatically. In its insistence on marriage and reconciliation, with political reconciliation constituting a kind of marriage itself, this play is almost a comedy, as has been more than once suggested,[10] one that requires at the end, if not elsewhere, the willing suspension of disbelief and also of time. Time and history will march on—no one knew that better than Shakespeare—but the artist stops them briefly, for our instruction, an invitation to grace, rejected.

But what about the claim itself? Henry V revived the claim to the French throne of his great-grandfather, Edward III, who claimed it in right of his mother, Isabella, eldest daughter and second child of Philip IV of France. Edward, with a noble French wife and a royal French mother, saw a gilded opportunity and made his claim on the female side, and the validity of that claim is the substance of Canterbury's nearly intolerable discourse on the Salic Law, a lawyer's dream but not, I think, lawyer's doubletalk—Shakespeare's, perhaps, because there seems to be more than one kind of succession at issue here.[11]

To counter Edward's claim, and then Henry's, the French revived the Salic Law, which purported to ban claims to the throne on the female side. The point of the Salic Law was not simply bloody-mindedness about women: it was designed, or used, to guarantee indefeasible hereditary right, the kind King Harry enjoyed in England. But whatever kind of legitimacy Edward's claim might have had, it is hard to believe that his principal motives were substantially different from those of other feudal monarchs: profit, and an excuse to busy giddy minds with foreign quarrels. Looting, pillaging, and kidnapping all paid well and distracted attention from domestic inconveniences. Thus Edward III started the Hundred Years' War (1337–1453), and his great-grandson revived it, with temporary success and, during the "reign" of Henry VI, total disaster.

As represented in the play and as known through the chronicles, the whole business was less outrageous to contemporary eyes than to modern ones. The connection and the rivalry between England and France were nothing new in 1337 and an old story in 1599. English kings from William the Conqueror to Richard III were of French or Norman French birth or French ancestry, and almost all of them had French wives. Richard II was born in Bordeaux and was known as Richard of Bordeaux. If we try to adopt the perspective of someone hearing the first performance of *Henry V*, we will perhaps remember some of the history of King Henry's claim; we will reflect that a dynastic claim to someone else's throne is credible in a fairly direct ratio to the claimant's ability to make good his claim (clearly not a problem for King Harry, we shall observe); we will hardly forget that the Queen of England is also—according to her offical titles, at least—Queen of France, Ireland, and Virginia. An elaborate English claim to the throne of France will not fall like a thunderbolt on astonished ears. And then of course there *are* the tennis balls.

If, sitting or standing in the Globe, we are not surprised to learn that Henry V has an acquisitive eye on France, we might be somewhat startled, or stupefied, by the way in which the longing of that eye is given legal sanction by the Archbishop of Canterbury. We will guess that something is up; something usually is in long speeches in Shakespeare, and Canterbury's is a long speech, although not so long as it seems (I.ii.33–95). It is interesting that although this speech goes on for over sixty lines, Canterbury never comes to grips with modern instances; he does not talk specifically about Edward III's claims or Henry V's. The main point of his long, tedious, obscure, and by now almost incomprehensible disquisition on the Salic Law is that it originally applied to an area of Germany and was "not devised for the realm of France" (55). Furthermore, although it bars claims on the female side, at seven points in these sixty-odd lines Canterbury alludes to or specifies female claims and claims on the female side, one of which he concedes was false, allowing us to assume the others were legitimate. And in response to the King's no doubt perplexed question, "May I with right and conscience make this claim?" (96), he clinches his argument with biblical support: "For in the book of Numbers is it writ:/'When the man dies, let the inheritance/Descend unto the daughter' " (98-100). This is a strange, but explainable, way to justify a man's claim to a throne: let the inheritance descend unto the daughter. Edward III was no one's daughter; neither was Henry V, although his great-grandmother was.

For most readers, Canterbury's speech is a nightmare, and some great actors and directors have not known how to deal with it. Olivier's turning it into a comic episode is notorious—with Canterbury reading it all from an enormous sheaf of loose pages, dropping some, with Ely officiously helping and getting his hands slapped for his pains. But it is seriously intended as a legal justification for making a claim on the female side—at least I assume this is the playwright's intention. Canterbury argues that the claim justifies war, and he says so in a notable passage of patriotic gore. No doubt he says what he thinks the King wants him to say; but I doubt that Shakespeare expected everyone in the theatre to follow the details of the argument, and I am sure he saved the famous tennis balls until after Canterbury's speech to provide the necessary patriotic and emotional underpinning for the French enterprise. As justification for war, however, the claim is flummery; it may be lawful enough, but it also points in another direction, and the war itself is not only justified but in effect legalized by something else, since the tennis balls constitute a challenge to a duel from the French Prince to the English King. The war is undertaken as a metaphorical duel, and the point of that we shall consider in the discussion of *Henry V*.

Obviously Shakespeare did not have to versify a tedious, pedantic, legalistic speech out of Hall to justify an English claim to the French throne. I would suggest that the tangled complexities of the long disquisition on the Salic Law represent an instance of the art that conceals something like subversion. We know very well how desperately important an issue the succession was by the time *Henry V* was written in 1599. We know that the Queen was pressed to name her successor and that for good and prudent reasons she did not do so. We know that she had forbidden public discussion of the subject and that she had ordered courtiers and councilors to stay away from it. And we know that Sir Robert Cecil and the Earl of Essex were among those committed to the claim of James VI of Scotland.[12]

A speech validating a claim to the *English* throne on the female side, particularly one that ends with "let the inheritance/Descend unto the daughter!" might possibly be taken as a windy, legalistic ratification of Mary Tudor's right to rule and of Elizabeth's legitimacy;[13] 1599, however, is very late in the day, impossibly late, to be offering such an argument in such tangled language, except, perhaps, as a superfluous act of bemused piety. But the speech can also be taken as an argument for the Stuart claim, and that, I believe, is why it is put into such intolerable language and why it says nothing at all specific about either Edward III or Henry V. It supports their claims in terms so abstract as to suggest that they are simply assumed. Everyone knew that Henry V was the great-grandson of Edward III; almost everyone knew that Mary Stuart was the great-granddaughter of Henry VII, granddaughter of that Henry's daughter Margaret, who married James IV of Scotland and whose descendants were barred from the English throne by the will of Henry VIII. There is a rough analogy between that will and the spurious Salic Law. Elizabeth was not the only woman with a claim to the English throne; Mary Stuart had one, too, until her accidental beheading in 1587. And her son James had a claim, on the female side, which was finally officially and triumphantly recognized. I believe that Shakespeare, in his pursuit of the idea of fair sequence and succession, was here, in Canterbury's speech, moving into forbidden territory and arguing, for the judicious spectator, the validity of James Stuart's claim to the throne of England (and possibly of France, which throne had once been his mother's).

Maybe there is a little more to it than this. Canterbury emphasizes female succession as well as claims on the female side. "When the man dies, let the inheritance/Descend unto the daughter" is a very specific statement although there is an obvious difficulty in applying it to the issue of the succession in 1599 (it is not a brief for the Infanta of Castile). What man? What daughter? My own answer to the first question is I don't know; I do not believe there is any intention to suggest that on the death of Henry VII the crown of England should have descended to his daughter Margaret. My tentative answer to the second question is Mary Queen of Scots. If Shakespeare is upholding the claim of James Stuart, I believe he is also cautiously suggesting that if James has a right to inherit, then his mother had also had such a right, one that was definitively canceled in 1587. Shakespeare had made a similar suggestion, also with great caution, in *King John*, where, on one level, Prince Arthur plays Mary Stuart to John's Elizabeth. If these conjectures are correct, Shakespeare nevertheless did not run any serious political risk since he did not specify James or Mary any more than he specified Edward or Henry. He is, I think, contemplating a double (or rather, unfortunately, bigamous) marriage: England and France, England and Scotland. Canterbury's complexities might well have appealed to Robert Cecil's subtlety; they might even have amused him. He was, after all, committed to the succession of James Stuart to the English throne and brought it about.

But it is a little hard to imagine that Shakespeare was in effect working for Sir Robert Cecil, writing subtle, if not incomprehensible, propaganda for Cecil's candidate; and both Cecils, father and son, found it well within their powers to restrain their affection for the candidate's late mother. He was probably giving a syntactically tormented version of his own views, which, on the subject of James VI, would have coincided with those of Essex as well as those of Cecil. If Shakespeare's company took sides in the rivalry between Essex and Cecil, they took sides with Essex.[14] At the time Shakespeare wrote *Henry V*, Essex was presumably still in Ireland, not yet in disgrace, although getting close enough, and the Prologue to act V pays him a reasonably gracious compliment. And it was Essex's friends who, in February of 1601, thought that a revival of *Richard II* would help stir up local (London) sentiment in favor of the Essex rebellion. It didn't, but they thought it would—a tribute to their naiveté as the Privy Council's refusal to do anything more than issue an admonition to the players was a tribute to its sophistication; the Council didn't care for sedition, but its members perceived clearly enough that a play did not and could not launch a rebellion. It is interesting, however, that the "tragedians of the city" who appear at Elsinore in a play perhaps written in 1601 and perform another subversive play are clearly identified as Shakespeare's company: "Hercules and his load, too."

I see no indication of any provable connection between Essex and the Bolingbroke of *Richard II* (some very dangerous allusions were made later, between 1597 and 1599); but the reference in *Henry V* is mildly suggestive, in the implied, and very discreet, comparison of Essex to King Harry. Unlike the unfortunate Hayward,[15] Shakespeare seems not to have thought of Essex as a likely, or desirable, successor to the aging Queen. I suspect that he did see in Essex, however, some qualities that a good ruler should have—affability, intelligence, personal charm, the ability to make people like him (charisma), great military talent, and personal flair and style. King Harry the fifth had the right to France that James Stuart had to England, and he had some of the qualities of the Earl of Essex, but none of his very striking defects.

The Essex question occurs again in *Julius Caesar* (Brutus), *Hamlet*, and *Troilus and Cressida*, and it is clear that Shakespeare did not see Essex consistently as a paragon—although perhaps a paragon *in potentia*. The question is decidedly *de trop* here except for one point: Hamlet has long been thought to have *something* to do with Essex; Fortinbras, I am convinced, has *something* to do with James VI. Fortinbras has "some rights of memory here in Denmark." Hamlet would have made a good king, Fortinbras observes; now that he is dead, he will have a soldier's funeral; Hamlet was not a soldier, but Essex was, and so was King Henry V.

In these history plays, the question of fair sequence and succession embraces a good deal more than King Richard's right to rule and to disinherit his cousin. And if Shakespeare glances discreetly at Queen Elizabeth in *Richard II* while dealing with the succession (she, in any case, thought he glanced at her, not necessarily discreetly), he seems also to look forward, and northward, to her successor, in *Henry V*. Most Englishmen looked northward, but they were supposed to look silently.[16]

III

The Troublesome Reign of King Henry IV

Prince Hal and Falstaff;

Some Famous Victories

It is the main business of Henry IV to record the painful reorientation of England from discredited and fatal notions of divine right and divine kingship to the triumph of man-centered kingship, to show the long transition from regal irresponsibility and anarchy under King Richard to the achievement of justice and something like an ideal commonwealth under King Henry V. It is not the function of *Henry IV* to demonstrate the unhappy fruits of rebellion and usurpation—not, certainly, in any cautionary sense—but to show how rebellion and usurpation led finally to something better than what they displaced.

The familiar argument that God punished King Richard with Bolingbroke and then punished King Henry with the Percys and an erring son, and then, after a brief holiday, punished all of England with the Wars of the Roses and Richard III,[1] and finally relented by giving England the beneficent reign of King Henry VII,[2] may not have strained Tudor credulity—although it certainly says something about official Tudor political ingenuity—but it does raise some questions. Historically it is ridiculous, and as an "interpretation" of the history plays it is equally unsatisfactory—because, after all, what is wrong with the England of King Henry IV is easily identifiable: a nearly unmanageable combination of Percys, Glendower, Scots, an apparently irresponsible and indifferent heir apparent, and Sir John Falstaff. All of these may demonstrate the busy and petulant workings of a God turned grumpy, behaving discreditably. The hand of God may be present here, but in a sense different from the one somewhat tendentiously described above.

Henry IV inherited the Glendower and Scottish problems and, in a special sense, the Falstaff problem; the Percy rebellion (actually three, telescoped, more or less, into one by Shakespeare) was bound to happen, not because of Fate but because of the Percys, who behave in the play as people like them always behave when they get the chance—a point made clearly by Warwick (*2HIV*, III.i.80-92) and accepted by the King. The estrangement of father and son may be providential, but if it is, so is their reconciliation.

Holinshed writes about Henry IV's harshness and his vindictiveness, and about taxation amounting almost to extortion. Tyndale and Foxe write about his, and his Lancastrian successors', persecution of Lollards. Shakespeare does neither; he shows us a beleaguered king trying to persuade his heir to get ready to rule, trying to put down a rebellion that no one can justify, trying to govern well, trying to create a strong and united kingdom. As great feudal lords, the Percys would prefer a disunited and fragmented kingdom, a loose federation of feudal baronies, even a kingdom divided into three. That is what the prisoner issue is about (*1HIV*, I.i and I.iii), and that is why the Percys pretend briefly to push the Mortimer claim (*1HIV*, I.iii) and why they rebel: their protégé has declared his independence and his determination to rule his kingdom—including them; their response is that of any kingmaker under similar circumstances. King Henry's problems, including in an important sense his difficulties with his son, are political problems to be dealt with by political means and, when necessary, by their familiar extension, war. And they finally are dealt with in a manner of which providence seems to approve.

Central to the whole complex business is the process whereby England and Prince Hal get ready for each other, so to speak, how King Henry helps that process and how Sir John Falstaff tries to hinder it. Toward the end of *2 Henry IV*, the new king makes a formal commitment when he takes the Lord Chief Justice, who also represents the Idea of justice, as his new father. This is a symbolic gesture, and we do not see the Lord Chief Justice hovering over King Henry V; but we should understand that he is there. Justice, we are told (2HIV, V.ii.77–79), had resided with the dead king; it now resides with the Lord Chief Justice; it will reside with the new king if he wishes it to. He does. It replaces that immortal corporation, the King Body Politic, and to be effective it must be consciously adopted by the succeeding king, as it is here. But for this king to adopt it in any meaningful sense, he must reach an understanding with his father, and he must be prepared to dismiss those kinds of injustice, disorder, and misrule represented most compendiously by Falstaff. As we shall see, he has in effect already dismissed Falstaff after the battle of Shrewsbury; but Falstaff takes a lot of dismissing, and the process must be repeated, for emphasis and for important political reasons.

Here I am primarily concerned with three principal characters of the *Henry IV* plays, the King, the Prince, and Sir John, and with the complex relationships that exist among them. I shall argue that the most important events in these plays are what I call the dismissals of Falstaff and that a large part of the major action is designed to prepare us for these dismissals and to give them particular significance. Prince Hal is more or less constantly dismissing Falstaff while Shakespeare often asks us to imagine an England ruled, improbably, by that Lord of Misrule; and the final, and famous, rejection shocks only because it is so obviously, and so coldly, final. Prince Hal had meant it all along, and Falstaff and the rest of us must finally believe it. It always made good sense, especially for someone who was going to become the mirror of all Christian kings. I am concerned with these three characters mainly in the context of an historical and political action the overriding point of which is the achievement of justice in a just civil polity, as Shakespeare conceives of them. I should perhaps add that I am not much interested in defending Shakespeare's idea of a just civil polity. I would insist, though, that there have been, and still are, far worse polities than that of Shakespeare's Henry V. Still, few people would be happy living in someone else's utopia—Aristotle makes the point in his remarks on *The Republic* in *The Politics*.

PROTEAN VICE:
RECONCILIATION AND REJECTION

A wide variety of critical approaches has contributed much to our understanding of Falstaff and the complicated relationship he enjoys, and finally endures, with Prince Hal. One approach, with which I mainly agree, is embodied in a classic statement that does not lend itself to paraphrase:

> But Falstaff, unimitated, unimitable Falstaff, how shall I describe thee? Thou compound of sense and vice; of sense which may be admired but not esteemed, of vice which may be despised but hardly detested. Falstaff is a character loaded with faults, and with those faults which naturally produce contempt. He is a thief and a glutton, a coward and a boaster, always ready to cheat the weak and prey upon the poor; to terrify the timorous and insult the defenseless. At once obsequious and malignant, he satirizes in their absence those whom he lives by flattering. He is familiar with the prince only as an agent of vice, but of this familiarity he is so proud as not only to be supercilious and haughty with common men but to think his interest of importance to the Duke of Lancaster. Yet the man thus corrupt, thus despicable, makes himself necessary to the prince that despises him, by the most pleasing of all qualities, perpetual gaiety, by an unfailing power of exciting laughter, which is the more freely indulged as his wit is not of the splendid or ambitious kind but consists in easy escapes and sallies of levity, which make sport but raise no envy. It must be observed that he is stained with no enormous or sanguinary crimes, so that his licentiousness is not so offensive but that it may be borne for the mirth.
>
> The moral to be drawn from this representation is that no man is more dangerous than he that, with a will to corrupt, hath the power to please; and that neither wit nor honesty ought to think themselves safe with such a companion when they see Henry seduced by Falstaff.[3]

C. S. Lewis, writing in the person of an infamous old devil, might have been glossing both Johnson and Shakespeare, although he wasn't:

> The real use of Jokes or Humour . . . is specially promising among the English, who take their "sense of humour" so seriously that a deficiency in this sense is almost the only deficiency at which they feel shame. Humour is for them the all-consoling and (mark this) the all-excusing grace of life. Hence it is invaluable as a means of destroying shame. If a

man simply lets others pay for him, he is "mean"; if he boasts of it in a jocular manner and twits his fellows with having been scored off, he is no longer "mean" but a comical fellow. Mere cowardice is shameful; cowardice boasted of with humorous exaggerations and grotesque gestures can be passed off as funny. Cruelty is shameful—unless the cruel man can represent it as a practical joke. A thousand bawdy, or even blasphemous, jokes do not help towards a man's damnation so much as his discovery that almost anything he wants to do can be done, not only without the disapproval but with the admiration of his fellows, if only it can get itself treated as a Joke. And this temptation can be almost entirely hidden from your patient by that English seriousness about Humour. Any suggestion that there might be too much of it can be represented to him as "Puritanical" or as betraying a "lack of humour."

But flippancy is the best of all. . . . Only a very clever human can make a real Joke about virtue, or indeed about anything else; any of them can be trained to talk *as if* virtue were funny. Among flippant people the Joke is always assumed to have been made. No one actually makes it; but every serious subject is discussed in a manner which implies that they have already found a ridiculous side to it. If prolonged, the habit of Flippancy builds up around a man the finest armour plating against the Enemy [God] that I know, and it is quite free from the dangers inherent in the other sources of laughter [earlier defined as joy and fun]. It is a thousand miles away from joy; it deadens, instead of sharpening, the intellect; and it excites no affection between those who practice it.[4]

Close enough. Falstaff doesn't boast of his cowardice, but he lies about his courage, knowing his audience knows he is lying; in effect, then, boasting of his cowardice. He makes an elaborate joke about the virtue of honor; he doesn't assume that the joke has been made, but he does assume, in a context that is to prove him wrong (Shrewsbury), that honor is a subject for joking. He makes his joke in a famous soliloquy; there is no one to be revealed but Falstaff, no one to be corrupted but the audience.

Having pressed one old master and one modern one into service, I should add that, like everyone else who has tried to understand Falstaff in the past twenty years, I am greatly indebted, and grateful, to another modern master, Professor C. L. Barber and *Shakespeare's Festive Comedy*.[5] The archetypal approach is not exactly Dr. Johnson's, but (although he would have denied it if presented with the notion) his approach and Barber's are complementary, not mutually exclusive. My general view of Falstaff is essentially theirs although I have of course gone my own way, not wholly without company, in the remarks that follow. The historical approach is also valuable, and, properly applied, it too complements the moral and the archetypal, and I have utilized it also, particularly in connection with Falstaff, who began life as a historical figure. Professor Alice-Lyle Scoufos has produced a splendid study of this very complex subject, to which I am happy to record my indebtedness.[6]

For present purposes I shall avoid any systematic use of Freudian and archetypal terms, although they certainly have their uses. Falstaff does, however, represent the spirit of carnival, of Shrovetide, even though he has an odd way of celebrating it and does not understand that it must end, or when, or how. He is also, as Prince Hal observes, a reverend vice, a gray iniquity, an old white-bearded Satan. With respect to Prince Hal, if not to the audience, he is a supremely inept tempter, no more gifted finally than C. S. Lewis's Wormwood. And he is, of course, a father figure of sorts, a substitute father and a surrogate king, a father who exists to be denied, a king who exists to be deposed. (In 2 Henry IV the Lord Chief Justice does become a genuine substitute for the new king's dead father—another story.) And he is a commentator on the play's historical and political action, but not an accurate or reliable one. He understands something about Prince John and about Hotspur, surprisingly little about King Henry or Prince Hal. And he is a gifted liar and raconteur, a fool, a jester, a licensed buffoon, and a soldier not so much cowardly or incompetent (something of both, however) as heartless and cynical: in one play he leads his wretched men into battle in circumstances that virtually guarantee that he will not be hurt and they will be killed, so that he can draw their pay. And in another he misuses the King's press more than damnably, drafting soldiers who cannot buy their way out and are most likely to be killed.[7]

Just before his death, the Hostess saw him "fumble with the sheets and play with flowers and smile upon his fingers' end" (HV, II.iii.14-15)—masturbating, perhaps, more likely than admiring the Hostess's embroidery. And, with his nose as sharp as a pen and a table of green fields, or babbling of green fields (it doesn't greatly matter

which: one is perhaps pornographic, the other certainly presump-
tuous), solicitously explored by the Hostess, who finds everything as
cold as any stone (the Folio reading here is attractive: "Then I felt to
his knees, and so up-peer'd, and upward, and all was as cold as any
stone" [II.846–847 in the Norton facsimile]), he dies in an excruciating parody of the death of Socrates. He had tried, with limited success, to corrupt the youth of the country; he had played the role of
tempter, and the Hostess's description of his genital frigidity neatly
and outrageously combines Socrates and the devil. It would be redundant to note that Falstaff has been very funny, less so to observe
that he has also been sinister. When he steps out of the subplot, out of
his senile delinquent's carnival, into the main plot, into the busy and
serious new world of King Henry V, only he can (or should) be surprised by his reception there.

We need not be surprised or distressed by the new king's treatment of his old acquaintance because we know, although Falstaff
does not, that Prince Hal has made his peace with his father, has received what is now an hereditary crown, and has taken the Lord
Chief Justice as his second father. There is no way for Falstaff and
Justice to move in the same sphere. I suspect that some of that army
of critics and readers who are perplexed, offended, or outraged by
King Henry V's cool dismissal of his old chum are in fact recollecting
the witty, cynical, occasionally engaging, inspired buffoon of *1
Henry IV*, where the prince finds him amusing and likable as a sort of
holiday companion, not the seamy, diseased, increasingly lecherous
and boorish character we find in *2 Henry IV*; few readers or audiences, coming to that play with no knowledge of its predecessor,
would be either surprised or offended by what happens to Falstaff.

RECONCILIATION

ALTHOUGH THE FINAL DISMISSAL OF FALSTAFF HAS BEEN SIGNALED ALMOST
from the beginning (*1HIV*, I.ii) and although Prince Hal in effect rejects him at least twice before the final and definitive dismissal, what
makes that final break absolutely inevitable is reconciliation—reconciliation of father and son and of King Henry V and Justice. The
Prince had made some basic commitments long before being reconciled with his father; the choice is sealed by the reconciliation, in

which the final dismissal of Falstaff is already silently effected. Both reconciliations deserve attention.

The old king is dying; his son thinks he is dead. What follows shows, better than any other single episode, the true values of the King and the Prince, what it was that "awak'd" Prince Hal from that dream he later says he despises. The words of the Lord Chief Justice in act V, scene ii make the awakening complete. Unlike Falstaff at Shrewsbury, playing dead, the King does not hear his son's words as he takes the crown:

> This sleep is sound indeed; this is a sleep
> That from this golden rigol hath divorc'd
> So many English kings. Thy due from me
> Is tears and heavy sorrows of the blood,
> Which nature, love, and filial tenderness
> Shall, O dear father, pay thee plenteously.
> My due from thee is this imperial crown,
> Which, as immediate from thy place and blood,
> Derives itself to me. Lo where it sits,
> Which God shall guard; and put the world's whole strength
> Into one giant arm, it shall not force
> This lineal honour from me. This from thee
> Will I to mine leave, as 'tis left to me.
>
> (IV.v.34–46)

It seems to me absurd to suggest that these words, spoken under these circumstances, mean anything but what they say; the commitment to father, crown, and country is total as is the commitment to lineal succession. Even more important, perhaps, is the King's desperate effort to retrieve his supposedly wild and erring son to a sense of his regal responsibility. The two long speeches tell us much about the Prince and his father. They are very well known, but I am not sure that their power and importance are always fully appreciated. They reconcile father and son; they underscore the son's commitment to duty; they relieve the father's mind, as much as it can be relieved; they demonstrate once more the father's and the son's primary concern for the welfare of England; the Prince's words convince the King that his work is in fact done so that he can, praising God, die in Jerusalem. And they make it impossible for King Henry V to deal with either Justice or Falstaff in any way other than those in which he does deal with them.

Prince.   I never thought to hear you speak again.

King.   Thy wish was father, Harry, to that thought:
I stay too long by thee, I weary thee.
Dost thou so hunger for mine empty chair
That thou wilt needs invest thee with my honours
Before thy hour be ripe? O foolish youth!
Thou seek'st the greatness that will overwhelm thee.
Stay but a little, for my cloud of dignity
Is held from falling with so weak a wind
That it will quickly drop; my day is dim.
Thou hast stol'n that which after some few hours
Were thine without offence, and at my death
Thou hast seal'd up my expectation.
Thy life did manifest thou lov'dst me not,
And thou wilt have me die assur'd of it.
Thou hid'st a thousand daggers in thy thoughts,
Which thou hast whetted on thy stony heart,
To stab at half an hour of my life.
What, canst thou not forbear me half an hour?
Then get thee gone, and dig my grave thyself,
And bid the merry bells ring to thine ear
That thou art crowned, not that I am dead.
Let all the tears that should bedew my hearse
Be drops of balm to sanctify thy head,
Only compound me with forgotten dust.
Give that which gave thee life unto the worms;
Pluck down my officers; break my decrees;
For now a time is come to mock at form—
Harry the fifth is crown'd! Up, vanity!
Down, royal state! All you sage counsellors, hence!
And to the English court assemble now
From every region, apes of idleness!
Now, neighbour confines, purge you of your scum!
Have you a ruffian that will swear, drink, dance,
Revel the night, rob, murder, and commit
The oldest sins the newest kind of ways?
Be happy, he will trouble you no more.
England shall double gild his treble guilt,
England shall give him office, honour, might:
For the fifth Harry from curb'd licence plucks

The muzzle of restraint, and the wild dog
Shall flesh his tooth on every innocent.
O my poor kingdom, sick with civil blows!
When that my care could not withhold thy riots,
What wilt thou do when riot is thy care?
O, thou wilt be a wilderness again,
Peopled with wolves, thy old inhabitants!

Prince. [*Kneels*] O, pardon me, my liege! But for my tears,
The moist impediments unto my speech,
I had forestalled this dear and deep rebuke,
Ere you with grief had spoke and I had heard
The course of it so far. There is your crown;
And He that wears the crown immortally
Long guard it yours! If I affect it more
Than as your honour and as your renown,
Let me no more from this obedience rise,
Which my most inward true and duteous spirit
Teacheth this prostrate and exterior bending.
God witness with me, when I here came in,
And found no course of breath within your Majesty,
How cold it struck my heart! If I do feign,
O, let me in my present wildness die,
And never live to show th'incredulous world
The noble change that I have purposed!
Coming to look on you, thinking you dead,
And dead almost, my liege, to think you were,
I spake unto this crown as having sense,
And thus upbraided it: 'The care on thee depending
Hath fed upon the body of my father;
Therefore thou best of gold art worst of gold.
Other, less fine in carat, is more precious,
Preserving life in med'cine potable;
But thou, most fine, most honour'd, most renown'd,
Hast eat thy bearer up'. Thus, my most royal liege,
Accusing it, I put it on my head,
To try with it, as with an enemy
That had before my face murder'd my father,
The quarrel of a true inheritor.
But if it did infect my blood with joy,
Or swell my thoughts to any strain of pride,
If any rebel or vain spirit of mine
Did with the least affection of a welcome
Give entertainment to the might of it,

> Let God forever keep it from my head,
> And make me as the poorest vassal is,
> That doth with awe and terror kneel to it!
>
> (IV.v.91-176)

The words of the father and son are both studied and heartfelt. Both men must use all their resources of language, not to deceive or mislead, but to get to the heart of the matter. They don't know each other very well—their mutual affection is according to their bond. With Hal and Falstaff there has been neither genuine affection nor meaningful bond. The King is heartsick about the future of his kingdom, wanting to believe, but unable to do so, that his son will be both willing and able to carry forward the prosecution of justice and the restoration of order. Enormous determination and strength must go into his long and, as he knows, last exhortation to his erring son. As strength and life ebb, he performs what must be for him the most important single act of his kingship. He believes in fair sequence and succession, and he is bound to try to make it work. He does not plead for personal reconciliation although he wants it desperately; he does plead, most emphatically, for good government in the only way he thinks possible: by describing his vision of England under King Harry the fifth.

Throughout the first three plays of this tetralogy we have seen language and rhetoric used and misused, working and not working, deceiving and not deceiving. The most splendid rhetoric, and superficially the most moving, is that of King Richard, dedicated to a cause that is lost and deserves to be lost. It is splendidly hollow. The rhetoric of the dying King Henry IV is, in every respect except the most superficial, effective and affecting because it is grounded in a personal and political reality of which Richard had no conception: Henry IV cares deeply for a kingdom that he has tried to govern well, and he has a son to whom he must bequeath his crown. This is his last chance to bring that son to the sense of duty and responsibility that might just make it possible for him to govern an unruly kingdom. He must put purely personal resentment aside. When he awoke to find that his crown was gone, his first thought was of sons stealing their patrimony before their fathers were dead. The crown was merely gold (IV.v.66). Fathers, like bees, "have engrossed and pil'd up/The canker'd heaps of strange-achieved gold" (70-71), "and like the bees/Are murder'd for [their] sins" (77-78). The sick and weary king, alone with his thoughts, is suddenly the merchant father of a rapacious prodigal son. It is all the more remarkable that when his son returns, the King can almost immediately banish from his speech the homely figures of merchant father and prodigal son and proceed to matters of state and kingship, although even here the idea of the gaping heir is discernible; King Henry is shrinking to ordinary manhood while his son is growing to kingship: "Then get thee gone, and dig my grave thyself,/And bid the merry bells ring to thine ear/That thou art crowned, not that I am dead" (110-112).

The Prince's response is equally revealing and again both genuine and studied. The "polish'd perturbation! golden care!" of his soliloquy to the crown (22), with its idea of gold in a different sense from his father's, is repeated when he tells his father what he said to the crown: "The care on thee depending/Hath fed upon the body of my father;/Therefore thou best of gold art worst of gold" (158-160).

It is, I suppose, inevitable that some modern readers should see consummate hypocrisy on both sides here. After all, why should King Harry, who has stolen a crown and the kingdom that goes with it, concern himself with a future he will never see and fret about giving his crown to an irresponsible son? And why should Prince Hal be so intent on persuading his father of his worthiness when he will get both crown and kingdom whether his father thinks him worthy or not? The answers provided by the text are that the father loves his kingdom and his son and the son loves his father and his kingdom. The fact that the Prince's account of what he said to the crown differs in language (but not in sentiment) from what he actually said indicates only that Shakespeare was not much interested in having a speech repeated verbatim in the same scene.

These sad and moving speeches produce something as close to a meeting of minds as this father and this son will ever get. King Henry IV is a man not easily persuaded; here, at least, he comes close enough: "O my son,/God put it in thy mind to take it hence,/That thou mightst win the more thy father's love,/Pleading so wisely in excuse of it!" (177-180). I say close enough, because the King's last speech to his son tells us he is still not sure what kind of king that son will be. He gives him some necessary advice but, I think, deliberately falsifies his own motives in the process.

The King's last long speech (177-199) is a kind of summation of his political difficulties, followed by some practical advice to his son, advice that seems cynical to many modern readers who tend to take an understandably dim view of politicians and are not greatly concerned with governing. But governing and problems of government are of obvious concern to a troubled and doubtfully legitimate ruler who is about to pass on his crown and kingdom to his legitimate heir, who, unlike his father, will rule by fair sequence and succession. He "met this crown" by "by-paths and indirect crook'd ways," and it was at best troublesome (he hadn't expected it to be *fun*, of course); but,

> To thee it shall descend with better quiet,
> Better opinion, better confirmation,
> For all the soil of the achievement goes
> With me into the earth.
>
> (187-190)

What he had taken falls upon his son "in a more fairer sort;/So thou the garland wear'st successively." The legitimacy of King Henry V is never an issue; nor, for Shakespeare, is the legitimacy of King Henry IV. The King nevertheless has his own heavy doubts: "How I came by the crown, O God forgive,/And grant it may with thee in true peace live!" (218-219). The Prince has no doubt on this score: "My gracious liege,/You won it, wore it, kept it, gave it me;/Then plain and right must my possession be" (220-222). Henry VIII could not have spoken truer or more orthodox words to his own father, who claimed the kingship "by right of conquest."

The dying king's practical advice includes what must be for many readers a remarkable statement. Prince Hal will be more sure, because legitimate, in his kingship than his father was, but he can anticipate trouble: all his father's friends, "by whose fell working [he] was first advanc'd," might well have wanted to replace him, "which to avoid,/I cut them off, and had a purpose now/To lead out many to the Holy Land,/Lest rest and lying still might make them look/Too near my state" (IV.v.206-212). Every student of these plays will have long since made up his mind about the genuineness of Henry IV's desire to make a pilgrimage, or lead a crusade, to the Holy Land.[8] The matter certainly can't be proved, but I at least am thoroughly persuaded, mainly by his language in *1 Henry IV*, I.i, at the end of act III, scene i of *2 Henry IV*, and particularly by his last words in that play, the "Laud be to God!" passage. Now his pilgrimage, which was also his crusade, is over. Henry IV's last sacrifice was to deny the validity of his own motives while giving his son some practical advice: "Therefore, my Harry,/Be it thy course to busy giddy minds/With foreign quarrels, that action hence borne out/May waste the memory of the former days" (IV.v.212-215). King Harry the fifth will conduct a famous foreign quarrel and win a famous victory, but he will not need to busy giddy minds—they are all well under control when the foreign quarrel is launched.

Prince Hal may or may not perceive the sort of sacrifice his father is making here, but he shares his father's dedication to the welfare of England; and when the time comes, he rules more effectively than his father could have thought possible—not only well but brilliantly and, as the playwright puts it, "most greatly liv'd." If Henry IV had had nothing more than a familiar political motive for a crusade, the motive would have been politically sound enough; but he would hardly have praised God and spoken as he does about dying in Jerusalem.

* * * * *

Meanwhile, back in Gloucestershire, Falstaff, not for the first time, doesn't know what is going on. There, knavery is the theme, as Justice Shallow agrees "to countenance William Visor of Woncot against Clement Perkes a' th' hill" (V.i.34-35). "Go to, I say he shall have no wrong" (V.i.49). And while Justice Shallow is promising injustice in Gloucestershire and Falstaff is planning "to keep Prince Harry in continual laughter the wearing out of six fashions" (V.i.75-76), King Henry V is meeting Justice, passing a test, and taking a new father. In *2 Henry IV*, the Lord Chief Justice is the King's true surrogate, and in act I, scene ii the Lord Chief Justice is also something like Prince Hal's surrogate in a wit combat with Falstaff—the somewhat mysterious figure of Justice replaces the Prince Hal of the parallel scene in *1 Henry IV*, no casual substitution. In act V, scene ii the new king speaks sharply to the Lord Chief Justice for having once rated him, rebuked him, and sent him to prison for striking him. (It wouldn't do at all to *show* the Prince striking the Justice: to talk about it, however, renders it suitable for a discussion of principles. Sometimes, as with Antonio's spitting on Shylock's Jewish gaberdine, the picture would ruin the poesy; and no one knew better than Shakespeare when to join them and when to keep them apart.) The reply is a masterpiece, enormously instructive; it provides one of the ethical centers of the play, establishing concretely the primacy of law and justice as Justice sets out to reclaim a prodigal prince:

> I then did use the person of your father;
> The image of his power lay then in me;
> And in th'administration of his law,
> Whiles I was busy for the commonwealth,
> Your Highness pleased to forget my place,
> The majesty and power of law and justice,
> The image of the King whom I presented,
> And struck me in my very seat of judgment;
> Whereon, as an offender to your father,
> I gave bold way to my authority
> And did commit you. If the deed were ill,
> Be you contented, wearing now the garland,
> To have a son set your decrees at naught?
> To pluck down justice from your aweful bench?
> To trip the course of law, and blunt the sword
> That guards the peace and safety of your person?
> Nay more, to spurn at your most royal image,
> And mock your workings in a second body?
> Question your royal thoughts, make the case yours,
> Be now the father, and propose a son,
> Hear your own dignity so much profan'd,
> See your most dreadful laws so loosely slighted,
> Behold yourself so by a son disdain'd:
> And then imagine me taking your part,
> And in your power soft silencing your son.
> After this cold considerance sentence me;
> And, as you are a king, speak in your state
> What I have done that misbecame my place,
> My person, or my liege's sovereignty.

(V.ii.73-101)

I see no possibility whatever of rationally assigning irony to this speech or to the equating of "the image of the King" with "The majesty and power of law and justice." We already knew the message, but we need the whole speech before us to grasp its power and authority. The Lord Chief Justice asserts the authority of the father and of the law, and the new king accepts this authority without question; and he adopts Justice as his new father (102). In act I, scene ii Falstaff has bandied words, metaphorically, with the King's image Justice. In act IV the Prince is reconciled with the dying king, his father. In act V he is reconciled with is father's surrogate, Justice, who becomes like a new father, "a second body" in a specialized metaphorical version of the doctrine of the King's Two Bodies.

What has now passed between the Prince and his father, the new king and his Lord Chief Justice, ought to prevent excessive astonishment and outrage at King Henry V's treatment of Falstaff, whose appearance in London would be almost an anticlimax were it not for the fact that Shakespeare asks us to anticipate it, teases us into imagining just how the rather large balloon is going to be pricked. The new king's meeting with the Lord Chief Justice is bracketed between the last two Gloucestershire episodes, in the first of which Justice Shallow promises injustice, in the second of which merry Shrovetide is being celebrated amid images of old age and death. In the world outside, there hasn't been much merriment; but now the emphasis is on the beginning of a new life and a new world. It is into that world that Falstaff intrudes, for the last time.

The pattern is perfectly clear: in act IV, scene v the father and the son are magnificently reconciled, and Prince Hal is ready to assume the responsibilities of kingship. In act V, scene i Justice Shallow assures Davy that the knave William visor of Woncot "shall have no wrong," and Falstaff promises to keep the Prince perpetually entertained. In act V, scene ii the new king is reconciled with the old justice, who becomes his new father. In act V, scene iii Master Silence, Shallow, and Falstaff celebrate merry Shrovetide; Pistol enters with the news that the old king is dead and tells the enthralled Falstaff, "Sir John, thy tender lambkin now is King;/Harry the Fifth's the man: I speak the truth" (113–114). Accompanied by his friends, Falstaff sets out for London, observing that "the laws of

England are at my commandment" and pronouncing a strange beatitude: "Blessed are they that have been my friends, and woe to my Lord Chief Justice!" (132-134). On the basis of his relationship with Prince Hal during this play, he has scarcely more reason than we do to expect that he will be warmly received. But even here Shakespeare is still piling circumstance on Sir John: in act V, scene iv the beadles are arresting Doll and the Hostess because "the man is dead that you and Pistol beat amongst you" (17-18)—a thoroughly ugly detail.

For five scenes, then, we have been getting concentrated preparation for, among other things, an absolute and final break between Falstaff and his former protégé, a break precipitated by Falstaff himself, not by the new king. For King Henry V, the sudden appearance of an old and bad dream must be nearly as uncomfortable as the arrival on stage of Exton with the body of King Richard had been for his father. Nothing in either of these plays can give objective justification to the assumptions upon which Falstaff decides to hurry off to London, and one must assume that his powers of self-deception, particularly where Prince Hal is concerned, are even greater than his power to deceive others. Falstaff's sudden appearance is wholly unexpected by the new king, and certainly uninvited. He is truly the ghost of an old, seductive, but finally bad dream, and the effect is in no way mitigated by "God save thee, my sweet boy!"—a world away from old Sir Thomas Erpingham's "The Lord in heaven bless thee, noble Harry!" (*HV*, IV.i.33). Falstaff can't quite accept the fact that he is addressing a king. Comprehension comes even to Justice Shallow, and although not every reader will accept the validity of Prince John's words on this subject, I believe they are intended to be an accurate summing up:

> I like this fair proceeding of the King's.
> He hath intent his wonted followers
> Shall all be very well provided for,
> But all are banish'd till their conversations
> Appear more wise and modest to the world.
>
> (V.v.97-101)

The fair proceeding, including the dismissal of Falstaff, is the first official act of the new king, and it has long been seen as a stage in the education of the Prince, even though critics have disagreed, almost violently, on the quality of that education. It seems to me that, considering the great reconciliations of acts IV and V, the education thus far has been notably successful: the King has rejected old vices, and he has chosen justice and order over their opposites. A call to duty has been uttered and answered in the only proper way. We should not be so skeptical about the claims and postures of politicians that we miss the point of what Shakespeare does with Falstaff and Prince Hal. The reconciliations with his father and with Justice, and the rejection of Falstaff, make it official: if we did not already know that Prince Hal had grown up, we know it now.

REJECTIONS

The reconciliations provide the moral ballast for the final dismissal, but, as everyone knows, already at the end of act I, scene ii of *1 Henry IV* Falstaff's status with the Prince has been very nearly settled: "If all the world were playing holidays,/To sport would be as tedious as to work" (I.ii.199–200). The words are familiar, and the Prince means them—within the sensible limitations described by Dr. Johnson: ". . . a natural picture of a great mind offering excuses to itself and palliating those follies which it can neither justify nor forsake" (*Samuel Johnson on Shakespeare*, p. 87). Falstaff dreams of a perpetual holiday; the Prince knows there is no such thing: an unsuitable companion for the Prince of Wales would be an impossible one for King Henry V, and even *1 Henry IV* warns us, if not Falstaff, that the friendship must be a temporary one: "Banish plump Jack and banish all the world./I do, I will" (II.iv.474–475).

Most revealing, still in *1 Henry IV*, are Hal's words after Shrewsbury, over the supposed corpse of Falstaff:

What, old acquaintance, could not all this flesh
Keep in a little life? Poor Jack, farewell!
I could have better spar'd a better man:
O, I should have a heavy miss of thee

If I were much in love with vanity:
Death hath not struck so fat a deer today,
Though many dearer, in this bloody fray.
Embowell'd will I see thee by and by,
Till then in blood by noble Percy lie.

(V.iv.101-109)

He is saddened by the supposed death of his "old acquaintance," and being saddened makes him a little uneasy, hence, the muted version of the jokes he had been accustomed to making at Falstaff's expense in Falstaff's presence. These mildly rueful words contrast vividly with his magnanimous elegy over the genuinely dead Hotspur. "Fare thee well, great heart!" implies a much stronger commitment than "old acquaintance" or "so fat a deer," and the double elegy, for Hotspur and Falstaff, indicates sufficiently just values.

Falstaff, still playing dead, hears, needless to say, a lot more than "embowell'd" before he "riseth up." His lonely ruminations are so amusing at the outset that we tend to overlook the cynicism and then the brutality that follow. In fact, his pseudo-philosophical puns on counterfeiting, and the action that follows them, suggest a new, sinister game, and a role for the old devil that is finally more ugly than funny. His values are characteristically upside-down ("for he is but the counterfeit of a man, who hath not the life of a man; but to counterfeit dying, when a man thereby liveth, is to be no counterfeit, but the true and perfect image of life indeed" [V.iv.115-119]), and the action to which they lead is atrocious. Anyone committed to the notion of an essentially lovable Falstaff must move fairly quickly over this passage. No doubt it is amusing that Falstaff is willing to attribute his own values to Hotspur and assume that he too may be a counterfeit—unlikely as that may seem to the audience; Hotspur is altogether transparent—but since Hotspur may be a counterfeit, "I'll make him sure, yea, and I'll swear I killed him. Why may not he rise as well as I? Nothing confutes me but eyes, and nobody sees me: therefore, sirrah [*stabbing him*, (but the stage direction is unnecessary)], with a new wound in your thigh, come you along with me. *He takes Hotspur up on his back* [S. D.]" (V.iv.124-128).[9]

Falstaff's fear of the dead Hotspur is amusing enough, and it is typical; and a wound in the thigh may well be superficial (unless one assumes, improbably, that Falstaff means to cut the femoral artery with surgical precision). But Falstaff's intentions are by no means superficial, however shallow his fear might be. It has often been noted, as a kind of joke, that when he takes up the body of Hotspur on his back, Falstaff is emulating a bad angel, vice, or devil in a morality play (like the Bad Angel in *The Castle of Perseverance*); but Falstaff is more complicated than that, and the degree of complexity is suggested by Prince Hal's words following his reentrance with Prince John just as Falstaff picks up Hotspur's body. What the Princes see is Falstaff with Hotspur's body on his back, just ready to leave the scene and claim his triumph. What Prince Hal says is almost self-explanatory:

> Art thou alive?
> Or is it fantasy that plays upon our eyesight?
> I prithee speak, we will not trust our eyes
> Without our ears: thou art not what thou seem'st.
>
> (V.iv.133-136)

Prince Hal is not so sophisticated a theatergoer as Prince Hamlet, who would no doubt find "nothing confutes me but eyes" somewhat shallow. Whether or not one agrees that Falstaff is not what he seems depends to a large extent on what one makes of what he seems. He seems to Prince Hal to be the dead Falstaff come to life and now carrying the body of Hotspur off the battlefield. If he seems to be a bad angel carrying a body off to hell, it is as Hotspur's bad angel: Falstaff's perversions of chivalry mock Hotspur's excesses.

But he is also Hal's bad angel, in this passage a truly diabolical tempter, for, having desecrated the body of a soldier who had died more honorably than he had lived, Falstaff, perhaps *"throwing the body down"* (the stage direction originates in the 1773 variorum), challenges the Prince to claim his legitimate, but now very tarnished, victory. The brutality here is astonishing: Take this body, with the gratuitous wound in the thigh (one recalls the "beastly shameless transformation,/By those Welshwomen done" to the bodies of dead Englishmen [I.i.44-45]), and claim the victory if you wish. Listening to Falstaff's lies, a good deal less entertaining than his account of Gad's Hill (where he had been engaged only in armed robbery), Hal can make his decision easily enough: "Come, bring your luggage nobly [!] on your back./For my part, if a lie may do thee grace,/I'll gild it with the happiest terms I have" (V.iv.155–157). That is to say, he rejects the temptation and throws the burden (almost literally) back on Falstaff. Falstaff's private vow to grow less if he grows great reduces him finally—the last we see of him in this play—to his own original, considerable stature; the unsuccessful tempter has this time failed in a much larger enterprise than he had attempted before, and the defeat is emphasized by Prince Hal's magnanimous decision to release Douglas because "his valours shown upon our crests today/ Have taught us how to cherish such high deeds,/Even in the bosom of our adversaries" (V.v.29–31). For Hal, at least, honor is more than a word.

This is in fact the end of their friendship, and after this last exchange, as *1 Henry IV* comes to an end, there will be no more merry interludes with Falstaff and the Prince of Wales. They will meet briefly and part bitterly in the tavern scene of *2 Henry IV*, and at the end of that play they will part forever. At Shrewsbury the Prince saves his father's life and rejects Falstaff's temptation. If we put the two plays together, it will be clear enough that Falstaff's feigned death was more than a bad joke: as far as Prince Hal is concerned, Falstaff *is* something like a dead man. He sees him now with eyes wide open, and he doesn't like what he sees. His descent on the tavern in *2 Henry IV* looks like incipient backsliding, but he does not slide very far, and his recovery is abrupt and complete. It would be only a slight exaggeration to say that, for the Prince, Falstaff died at Shrewsbury. It is someone else he sees after his coronation, sees and quickly dismisses. Falstaff's last temptation presents no problems at all: the new king sees him, sees into him, sees through him; the bad dream is exorcised.

But the wound in Hotspur's thigh: certainly Falstaff the tempter and *miles gloriosus* is desecrating the body of a soldier honorably dead; but I should think he is doing something else as well, a special kind of mutilation. The wound in the thigh must, I suppose, be a symbolic castration, a grim parody of the activities of the wild Welshwomen, more shocking because shown on the stage. The symbolic castration is an act of sexual jealousy. Falstaff was, after all, only playing dead, only counterfeiting, as he heard the words spoken by his putative protégé over the body of Hotspur and then over his own very much alive body. "Great heart" and "old acquaintance," "this earth that bears thee dead/Bears not alive so stout a gentleman," and "Death hath not struck so fat a deer today,/Though many dearer, in this bloody fray." Prince Hal's values are stable, rational, and, it seems to me, admirable. His "Come, bring your luggage nobly on your back" is almost as devastating in its implications as "I know thee not, old man," a denial well anticipated by "thou are not what thou seem'st": I know what you are; you are not what you seem to be; therefore, I know *you* not.

Falstaff is probably almost everything that he has been said to be (with some qualifications): tempter, bad angel, devil, surrogate father (of a highly specialized sort), *miles gloriosus*, rejected lover, lord of misrule, merry Shrovetide itself, licensed buffoon, clown, and jester. He is also, I suppose, a spirit of freedom and liberation, of a sort, from duty, responsibility, the civil polity, civilization.

He is very good at most of what he does, but he is not good at all as the tempter of Prince Hal. There he fails because his "subject," his intended victim, although he is certainly tempted from time to time and occasionally seems rather close to coming over, is able to resist and reject the Old One under circumstances in which he could hardly have done anything else. The Prince who can resist this temptation is already very close to the King who will dismiss Falstaff as easily as the recollection of a bad dream.

If the Prince's rejection of the temptation of Hotspur's corpse does not constitute an out and out rejection of Falstaff, it is certainly a rejection of Falstaff's values, a final declaration of independence. He has proved himself in battle, saved his father's life, killed Hotspur honorably; and these achievements tend to make Falstaff's blandishments somewhat redundant. When Hal next comes to be entertained by Falstaff, he is first annoyed, then disgusted—with himself as much as with Falstaff.

In *1 Henry IV*, there are several merry meetings between Falstaff and the Prince, every one of which carries some edge of foreboding for Falstaff. But in *2 Henry IV*, there are only two meetings between them; in one, Falstaff's final dismissal is begun ("Falstaff, good night"); in the other it is accomplished. No one coming to this long, complex, heavily symbolic play need be surprised by the dénouement. It is only a question of how the grey iniquity is to be dismissed; and when the time comes, Shakespeare has arranged matters in such a way that even if the new king had any tender feelings toward his old chum (not likely), the old chum asks to be violently rejected. His sudden, uninvited, unexpected reappearance hardly invited a cordial reception.

It has often been noted that the structures of the *Henry IV* plays are to some extent parallel. In each play, act I, scene i establishes a theme and act I, scene ii introduces Falstaff and the subplot. Act II, scene iv of each play is a splendid tavern scene, radically different from each other in tone, but equally brilliant. And the last scene of each play brings Falstaff and Hal briefly together, one scene ending with a rejection, the other with a dismissal. Act I, scene ii of *1 Henry IV* is a wonderfully engaging, funny, ironic, portentous debate between Falstaff and the Prince, ending with the famous soliloquy in which Hal assures us, and tries to assure himself, that he can resist temptation and will finally do so. His vocation, at which he succeeds stunningly, is kingship. It is pleasant enough to pass the time in taverns with Falstaff, but that pleasure is simply incompatible with the vocation.

It is not surprising that Shakespeare presents a good part of Prince Hal's life as a series of tests to be met and temptations to be overcome; they are preparations for his vocation. Act I, scene ii of *2 Henry IV* begins and ends with suggestive observations about Falstaff's diseases, these passages elegantly enclosing another debate, ironic and portentous but not wonderfully funny, between Falstaff and the Lord Chief Justice, who is also Justice and will become King Henry V's substitute father. The point is not obscure: in *1 Henry IV* it is Falstaff the unsuccessful tempter with his intended but impervious victim; in *2 Henry IV* it is a sick, seedy, boorish Falstaff, this time not with the Prince but with Justice, unnamed otherwise and emblematic, one of Falstaff's rivals and finally one of his conquerors.

In the first tavern scene, if Falstaff is not exactly in charge he nevertheless plays his part superbly, entertaining both audiences with his preposterous, outrageous, inspired, and mendacious account of his heroism at Gad's Hill. And he is told that he will be banished. In the second tavern scene (*2HIV*, II.iv) the emphasis is on old age, disease, impotence, lechery, sloth, envy, wrath (against Pistol), gluttony. The dialogue with Prince Hal (the only one before the final scene of the play) is brief, bitter, and pointed. The Prince and Poins look in to view the withered elder and his whore. Their stay is brief, their departure emphatic: "Falstaff, good night."

Henry IV, Part 1 closes with Hal rejecting the most serious and dangerous temptation offered by the old, white-bearded Satan. *Henry IV*, Part 2 ends with the famous and utterly predictable dismissal—so predictable that it is almost a mere formality, although not quite an anticlimax. In the earlier play some bewilderment precedes Hal's resisting Falstaff's temptation: "Is it fantasy that preys upon our eyesight?/ . . . thou are not what thou seem'st." In *2 Henry IV* there is no such doubt or bewilderment: "I have long dreamt of such a kind of man,/So surfeit-swilled, so old, and so profane;/But being awak'd I do despise my dream" (V.v.49-51). The counterfeit of the first play has become the idle, impertinent, annoying dream of the second play—now *recognized* as a dream.

It is easy enough to see a calculating cynicism and opportunism in these lines of the new king's and in the entire dismissal speech. But I think this view misreads the speech and partly misreads the whole play. I have no doubt that King Harry the fifth means exactly what he says: "But being awak'd, I do despise my dream." It is true that much earlier he had said, "I know you all, and will awhile/Uphold the unyok'd humour of your idleness" (*1HIV*, I.ii.190-191), and "I'll so offend, to make offence a skill,/Redeeming time when men least think I will" (211-212). He speaks with perfect seriousness but not with full maturity and understanding. At the end of *2 Henry IV* the audience has a decided advantage over the other princes and the Lord Chief Justice: they are surprised, we are not (or should not be), by the apparent transformation that occurs when Prince Hal becomes King Henry V—the same apparent transformation discussed at length by Canterbury and Ely in the opening scene of *Henry V*; we have an advantage over them, too.

It is also true that Hal had a fairly clear idea about what Falstaff, Bardolph, and the others were really like and about the sort of dan-

gers that would come to England if its King cherished, or even toler-
ated, their company—but perhaps not quite clear enough. It was no
doubt politic to offend, to spend more time in the tavern than at the
court, to spend more time with Falstaff than with his father, even
though he was able to save his father's life and win the battle of
Shrewsbury. But it also seems clear enough that, although he knew
them all, he also found their company both interesting and amusing,
if not edifying. And he certainly enjoyed the wit combats with Falstaff in *1 Henry IV*. He knows them all, but he can't quite shake them
and is not ready to. When we see him in *2 Henry IV* he knows a great
deal more; by the time he is King he knows yet more and he knows
what to do about it because he has awakened from his dream: "I
know thee not, old man. Fall to thy prayers." A dream come true. An
awakening.

It is a critical commonplace that the shock value of these lines is
tremendous. They certainly shock Falstaff, and it is hard to see how
anything less could have cooled his ebullience. And yet, as many
critics have seen, Shakespeare has gone out of his way to prepare us
for an emphatic dismissal; almost, one feels, he has attempted to
make us shockproof. For example, we are treated to Falstaff's remarkable notion that the new king will make him Lord Chief Justice
(perhaps paralleling his fond view in Act I, scene ii of *1 Henry IV* that
he would become a judge and hang people). By act V, scene v of *1
Henry IV* Prince Hal has seen all he needs to see; in *2 Henry IV* he
spends far more time with his father than he does with Falstaff, and
he has a crucial interview with the Lord Chief Justice. It is what the
Prince sees of his father, of kingship, of his own duties, and of Justice
that makes him despise his dream. And it is Falstaff's somewhat in-
delicate behavior on arriving in London right after the coronation
that briefly revives the dream, makes it all the more despicable, and
helps explain and justify the cold dismissal—shocking, perhaps, but
not discreditable.

The whole dramatic action of both plays prepares us for the most
emphatic dismissal. The cumulative effect is strong, beginning with
1 Henry IV, I.ii, and becoming irresistible in the reconciliation of
father and son in *2 Henry IV*, IV.v, and the reconciliation of King and
Justice in act V, scene ii. After the great reconciliations we know

perfectly well that Falstaff can do nothing more useless to himself (and to the King) than to steal horses and ride to London to depose Justice. The notion that Falstaff's intentions here are merely high spirits and good fun, or that he is giving the King one last chance to display his warm humanity, strikes me as naive: he has real mischief in mind, the utter corruption of the kingdom and the King.

The dismissal of Falstaff is of course Shakespeare's inspired version of an ancient, effective, and familiar comic device, the explosive pricking of the balloon of fraudulent or pretentious pride and arrogant expectation. Plautus had done it well enough, Jonson incomparably better—particularly with Mammon. But Jonson was a satirist and Shakespeare was not—he never seems quite at home when writing satirically simply because he wants us to see more of a character than the satirist can allow, hence, our embarrassment at some of Troilus's more fatuous displays, our uneasiness with Shylock, our difficulty in accepting the total, cold finality of King Harry's definitive dismissal of Falstaff. It is a satirist's situation, involving a character who might himself be described as a satirist of sorts. We have no such trouble with Sir Epicure Mammon: we merely wait with eager anticipation to see how Subtle, Face, and Doll will annihilate him; and when it happens, we certainly don't pity him. What happens with (or to) Falstaff is that he steps irrevocably out of the subplot, where he can flourish, into the main plot, in which there is no room for him at all, in which he can have only one function: to be dismissed. I do not find the dismissal, or the language in which it is put, shocking, but many readers—most readers—do. But surely the shock would have been greater if King Henry had, after all that has been happening in acts IV and V, warmly embraced his old acquaintance and welcomed him to affairs of state. That Shakespeare's version of the pricked balloon should have more humanity than others ("Master Shallow, I owe you a thousand pound"), as well as more inhumanity, as some would say, is hardly surprising. The coldness is psychologically necessary—you have to be emphatic with Falstaff—and also necessary for the ritual casting out, or off, of the substitute king, father, and justice: it's something like an exorcism.

This sort of balloon exists, and is inflated, in order to be pricked;

this surrogate father must go, like any impostor, so that nature and the body politic may go their ways. To think of the King as playing a savage trick on Falstaff is to turn the whole matter upside-down because Falstaff has been guilty of at least a potentially very dirty trick. The man who has spoken with his father, and then with Justice, as this one has, cannot be expected to embrace Falstaff—false father, perverter of justice, would-be corrupter of youth—or to be any more eager for his presence than he had been at the end of their last meeting, late in act II, scene iv. At the moment of Falstaff's atrocious "God save thee, my sweet boy!" no one could be further than Falstaff from the thoughts of the new king so recently reconciled with everyone who counts—father, brothers, Justice. If he had invited Falstaff to come up to London with some hint of a warm welcome and then coldly and publicly dismissed him, then there would be cause to complain. But he didn't do that, and at the end of act II, scene iv he had already pretty thoroughly dismissed his old acquaintance. According to Holinshed, he simply dismissed all of his "unruly mates" and banished them from his company (Hosley, p. 118). Professor Campbell calls attention to "a rather curious book called *Newes from the North*," perhaps by Francis Thynne, published in 1579, in which the newly crowned King Henry V does indeed play a savage trick: "he sent for all his olde companions, who were not a little glad thereof," and when they appeared, he rebuked them sharply and forbade them to come within twelve miles of the court (Campbell, p. 242). Such a device would of course have been acceptable in a morality play, but it would be wholly unacceptable coming from a Shakespearean monarch soon to be described as "the mirror of all Christian kings." I know of no evidence that Shakespeare read *Newes from the North*. If he did, however—certainly it was not impossible— he made the King innocent and Falstaff guilty of dirty tricks. In any case, he arranged matters so that Falstaff invited his own dismissal and disaster. Coming to London with absurd expectations and equally absurd companions was Falstaff's idea, not the King's.

In view of what has gone before, particularly in *2 Henry IV*, Falstaff's action in riding up to London to greet his tender lambkin and bring woe to my Lord Chief Justice must rank very high in any catalogue of ill-advised fatuities. But as we know, it is not Shakespeare's view that Falstaff should merely be dismissed: the dismissal must be as unequivocal and brutal as possible. How else could it be done? There is no other way. Falstaff is not the type to bow to mere reason (except of his own devising); and he has an astonishing notion of his hold on his young acquaintance, as is indicated by his rather unrepentant response to "Falstaff, good night" and by the assumption under which he leaves Gloucestershire for London. Prince Hal had never been much in love with vanity, in spite of Hotspur's opinion, and King Henry V doesn't care for it either. But Falstaff has come close to being its very embodiment, most immediately revealed in his journey to London and in his somewhat indecorous way of greeting his new king.

From another, and familiar, point of view, one can say that with his "real" father dead, the new king must choose between two surrogates, and choosing one necessarily requires rejecting the other. Here it is not a matter of choosing between two roughly comparable candidates: they are wholly antithetical, and choosing one means absolutely rejecting the other. Clearly enough, the choice is between Justice and Misrule, a point heavily underscored by the Lord Chief Justice's speech, V.ii.73–101, and by Falstaff's last speech in act V, scene iii: "Let us take any man's horses—the laws of England are at my commandment. Blessed are they that have been my friends, and woe to my Lord Chief Justice!" But Justice is what remains of King Henry IV:

> Whiles I was busy for the commonwealth,
> Your highness pleased to forget my place,
> The majesty and power of law and justice,
> The image of the King whom I presented.
>
> (V.ii.76–79)

With the new king's cold dismissal, the long holiday is over. Falstaff may or may not know that; but in fact he has no place to go (after prison) but back to the tavern, where, apparently, he dies—not that it hadn't been fun, but for Falstaff all the year was playing holidays.

Modern readers may be justified in wishing that King Henry V had been kinder to his old acquaintance. But the standards and attitudes at work in the play are not those of the late twentieth century. Our own sensibilities make it difficult to accept without question what Shakespeare did with (and to) Falstaff. I do not suggest that the terms of the dismissal are designed to make the King lovable. But it is important to see that Shakespeare did not anticipate *our* attitudes and did not intend to have his audience detest Henry V. Shakespeare has arranged it so that there is scarcely any other way for the dismissal to take place. Imagine the plays as they are, with the reconciliations of Prince Hal and his father, with the reconciliations of King Henry V and his brothers and Justice, and with Falstaff's setting out for London under the misapprehension that "the laws of England are at my commandment"; then imagine something different in sentiment from "I know thee not, old man." One can imagine different words, but in view of everything that we have seen until this point, I find it hard to imagine a different message; how else is the swollen bladder to be pricked, the perpetual ebullience cooled?

We have seen, particularly in the work of C. L. Barber, how closely Falstaff's function is modeled on that of the traditional Lord of Misrule. In connection with the plays' political and ethical action, it is important to see not only that Shakespeare uses this identity as a source of extraordinarily rich comedy but also that in doing so he asks us to imagine an England ruled by this Lord of Misrule, from "By the Lord, I'll be a brave judge!" (*1HIV*, I.ii.62) through the great tavern scene, with Falstaff playing the King's role, through Falstaff's performance as a military commander in both plays, right down to his rather grim plans for "my Lord Chief Justice." We are all familiar with the argument, offered with varying degrees of cogency, that Falstaff represents a continuing ironic commentary on the political world of the plays and particularly on the reign of a usurping king who must now reap the fruits of his criminality. The argument may be true—at least it would be indiscreet to insist that every Shakespearean ambiguity exists to be resolved. On the other hand, it is *very* easy to see the Falstaff episodes existing in ironic counterpoint to those of rebellion; the plans for the Gad's Hill robbery and Falstaff's subsequent role in that adventure have more to do with Northumberland and Worcester and Hotspur than with the business of King Henry, except insofar as *those* three are part of his business. Appropriately, the great tavern scene in *1 Henry IV* is preceded by the desertion of Hotspur by an unnamed follower and is followed by a detailed exposition of the plans of Hotspur, Glendower, and Mortimer to divide the kingdom among them. Where more or less direct comparisons between Falstaff and the King *are* invited, as in the same tavern scene, they hardly cast Falstaff in a favorable light and the King in an unfavorable one unless we choose to adopt Falstaff's general view of the world. We are not asked to view Falstaff as a desirable, if satirical, version of the King or as a satirical commentator to be taken seriously, but as an absurd substitute. If we imagine an England ruled by Falstaff, we can see easily enough that he is potentially more dangerous to the body politic than are the rebels. The fact that Falstaff is more *fun* than the King may represent a commentary on kingship, but not a derisive one. Shakespeare does not present Henry IV as an object of satire, but as a potential subject for tragedy.

This is not to say that the Falstaff episodes have no direct bearing on the role, and rule, of King Henry IV; they have a lot to do with it, mainly by implying impossible alternatives: Falstaff or Henry as king and father, Falstaff's flippancy about everything from the immediate heir of England to England itself or the King's desperate seriousness about the same range of subjects. Falstaff would no doubt make a better drinking companion than the King, but the subject is governing, not drinking. I agree that there "is unconscious humor in the fugitive and cloistered vice of literary scholars who condemn Hal for repudiating the free life of a tavern roisterer and highway robber; one explanation of such a view is the absence in our day of much feeling for the importance of calling. Hal is called to be the next king of England, and so he cannot be an ordinary man. He is not denying his humanity in accepting his duty to prepare for royalty, because a man's vocation is the center of his manhood."[10] If Falstaff were king, or Lord Chief Justice, the body politic would have a fearful, and permanent, hangover; and it is the body politic that concerns Shakespeare. The rejection and dismissal of Falstaff, at Shrewsbury and at

the end of *2 Henry IV*, are famous victories for Prince Hal, on behalf
of himself and on behalf of the commonwealth, and to that subject
we shall return.

GREY INIQUITY:
IT MEANS MISCHIEF

Falstaff began his spectacular dramatic life as an historical
character with strong religious and political overtones. Religion and
politics were inseparable in Shakespeare's time, and the potent
combination of Reformation, Counter Reformation, and erastianism
made the question of conscience a political as well as a religious one.
For Shakespeare, Falstaff represents a rank disorder with roots deep
enough. They flourished mightily in the soil of sixteenth-century
England (and Europe), and Shakespeare performs a symbolic eradi-
cation.

As everyone knows, Falstaff was originally called Sir John Oldcastle, and the name Oldcastle, for Falstaff, is found well into the
seventeenth century.[11] It is possible, although I think it very unlikely,
that Shakespeare simply took the name from one of his sources, the
anonymous play called *The Famous Victories of King Henry V*, in which
Oldcastle, usually called Jockey, one of the prince's companions in
debauchery, is a minor character.[12]

Since Oldcastle was a celebrated figure and was the subject of
much controversy, and since he had extremely influential descendants at court in the last decade of the sixteenth century, it would
seem, I think, that Shakespeare did not choose the name casually. Sir
John Oldcastle, Lord Cobham, was a lay leader, and patron, of the
Lollards, the pre-Reformation protestants who flourished in the
later fourteenth, fifteenth, and earlier sixteenth centuries, merging
with the Reformation when it came to England. He died a singularly
disgusting death for heresy in 1417, early in the reign of King Henry
V. Oldcastle died a martyr, and Foxe described his death in detail.

By Shakespeare's time there were two clearly defined and well-
developed traditions about Sir John Oldcastle. The Catholic view
was that he was a riotous debauchee, a corrupter of the innocent, a
traitor, and a heretic. I do not know precisely what sort of access
Shakespeare had to the Catholic tradition; it is at least possible that

he made his own contribution to it. The Protestant view, more widely known in Shakespeare's time, saw Oldcastle as a loyal Protestant hero and martyr, hounded to his dreadful death by the bishops of a bigoted church. This is the view found, perhaps somewhat decorated, in Foxe's *Acts and Monuments of the English Church*. To the extent that Shakespeare's Oldcastle is related to the historical figure, it is via the older tradition, which, in its literary manifestations, included puns on Oldcastle not unlike Prince Hal's reference to "my old lad of the castle" in *1 Henry IV*, I.ii.41. For example, the sermon topic of "the devil's castle" could be developed this way:

> The Castle of Righteousness can become conveniently enough "the Castle of Religion", in the narrower, monastic sense of that term. The Devil's Fortress, on the other hand, *by the kindly fortune of History* [emphasis added here], provides excellent scope for an attack on current heresy. "The Castle of Sin and Misery, the Devil's Castle", is now—*'Oldcastell* and his sect, who were leagued in malice and were united against the Lord God, against our noble King [Henry V] and the ministers of Holy Church. The *sowdioures* of this *synful* fortress made many sharp attacks upon the fort of God. First, they shot the arrows of many wicked words at the poor friars. They slandered and rebuked their poverty and the Order which the Church approves, concerning which many excellent clerics, many perfect priests and virtuous men say that it is a great charity to succour and support them—whatever Lollards may gabble to the contrary. . . . The strength and valour of this sinful castle terrified the hearts of many brave men. It began to be so strong in this kingdom that, if our liege lord had not made a timely and manly attack upon it, it would in very truth by that time have either conquered or plundered the realm [a reference to the Lollard Bill discussed by Canterbury and Ely at the beginning of *Henry V*], according to men's reckoning.[13]

These charitable sentiments were echoed in an inelegant piece of satirical verse:

> Hit is unkyndly for a Kni[gh]t
>   That shuld a kynges castel kepe,
> To bable the Bibel day and ni[gh]t
>   In restyng tyme when he shuld slepe;
>   And carefully awey to crepe,
> For alle the chief of chivalrie.
>   Wel aught hym to waile and wepe,

That suyche lust hath in lollardie. . . .
An old castel, and not repaired,
  With wast walles and wowes wide,
The wages ben ful yvel wared
  Sith suiche a capitayn to abide;
  That rereth riot for to ride
Agains the kynge and his clergie,
  With prive payne and pore pride;
There is a poynt of lollardie. . . .
An old castel draw al down,
  Hit is ful hard to rere hit hewe,
Sith suyche a congregacioun
  That cast hem to be untrewe.
  When beggers nether bake ne brewe,
Ne have therwith to borow ne bie,
Than mot riot robbe or reve,
Unde[r] the colour of lollardie.[14]

Sweet reasonableness was not the dominant tone of English religious controversy before Hooker (nor afterwards much either). The "manly attack" on the devil's castle, mentioned by the preacher, presumably refers to the burning of Oldcastle. These allusions are particularly important because of Shakespeare's use of the morality-play figure of the vice as part of Falstaff-Oldcastle's ancestry ("that reverend vice, that grey iniquity, that old white-bearded Satan") and because Falstaff is a soldier of sorts, like the Old Castle of the two extracts, and a captain, "suiche a capitayn."

Although Sir John Oldcastle, Lord Cobham, was burned as a heretic, his descendants managed to thrive, and one of them apparently had enough influence at court to force a change of the name of Shakespeare's character (although Falstaff is in itself not a particularly flattering name for a soldier; it was taken from the cowardly Sir John Fastolfe, or Falstaff, of 1 Henry VI). In July of 1596, Henry Carey, Lord Hunsdon, the Lord Chamberlain and nominal patron of Shakespeare's company, died and was briefly succeeded in his office by William Brooke, Lord Cobham, a descendant of the original Sir John Oldcastle. He, however, died on 6 March 1597 and was succeeded as Lord Chamberlain by Lord Hunsdon's son Sir George Carey. Cobham was the father-in-law of Sir Robert Cecil, already perhaps the most powerful man in England; and his son, Henry Brooke, who succeeded to his father's title as Lord Cobham, was allied with the Cecil faction at court and hence against the Essex faction, with which Shakespeare and his company apparently had some sort of political understanding.[15] Thus for about eight months Shakespeare and his company had a "patron" with whom their relationship could only have been uneasy although it seems highly unlikely that Shakespeare used the name Oldcastle *merely* to annoy a contemporary Lord of Cobham. Clearly he wanted the name to stick—hence, Prince Hal's pun—and apparently it did, for a while. (The process was reversed, also: in February 1598, Essex, in a letter to Cecil, refers to Henry Brooke as Sir John Falstaff (Humphreys 1, p. xii).

In 1611 the issue was joined rather dangerously by the Protestant historian John Speed in his *History of Great Britain* (9, XV):

> N. D., author of the *Three Conversions*, hath made Oldcastle a ruffian, a robber and a rebel, and his authority taken from the stage-players is more befitting the pen of his slanderous report than the credit of the judicious, being only grounded from this papist and his poet, of like conscience for lies, the one ever feigning, and the other falsifying the truth . . . I am not ignorant.[16]

"N. D." is Dolman, a pseudonym adopted by Fr. Robert Persons, the Jesuit priest who returned to England with Fr. Edmund Campion in 1580 but was ordered by his superiors to return to the continent after Campion's arrest in 1581. He spent the rest of his life (he died in 1610) writing about English affairs and doing everything in his considerable power to arrange the deposition of the heretic Elizabeth and to return England to the Old Faith. *The Three Conversions of England*, probably Persons's work but possibly not, was published in 1603, smuggled into England in large numbers, and read as avidly as were most works attributed to him. It addresses itself to a question that burned more brightly then than it does now: Was England first converted to Christianity by missionaries from Rome (as Geoffrey of Monmouth had said), by Joseph of Arimathea, by missionaries from Greece? It has little to say about Oldcastle beyond what is reported by Speed; but it is interesting and important that Speed should have said that "N. D." took "his authority from the stage-players," who could scarcely be any players but the Chamberlain's company (by then the King's Men); and his reference to "this papist and his poet" is even more interesting, because the most likely candidates for those titles would surely seem to be Persons and Shakespeare, although the proprietary epithet "his poet" does seem a bit much.

In any case, if there was a plot afoot to denigrate, for any reason, the historical Oldcastle and his Elizabethan descendants, it is at least arguable that Shakespeare had something to do with it—right down to the Hostess's "but then he was rheumatic [i.e., "rome-attic," which also goes rather horridly with the parody of the death of Socrates], and talked of the whore of Babylon" (*HV*, II.iv.38-40). But in fact more than a decade before John Speed made his charge, there had already been a remarkable response to Falstaff-Oldcastle: the Brookes (apparently) commissioned a play, *The First Part of Sir John Oldcastle*, printed in 1600 and apparently performed by the Chamberlain's chief rivals, the Admiral's company. (The second part has not survived; possibly it was never written or never printed.) The relative lateness of the date of publication suggests that the issue was far from moribund four years after the first performance of *1 Henry IV*. The purpose of the play was to rehabilitate Oldcastle's reputation after what it had suffered at the hands of "the stage-players." And he was rather handsomely rehabilitated; Michael Drayton and the talented but utterly unprincipled Anthony Munday were among the committee of five that wrote the play. The Prologue assures its audience that

> It is no pampered glutton we present,
> Nor aged counsellor to youthful sin;
> But one whose virtues shine above the rest,
> A valiant martyr and a youthful [*N.B.*] peer
> In whose true faith and loyalty expressed
> Unto his sovereign and his country's weal
> We strive to pay that tribute to our love
> Your favors merit. Let fair truth be graced,
> Since forged invention former times defaced.[17]

It is hard to imagine a more specific response to Sir John Falstaff-Oldcastle.

But much more interesting than the Prologue, much more revealing, and entertaining enough in its own right, is the fact that the authors of *Sir John Oldcastle*, in addition to rescuing their hero from the Blatant Swan, provided their own version of the character of Falstaff. He is also called Sir John, Sir John of Wrotham; he is old, fat, lecherous; he has a doxy named Doll; he is a glutton, a drunkard, a highwayman, a would-be corrupter of the youthful king, and, just to round out a picture that surely teems with quiet fun, he is a Roman Catholic parish priest. Now it may be, as is sometimes argued, that the Brookes and their squad of playwrights were overreacting to what they saw in Falstaff-Oldcastle. Personally, I doubt it.

I strongly suspect that for Shakespeare young King Harry the fifth must not only accept Justice as his new father but he must also reject heresy and other kinds of moral and spiritual disorder in his realm, as represented by the riotously irrepressible Sir John Falstaff-Oldcastle—the one who said, "The laws of England are at my commandment." I also suspect that the words of the Epilogue to *2 Henry IV*, spoken by an exceedingly rude dancer, "for Oldcastle died a martyr, and this is not the man," are flummery: "this is not the man to die a martyr; neither was Oldcastle." In his own rather special way, "our humble author [*does*] continue the story with Sir John in it," at least an account of his death that manages to revive many of the old jokes about Falstaff and includes enough references to fire and burning to remind us of Oldcastle's dreadful death. The tone of the Epilogue is not so much satirical as sarcastic; I believe that Shakespeare continued the story with Sir John in it exactly as far as he intended to, with Falstaff dying of a sweat, not, to be sure, in France, but in England, where "Oldcastle died a martyr" in a greater and drier heat. The cool dismissal of Falstaff-Oldcastle the Lollard heretic also prepares us for the curious discussion, never really settled, with which *Henry V* begins. The bill that Canterbury and Ely are discussing with some apprehension was, after all, called the Lollard Bill, and Canterbury and Ely have high hopes that the King, "full of grace and fair regard" and "a true lover of the holy Church," will not countenance a bill that "would drink the cup and all." (For more detailed discussion, see chapter IV, below.)

What we have at the end of *2 Henry IV* is, among many other things, a dismissal of heresy pending an unlikely recantation. If we think the picture is not a pretty one, we may nevertheless reflect that it is not quite so ugly as the reality to which it probably alludes—although the tone is certainly disagreeable. This aspect of Falstaff is not at all casual or incidental in the context of the entire tetralogy. Shakespeare was notoriously careful when dealing with religion, the central issue of his age. He had to be. In *Richard II* he was so careful that we are unlikely to notice that he dealt with it at all. But in "killing" divine kingship, he was also killing, as we have seen, a favorite medieval antipapal phenomenon—as well as something offensive on general principles. In *Henry V* he represents a scrupulously Catholic monarch who seeks, and heeds, the advice of the Church and ignores a parliamentary bill designed to weaken it. In the *Henry IV* plays, he personifies the incipient Protestant Reformation in the goodly bulk of Sir John Falstaff—and coldly dismisses it. In *Henry V*, Falstaff-Oldcastle dies "of a burning quotidian tertian . . . most lamentable to behold" (II.i.119-120). We should recall that Wycliffe began developing ideas of divine right and that Tyndale, and then Foxe, highly approved of King Richard's ideas of kingship precisely because they were antipapal and that Foxe virulently attacked both Henry IV and Henry V for their persecution of Lollards (Aston, pp. 291-299). Shakespeare plays a very dangerous game, with considerable finesse, when he deals with Sir John Oldcastle (as he had done earlier when he dealt with Richard II): good kings do not countenance (Protestant) heresy, and they certainly don't want to see the spoliation of the Church—or to have their soldiers stealing objects from churches. The mirror of all Christian kings reflects quite a bit, not all of it necessarily attractive.

It should go without saying, but probably doesn't, that in jesting about the burning of a heretic, gentle Shakespeare reflects some of the religious beastliness of the bigoted age in which he lived. He did something similar with Shylock.

ANOTHER FAMOUS VICTORY

The great public issues of the Henry IV plays are of absorbing interest even though we know the story. We know that the rebellions will not succeed, and we can see that a large measure of political and social order is restored—perhaps instituted would be more accurate—by the end of King Henry's reign. Shakespeare has kept our sympathies consistently on the King's side, except perhaps at Gaultree Forest (see below); but at that point the King is sick, not in the field at all, as he had been at Shrewsbury, treating with the rebels and fighting his battle. Alone among the rebels, Hotspur, Prince Hal's foil, is personally attractive and entertaining, but I doubt that many of us want the rebels to win at Shrewsbury on that account— and we need to see Prince Hal winning his own spurs. What sympathy we have for Hotspur is partly the result of his own (somewhat incomplete) domestic charm, his amusing Glendower-baiting, partly the result of Shakespeare's representation of his unscrupulous manipulation by his father and his uncle, Northumberland and Worcester. We see what is happening to him, and we can sympathize. He is far from perfect, but he is much less imperfect than his father and uncle. We see agreeable human qualities manipulated and finally destroyed, with great treachery, for political purposes.

It is important to recall, in view of the elegant patterns of fathers-sons-surrogates in these plays, the striking contrast between Northumberland-Hotspur on the one hand and King Henry-Prince Hal on the other, and the relationship of both to the health of the body politic. The King's feelings about his son are largely an effect of his concern for England, and he tries, whenever he gets the chance, to persuade his son to share that concern and prepare himself to make England's welfare his principal occupation. He also loves his son. Northumberland is anarchy personified, a thoroughly terrible man (and much worse in the plays than he was historically).[18] For him and for his brother Worcester, betrayal is a way of life; it is their vocation in which they do indeed labor. They betrayed King Richard and supported Bolingbroke for their own personal gain. They use the Mortimer claim solely to keep Hotspur warm (after the Scottish prisoner issue) in their plotting against Henry IV. Northumberland betrays both his brother and his son by witholding his forces from Shrewsbury, and Worcester betrays his nephew by refusing to tell him about the King's genuine offer of pardon. Northumberland betrays his son in 1 Henry IV and then manages to betray his memory in 2 Henry IV (although of course his daughter-in-law is not thinking of betrayal when she urges him to seek refuge in Scotland). It is appro-

priate that he is the one to shout the magic slogan, "Let order die!" in
2 Henry IV (I.i.154).

Unlike the King, Northumberland doesn't have trouble with his
son, and he doesn't worry about him until it is much too late—not
until after he has betrayed him and is waiting, at the beginning of *2
Henry IV*, for the news from Shrewsbury. When he gets the news, his
rage is real enough, but rather misdirected. He doesn't have trouble
with his son: he merely betrays him to his death; and one of the things
that is attractive about Hotspur is his lack of rancor toward his
father, whose defection he thinks of only in military terms. Guileless
himself, no strategist and certainly no politician, he apparently cannot conceive guile in his father or his uncle (even though he easily
imagines that he sees it in the King): he does not say, "My father has
betrayed me." He is a victim in a great political struggle almost as
much as he is a participant, and after his death Prince Hal's generous
epitaph may well reflect the sentiments of any audience. Hotspur is
an instance of the extent to which all issues are political issues, as
well as an indication of how political considerations and ambitions
and the love of power can subvert human values. Bolingbroke is
often seen as nothing more than an ambitious and unscrupulous politician. I have already registered one or two reservations about this
view, but it applies without qualification to Northumberland and
Worcester, two thoroughly bad men.

But this is not to say that Hotspur is simply a victim, an agreeable
and likable pawn in the political context in which he finds himself:
he is also irresponsible, imperceptive, treacherous, and destructive.
He hates "this vile politician Bolingbroke," to whom he had earlier
(in *RII*) enthusiastically offered his services; and the original cause of
his hatred, as far as we can determine, was the prisoner issue. The
implications of that issue are clear enough: Is England to become a
strong national state, or is it to be a rather loose confederation of
feudal baronies? It is a political issue brought to a head by Hotspur's
impetuous arrogance and his solipsistic notion of honor. His willingness to see the country divided into three (*1HIV*, III.i), as long as he
has *his* third, is consistent with his stand on the prisoner issue. War is
for personal glory ("honor") and profit, and the idea of a united
kingdom is utterly foreign to his thinking—such a notion would sim-

ply not occur to him. Nor is he really much interested in the *principle* of the Mortimer claim. The raising of that claim by Northumberland and Worcester in act I, scene iii of *1 Henry IV* confirms his opinion of Bolingbroke and gives him a Cause: to bring down the usurper and restore the rightful ruler. By act III, scene i, he and the allegedly rightful ruler are partners, along with Glendower, in an enterprise designed to divide the kingdom into feudal baronies. In the parley with Blunt before Shrewsbury (IV.iii), he mentions the King's alleged treachery to Mortimer and, parenthetically, Mortimer's claim; but by then Mortimer is out of the picture, and the substance of his complaint is very different: Bolingbroke violated the "Doncaster promise"—the promise that he was returning from exile only to claim his own as Gaunt's heir (a promise that, in the play at least, he did not make)—"disgrac'd me in my happy [profitable?] victories" (97), dismissed Worcester from the Council (Worcester had not exactly been a very Nestor among councilors) and Northumberland from the court, and drove the Percys "to pry/Into his title, the which we find/Too indirect for long continuance" (103-105)— so we will chop up the kingdom for ourselves.

The complaint is that the King has been acting like a king, rather than like another feudal lord. The Percys' response to the unexpected independence of their protégé is very much like that of the last of the great feudal barons, Warwick the Kingmaker, on discovering the independence of *his* protégé, Edward IV, a similar situation with which Shakespeare had already dealt, somewhat less effectively.[19] Hotspur does not propose to make Mortimer king. (Worcester, in his recital of grievances [V.i.30-71], is superficially more plausible, twice citing the Doncaster promise, with the credibility that one might expect. He is talking for the record, very shrewdly; the sum of his complaint is "unkind usage, dangerous countenance,/And violation of all faith and troth/Sworn to us in our younger enterprise" [V.i.69-71]. It was Northumberland who arrested Carlisle for treason, for speaking out for Richard; and it was Bolingbroke, the vile politician, who pardoned him. No doubt that pardon, and Aumerle's, were politically motivated, but not all political motives are obscene—a notion very difficult to knock into some folks' heads.)

But for Hotspur, the heart of the matter is his obsessive notion of
honor, which is partly attractive, like King Henry V's, and partly
absurd. His response to the news, first that his father's troops will not
appear and then that Glendower's won't either, is very different
from King Richard's reaction to similar (although perhaps worse)
disasters. If we lose, we can count on them next time (the assumption
of a next time is rather gallant, too); if we win, our victory will be all
the more impressive—a little like King Harry the Fifth before Agincourt (*HV*, IV.iii.18-67), but with a radically different emphasis:
"God's will" is hardly a concern of Hotspur's. It is probably inevitable that, in retrospect, we think of Henry V when we hear Hotspur's reasonably gallant and high-spirited words about bucking the
odds, or about plucking bright honor from the pale-fac'd moon
(source of lunacy); but it is more important to notice that Prince Hal,
as described by Vernon (*1HIV*, IV.i.104-110; V.ii.51-68), is already
like a piece of Henry V—just emerged from the chrysalis—not
Henry V in embryo, but Henry V not quite fully revealed: he was
ordained to that end. What Vernon described is something that
Hotspur cannot believe and will not accept. The source of his disbelief is, on the first level, what he thinks of as Prince Harry's "vanity." That the "nimble-footed madcap Prince of Wales" (IV.i.95), a
prince of "so wild a liberty" (V.ii.71), should come to do battle with
Harry Percy is a source of annoyance as well as a frivolous challenge.
Chivalry is not exactly dead:

> *Prince.*   I am the Prince of Wales, and think not, Percy,
>   To share with me in glory any more:
>   Two stars keep not their motion in one sphere,
>   Nor can one England brook a double reign
>   Of Harry Percy and the Prince of Wales.
> *Hotspur.* Nor shall it, Harry, for the hour is come
>   To end the one of us, and would to God
>   Thy name in arms were now as great as mine!
> *Prince.*   I'll make it greater ere I part from thee,
>   And all the budding honors on thy crest
>   I'll crop to make a garland for my head.
> *Hotspur.* I can no longer brook thy vanities. [*They fight.*]
>   (V.iv.62-73)

We can easily see where Harry Monmouth's chief vanity lies: it is in his announced intention of cropping all the budding honors from Harry Percy's crest. Before they fight, and after, the thought is intolerable to Hotspur:

> O Harry, thou has robb'd me of my youth!
> I better brook the loss of brittle life
> Than those proud titles thou hast won of me;
> They wound my thoughts worse than thy sword my flesh.
>
> (V.iv.76–79)

But of course the vanity is really Hotspur's, and finally it is fatal (but not before some fetching alliteration). Prince Hal was not in love with vanity at all. His words to Hotspur (70–72) were a form of courtesy from one noble Harry to another; and when the vain Harry dies, the one who wasn't vain covers him, and himself, with chivalric honor. He doesn't need Hotspur's budding honors; and if Plump Jack thinks *he* can use them, he is welcome to them. A good man triumphs over one not so good but better than most, and in doing so he saves his father's life and most probably his kingdom. All this is part of the revelation, not the education, of the Prince. On the basis of his words over the fallen Hotspur and the supine Falstaff, we should not be surprised by the nonmiracle (strictly speaking) of King Henry V; all the important signs point to a winner.

Hotspur has been a foil to the Prince but one formidable enough so that his death gives incalculable support to the credentials of the immediate heir of England; supporting the Prince's credentials is one of Hotspur's main dramatic functions in *1 Henry IV*. His role underlines the indecency of Northumberland and Worcester, and it helps to give public credibility to the Prince—if he can manage Hotspur. . . . Shakespeare establishes the uneasy Hal-Hotspur symbiosis early in the play, with the King's wish that "some night-tripping fairy had exchanged/In cradle-clothes our children where they lay,/And call'd mine Percy, his Plantagenet!" (*1HIV*, I.iii.86–88). It is strengthened by Hal's amusing parody of "the Hotspur of the north" (II.iv.100) and heavily reenforced by the explicit comparisons drawn by the King and the Prince in their long and painful conversation (III.ii.93–159). And it reaches its culmination at Shrewsbury.

The political considerations of the Percy rebellion thus serve to support another theme, what might be called the revelation of Prince Hal; not "the education of the prince" like a courtesy book but the revelation of qualities that are there to be drawn on as needed, not to be displayed when they are not needed. When it was time to kill Harry Percy, he was able to do so, and he did not learn in an afternoon how to be a soldier (Vernon's descriptions of him, mentioned above, tell us that). When he says he will redeem the time "when men least think I will" (I.ii.212), he is merely stating a fact: he knows well enough how to redeem the time—his erected wit can easily correct his partly infected will. "When men least think I will" are important words; how could the Hotspur of the north imagine that the madcap, nimble-footed Prince of Wales would pull down Percy's vanity while displaying none of his own? The victory over Hotspur immediately precedes another, even more important, victory, as we have seen—the victory over the Tempter that comes when Hal refuses to take credit for Hotspur's mutilated corpse. The second victory seals the first.

In fact, Shrewsbury settles more than one issue: Falstaff's playing dead is a kind of symbolic death followed by a false resurrection, and the Prince's words over the hulk of his old acquaintance are a symbolic farewell. Metaphorically, Falstaff *is* dead when the Prince sees him lying (and hears him lying) at Shrewsbury; and he is rejected when Prince Hal refuses to claim credit for the mutilated body. Obviously, Hal's victory over Hotspur reveals more than his skill with weapons. There are some famous victories in *1 Henry IV*; in *2 Henry IV* there is an infamous victory, and it would have been very different had Prince Hal and his father, instead of Prince John and Westmoreland, been there.

An Infamous Victory

We are bred up to feel it a disgrace ever to succeed by falsehood . . . we will keep hammering along with the conviction that honesty is the best policy, and that truth always wins in the long run. These pretty little sentiments do well for a child's copy book, but a man [i.e., a soldier] who acts on them had better sheathe his sword forever.[20]

These sentiments of a Victorian general (although they don't *sound* Victorian) might have been spoken by Prince John of Lancaster, or by Westmoreland, to justify their betrayal of the rebel leaders at Gaultree Forest (*2HIV*, IV.ii). They represent a fact of military life well enough known, seldom so bluntly stated, and still officially regarded as rather bad form in Shakespeare's time and even, occasionally, in ours. Gaultree Forest established no precedents and should hold no surprises, although it has elicited considerable outrage. The kind of treachery displayed in Gaultree Forest is one way in which battles are won, or averted in such a way as to produce the effect of victory without the inconvenience of fighting. The rebels have no easily discernible cause (Mortimer, Scottish prisoners, Hotspur are all far behind) except detestation of the King, and the grievances to which they allude are unspecified: in the closest thing to a formal statement of cause, the Archbishop proclaims that England is sick and must be bled (IV.i.53–58), a sufficient reason for discontent but a rotten motive for civil war, particularly since the Archbishop is part of the sickness. England, or part of it, is bled, but the leeches are Prince John and Westmoreland, and this bleeding prevents the greater bloodshed of a battle (not much greater, perhaps, since a number of rebel soldiers are treacherously hunted down and killed). It is a successful Machiavellian operation and brings measurably closer the peace so desperately desired by the dying King. The rebel leaders will perforce sheathe their swords forever. With rebels so easily, if outrageously, duped, it is not surprising that another rebel, Sir John Colevile, seriously misreads Sir John Falstaff's reputation for valor. It seems doubtful that in all England another knight would consider surrendering to Falstaff, especially for Colevile's reasons. Rumor has certainly done its work.

Now, if one wished to justify the betrayal of the rebels, one might do so along the lines sketched above. Prince John is, after all, no Tamburlaine, although he is a good deal less straightforward. But such a justification, while it seems to fit the facts, more or less, simply does not "feel" right. The episode is ugly, the killings gratuitous:

the rebel troops have dispersed, and Prince John has promised redress of grievances—and continues to do so even while ordering the executions of the three rebel leaders. The rebels, to be sure, have a dubious cause consisting largely of unspecified grievances, and peace is now much closer; but it would not be easy to argue, much less to demonstrate, that Shakespeare expects much approval of this sort of proceeding, that he suggests that the end justifies the means.[21]

The whole episode, with its comic Falstaff-Colevile epilogue, is striking and memorably unpalatable, the aftertaste not improved by Prince John's insufferable "God, and not we, hath safely fought today" (IV.ii.121). One must probably agree with the author of *The Soldier's Handbook*—chivalry has not always been war's most familiar characteristic. The chivalric episodes and heroic figures are what we like to remember, but although they are often edifying and inspiring, they don't usually produce the great victories (Hal's killing of Hotspur might be an exception—kill the enemy's leader or ablest soldier, and the enemy will lose enthusiasm for battle). Only a very gifted commander can keep the killing clean, or even appear to.

The betrayal of the rebels is a negation of chivalry and honor; the submission of Colevile is a parody of chivalry, and his execution is both gratuitous (why kill so grotesquely harmless an enemy?) and a parody of justice (even if Colevile is only a parody of a prisoner of war, killing prisoners of war has always been bad form: Henry V mistakenly thought it was necessary to do so in the battle of Agincourt). The negation and the parody (or travesty)·mean that in the world of Prince John, Westmoreland, and the two Sir Johns (the lesser and the greater), chivalry is dead or dying or being killed. Can the same thing be said about chivalry in the larger world of these plays? Has a sordid but efficient Machiavellianism replaced honor and high achievement in the world of King Henry IV and his heir? The majority answer is a fairly emphatic yes: chivalry is dead, long live politics. But that answer oversimplifies.

The betrayal is entirely the doing of Westmoreland and John of Lancaster. It is not at all the style of Prince Hal, whose genuine chivalry has already been shown at Shrewsbury in his single combat with Hotspur and his generous epitaph for his fallen enemy. And certainly it is not a device of the King's; he is dying, and he has been assured by Warwick (III.i) that he need not concern himself with military affairs. Shakespeare is very careful to keep the King at a good distance from the dirty work here; in Holinshed, King Henry is actively engaged in the campaign, and the captured rebel leaders are taken to him at Pomfret and then on to York, where they are executed (Hosley, p. 113). These are important details: Shakespeare has made the betrayal of the rebels look very bad indeed, and he has carefully kept Prince Hal and his father out of it—but to what end?

If we assume that the tetralogy's first three plays in effect look forward to the triumphant reign of King Henry V, then some sort of answer to the question is relatively simple. The Gaultree Forest episode shows us a danger to the kingdom, partly from the rebels, whose malice, however, is more than balanced by their incompetence, but also, and perhaps more important, from the King's friends and kinsmen, from Lancaster and Westmoreland, who are too efficient by half and thoroughly unscrupulous. When such tactics as theirs become institutionalized, you have a Machiavellian state, with the kind of systematic betrayal that characterized, for example, Henry VIII's and Norfolk's handling of the Pilgrimage of Grace in 1539 or the government's disposition of the Babington Plot in 1585-1586. (The plot was real enough; the "intelligence overkill" used by the government was designed to do something more than get the goods on the inept Babington and his friends. It succeeded, too.)

One does not find many benign Machiavells on the Elizabethan and Jacobean stage (Jonson's Cicero is one, based on the character of Sir Robert Cecil). Machiavellian governments like Elizabeth's are in no position to encourage public support of Machiavellian practices, practices for which Shakespeare, in any case, had massive contempt. Neither his Henry IV nor his Henry V is notably Machiavellian (this view is not universally held), but at Gaultree Forest Lancaster and Westmoreland are, and the effect is unpleasant as well as unchivalric. The episode is another step in preparing us, through contrast, for King Henry V. Here is the sort of thing that just might become institutionalized under another regime; and it occurs at a critical point, with the King dying and his lawful heir momentarily away from the scene. Those of us who dislike the idea of conquering France, or anyone else, need to remind ourselves that what King Harry the fifth does is to set out, in response to an irresistible challenge, on a high chivalric adventure that he carries off with dash and style—not what his historical counterpart did, but that is for the moment another story. At Gaultree Forest we can look back to Shrewsbury and ahead to Agincourt and reflect that in *that* context, in any context perhaps, Lancaster and Westmoreland do not exactly cover themselves with glory and that they indicate a direction in which England might turn under the wrong auspices.

In the tricking of the rebel leaders we get a reprise, with variations, of the King's offer of peace before Shrewsbury. But there the treachery was Worcester's, who refused to relay the King's offer to Hotspur because, although he was willing to believe the King might pardon Hotspur, he could not believe the King would pardon *him*. Whether he was right or not we cannot be entirely certain, but we can make a fairly safe assumption; Worcester, after all, and his brother Northumberland are the Machiavells in *1 Henry IV*, and every action Northumberland takes in *both* plays is both treacherous and a denial of chivalry; Northumberland's repeated strategic retreats, beginning with his desertion of his son, are the most familiar examples.

Falstaff's taking of Colevile is a parody (or a travesty) of chivalry, and it too is a kind of reprise, with an amusing variation. This is that Falstaff who had spoken so edifyingly of honor at Shrewsbury while covering himself with disgrace; who played dead to avoid the fatal inconvenience of fighting Douglas; and who mutilated, symbolically castrated, the corpse of Hotspur; the Falstaff who managed to get most of his men killed at Shrewsbury (so that he could collect their pay) and who in this play entertainingly drafts the least likely soldiers he can find, letting their superiors buy their way out. Colevile surrenders to Falstaff because he is even less perceptive than his leaders and because Rumour, painted full of tongues, has brought off the ultimate triumph: persuading someone that Falstaff is a valiant captain, one to whom it would be no disgrace to surrender, discretion being (by far) the better part of valor. Another entertaining variation is played out at Agincourt (*HV*, IV.iv) when Pistol, in a role just possibly designed originally for Falstaff (Walter, pp. xxxviii-xxxix), takes the cautious French soldier. (The French provide an amusing parody of chivalric language and attitudes the night before Agincourt and a grim perversion when they kill the English boys during the battle itself.)

Shakespeare neatly disposes of both Lancaster and Falstaff in these scenes and wraps up the business with Lancaster's wholly accurate assessment of Colevile's surrender and Falstaff's reasonably accurate assessment of Lancaster (although it is doubtful that Lancaster would be much improved if he were to take up drinking seriously).

In addition to unjustifiable, if not wholly inexplicable, rebellion, Machiavellian betrayal, and denial and parody of chivalry, the Gaultree Forest episode raises an extremely touchy issue, very briefly, the only time it is raised in these plays after *Richard II*. If Lancaster, who raises it, were not such a cold and heartless young man (however loyal to his father), if it were raised by the King himself, or by Prince Hal, it would be sinister and dismaying. Ticking off the rebels' offenses, Lancaster observes:

> You have ta'en up,
> Under the counterfeited zeal of God,
> The subjects of his substitute, my father,
> And both against the peace of heaven and him
> Have here up-swarm'd them.
>
> (IV.ii.26–30)

Only King Richard, a handful of his followers, and John of Gaunt (briefly) have spoken of the king as God's substitute, with what cogency and effect and with what implications for Richard and his play we have already seen. Henry IV makes no such claim for himself, nor do any of his followers and supporters except the cool and opportunistic Lancaster. It is hard to see how Shakespeare could have had Henry IV make such claims in any case, not in view of the circumstances under which he became king, not in the political milieu in which the play was written and acted. But Henry V makes no such claim either, and Shakespeare could easily have had him do so, particularly when he discovers the treason and lectures the traitors before sending them off to execution (*HV*, II.ii). In Shakespeare's time, if not in ours, Henry V was after all a great national hero, and what better spot than this to slip in a couple of allusions to Tudor notions of the crown's divinity and the subject's duty?

In addition to being unchivalric, Machiavellian, ruthless, and no gentleman, Lancaster is politically regressive. He believes, or appears to believe, that the King is God's substitute and *for that reason* not liable to chastisement by his subjects, and this part of the episode carries on the demolition of divine right by bringing it up in a context in which it must appear to justify treachery, dishonor, betrayal. The idea of the King's divinity, or of his divine provenance, is by now not much of an argument, and it is impossible to be sure whether Prince John really believes it or merely uses it. It is, in either case, a notion that is being banished from the kingdom in these plays.

The Gaultree Forest episode is not merely an unpleasant interlude in a very busy play, nor is it only a chapter in the history of military-political strategy, nor is it simply an instance of what is wrong with King Harry and his kingdom. It represents present dangers and, by contrast, anticipates future achievements. The rebellion is almost the last gasp of civil discord in the kingdom of Henry IV, and the betrayal represents the sort of thing that will not be permitted in the England of Henry V. It reminds us of how much depends on Prince Hal, and it occurs just before the Prince is given the final push, or takes the final step, into political maturity and responsibility. The high adventure of Agincourt wipes out the misadventure in Gaultree Forest. In the meantime, the kingdom will not be discommoded by the absence, or the reformation, of these three Johns—Lancaster, Colevile, Falstaff. The fate of the last of them is about to be definitively sealed in London.

IV

The Mirror of All Christian Kings

WITH HENRY V THE GREAT TETRALOGY COMES TO A TRIUMPHANT CLOSE, with a king who is, whether we like him or not, the precise antithesis of King Richard II. Richard was utterly undone by the assumptions he made about kingship. He put his faith in divine right (although he was a little careless about his accountability to God and didn't understand the full meaning of hereditary right, even when it was explained to him); he had some idea of himself as a mystical corporation (King Body Politic); and he tended to think of his office in terms of a corrupt version of divine, Christ-centered kingship. His assumptions made it impossible for him to act once his authority was seriously challenged; they contained their own pathology; and the rhetoric of divine kingship proved to be stirring but hollow. The realization that his needs and desires were identical to those of other humans led him to the conclusion that he was, by definition, no king. When he looked in a mirror and saw a merely *human* face, any illusions he may still have had were shattered. The dramatic action of *Richard II* undermined and destroyed some official (and unofficial), mystical, religiously oriented Tudor doctrines on monarchs' rights and subjects' duties.

If Shakespeare's King Henry is the antithesis of his King Richard, what has happened to the four cardinal principles of the doctrine of the divine right of kings? If monarchy is ordained by God, here is a king who seems to have been born for just that sort of ordination; if hereditary right is indefeasible, here is a king who rules by hereditary right (a point vigorously made in *2 Henry IV*); if the king is accountable to God alone, here is a king who says that the success of his

143

ventures lies in God's hands and who thanks God when his ventures succeed; if passive obedience is enjoined by God, here is a king who enjoys the loyal obedience of the overwhelming majority of his subjects, including those who must follow him into battle. In fact, here is a king who seems to enjoy all the advantages of divine right without making any of its claims and without having anyone else make them for him, a king with no professional problems, so to speak, whatever, who seems to have no notion of the King Body Politic or of divine kingship.[1] It is almost as though Shakespeare were saying, "Let a king do his work well and the prerogatives will take care of themselves, or they will become irrelevant." Richard invoked divine right and divine kingship to buck himself up; Harry doesn't need to and wouldn't care to.

Shakespeare has been sorting things out, and mainly he has been sorting out the tangled relationships between the temporal and the spiritual worlds, especially as they are connected with ideas of kingship and the body politic. A king who falls into the habit of thinking of himself as the deputy elected by the Lord is likely, when challenged and in real danger, to think of himself as the Lord betrayed, as a spiritual figure and not a temporal, political figure at all. This at least is what happens to Richard: when he "disanoints" and "unkings" himself, he is more priest than king. Henry V is a Christian king whose religion is genuine, humble, and orthodox; but he is also a strictly temporal ruler whose work is exclusively in and of the temporal world. He has none of Richard's illusions and none of Richard's problems. (It is, I know, an odd thing to say about a major Shakespearean character, but King Harry *seems* to be absolutely normal psychologically.) *Richard II* (Dover Wilson's "gorgeous dramatic essay on the divine right of kings") is a veritable ocean of political mysticism (in which, one should add for consistency, the principal celebrant drowns). The mirror of all Christian kings has nothing whatever to do with mystical doctrines of kingship.

If Shakespeare demonstrated the dangers of mystical, religiously oriented theories of kingship in *Richard II*, he replaced them with something far more satisfactory in *Henry IV* and *Henry V*. The notion of the king as God's substitute is raised briefly, only to be discredited, in Gaultree Forest (*2HIV*, IV.ii.26–30); and it *is* discredited, by John of Lancaster's insufferable "God, and not we, hath safely fought today" (121), a mere hypocritical gloss on his own treachery. There is otherwise no hint of divine right, divine kingship, of the King's Two Bodies in *Henry IV*. *Henry V* represents the triumph of man-centered kingship, in which the standard by which a king is measured is human.[2] He is not a god, not like a god, not compared to a god; he is not God's substitute, deputy, or lieutenant. He is, for Shakespeare anyhow, someone who inherited a crown: a king, the one we have in England. Again, we're a long way from Richard II, a little closer to Henry IV.

King Henry himself has no identifiable theory of kingship, only a series of pragmatic observations: kings are like other people except that they have greater responsibilities, wear better clothes, (probably) eat better, work harder, are flattered, sleep less, and are burdened with "ceremony" (most of this emerges in act IV, scene i). Such a theory, if that's what it is, does not guarantee a good king, but it increases the likelihood of a reasonably responsible one; and it prevents the misuse of religion to cow subjects into accepting, or enduring, tyranny or gross incompetence. King Harry is of course rather special, and Shakespeare holds him up for special examination.

The great tetralogy began with a fascinating account of a king so obsessed with notions of his own divinity that he was unable to take the sort of actions one might expect of a mere prudent man or politician. It ends with an equally fascinating account of a man who is a king and who seems clearly to have worked hard and successfully to achieve the image and the qualities of a great king.

*   *   *   *   *

But, as all the world knows, there is radical disagreement over what we are to make of Shakespeare's King Henry V; he is Shakespeare's ideal king, or a hero-king; or he is just slightly better than Tamburlaine. He is a thoroughly attractive figure; he is wretchedly unattractive. Or he occupies some station or other between these wildly irreconcilable alternatives. It would not be unreasonable to complain that these views cannot all be right. But neither is it *wholly* unreasonable to base one's response to King Harry on one's own social, political, and moral principles. The so-called Hal-haters have their reasons: it is a lot easier to like Prince Hamlet than to love King Harry, although I don't doubt for a minute that Shakespeare expected his audience to love him. I happen to have a strong affection for both, and no interest at all in acting as a referee in this particular debate. I believe that Shakespeare intended King Harry to be seen as a model, that the Chorus's description of him as "the mirror of all Christian kings" (II. Chorus.6) is meant to be taken seriously, that the high adventures of this king are designed to bring the tetralogy to a triumphant close. It does seem to me that if Shakespeare had intended a contemporary audience to dislike King Henry, or to disapprove of his activities, he set about achieving his intention in a very strange way.

He gives us a King Harry who is frankly a winner (this is no doubt part of the problem), is seen by virtually everyone else in his play as a winner, and is almost universally applauded for it. He achieves everything he wants, on a superlative scale, with dash and flair; he wins the war, gets the girl, and will inherit her father's estate. In view of the status of Henry V in Shakespeare's time, this is not, on the face of it, surprising. He was, after all, a great national hero, perhaps England's greatest national hero, and he won one of England's two greatest military victories. In contemporary eyes, his greatest achievement was the victory at Agincourt, and so it was, in a special sense, for Shakespeare. Agincourt was light years from Gaultree Forest, and Agincourt is the center from which nearly all the action of Henry V radiates.[3] Anyone writing a play about Henry V in 1599 would have seemed more than a little eccentric if he did not deal with the famous victory and did not represent on the stage some of the qualities, kingly and military, that made it possible. Shakespeare was, after all, "an English dramatist writing for a fiercely assertive young nation. It would have been impossible for him to write of Agincourt as anything other than a victory for the right side; nor, I am sure, did he *want* to write otherwise."[4] We are speaking of prior probabilities, of course, but I see no evidence that Shakespeare was chafing under the mandate of a restrictive and inhibiting tradition. Quite the contrary: the play begins with high praise for the King, and Chorus and players maintain it until the end, and past the end, into the Epilogue.

And as villain, even as flawed hero, Henry would have been a very unusual Shakespearean character. Shakespearean characters who seriously misbehave come to grief or are reformed or are pardoned or are let off in the hope that reform might eventually come (Bertram and Angelo). And sooner or later everyone else in the play knows that the character has misbehaved. In *Henry V*, no on expresses really serious dissatisfaction with the King except the Dauphin, whose opinion we can perhaps discount. The tavern crowd is disappointed in him. The admirable soldiers, on the night before Agincourt, have some grave doubts and serious questions. But sooner or later everyone admires him, and the admiration begins in the first scene of the play. Throughout three plays, in fact, Shakespeare has given us a character admired and respected by virtually everyone except his father and Hotspur; his father loves him, and Hotspur is wrong.

At the very end of the Battle of Agincourt, Montjoy, the French herald, addresses Harry as "great king"—not surprisingly. He *is* now a great king, as Montjoy well knows, and he has demonstrated his greatness in a traditional way, by proving himself, and his men, in battle, against fearful odds. (No point in complaining that he doesn't fight and kill another Hotspur at Agincourt; Shakespeare and history took care to see that there were no Hotspurs recorded among the French, and Agincourt is in any case a different kind of duel [see below]. His triumph lies in holding together an army and inspiring it to fight and win. Under the circumstances so clearly defined here, this is a greater achievement.) The fact is that no matter how much we detest imperial adventures (and "imperial" in Shakespeare's time had a rather different meaning from its modern one), the heroism of Shakespeare's King Harry arises largely from the achievement that makes him downright repellent to some modern readers—the great victory at Agincourt. It is not surprising that most of the aggressively patriotic population of a small sixteenth-century western-European nation whose Queen laid at least *pro forma* claim to the French crown should have been delighted at the spectacle of an English king leading a fearfully outnumbered army to victory against the French. It *would* have been surprising if Shakespeare had taken a national hero and made him into a second-rate opportunist, like John of Lancaster at Gaultree Forest. (John is an oddly unformed character: he did well at Shrewsbury, very well at Agincourt, miserably at Gaultree Forest.) It would have been even more surprising if, after writing *Henry IV*, Shakespeare had decided to present Hal not only in a new light, which he does, but in a bad one, which he does not. It would have made a shambles of the tetralogy, reduced it to ruin. Shakespeare is full of surprises, but not that kind. The young king who adopted Justice as his father at the end of one play has not sneaked off for a liaison with Injustice before the next one. And *Henry V* is no anticlimax: it is the logical conclusion to the tetralogy.

* * * * *

Whether we take it as an isolated play or as the logical ending of the tetralogy, however, there is one particularly striking fact about *Henry V*—a fact so obvious that it is easily overlooked or easily misinterpreted. Everyone knows that the reign of Henry V—still often described as one of the most successful in English history, although it wasn't—was followed by a series of disasters. Elizabeth claimed to be Queen of France, but by 1453 the English in France had already been thoroughly defeated. If that wasn't bad enough, Tudor historians invented the Wars of the Roses to justify Henry VII's claim of a mandate to restore order and unity (he did restore order, in the usual way, after destroying it). Shakespeare had already written about the disasters that followed the death of Henry V, and his first tetralogy no doubt made its own contribution to the notion that the years from 1422–1485 were total chaos interrupted only by a brief idyllic interlude in a garden in Kent. The Epilogue to *Henry V* reminds anyone who needs reminding that things did not turn out well and gives a reason more plausible than that advanced in the chronicles. But *Henry V* ends not only on a most emphatic note of triumph but also with a sense of finality and completion, like a comedy—as though, if we were ignorant of history, we might expect them all, Harry and Kate, England and France, to live happily every after, like Rosalind and Orlando, Celia and Oliver, in a play written at about the same time. Well, if Henry V is to be Shakespeare's ideal king (even if Wisdom cries out in the streets against it), or merely his most successful king, his play cannot end on too dreary a note. But each of the two preceding plays, although both can stand by themselves, ends with an implied invitation to come back for more, to anticipate what comes next. But, in spite of the efforts of Tillyard, Wilson, and others to persuade us to read the plays in their historical order rather than in their Shakespearean chronology, there is no sequel to *Henry V*. Something has been extracted from history—which does not stop—and has been given a beginning, a middle, and an end (the statement can apply both to *Henry V* and to the tetralogy as a whole). Now, in 1599, we are *not* invited to look ahead to the time of Henry VI because it is already in the past. Instead, the play ends with preparations for marriage—the subject of its closing speech—and an Epilogue, appropriately a sonnet, asks us to contemplate the life of this star of England, who lived a short time but lived most greatly. One may well observe that a play has to end *somehow*, but I should think it is obvious that the way *this* play ends seems designed to separate history from its movement, time from its flowing; and the reason must be that if we contemplate *this* history, and are properly instructed by it, then what followed need not necessarily repeat itself. Scholars have sometimes taken the historical events following the death of Henry V as providing evidence of sorts that Shakespeare could not have intended *his* King Henry to be seen as a paragon or that he intended to impress on his audience an inevitable historical irony. But would anyone seriously argue that the achievements of great national heroes, or epic heroes or folk heroes or culture heroes, are *permanent*? Nothing is. Their permanence lies in tradition, in historical records, in literature—a view that would surely be granted by most students, for example, of Renaissance literature. For reasons that presumably seemed important, Shakespeare chose to preserve what he took to be the best of the career of Henry V, to make a living record that neither Mars his sword nor war's quick fire would burn. And I suppose it was not accidental that he made this choice toward the end of the sixteenth century.

* * * * *

As Professors Campbell and Jorgensen have shown, this is a "war play," at least in the sense that its author knew a great deal about warfare, soldiers, officers, armies, policies, motives, and methods, and put much of what he knew into the play (Campbell, pp. 255–305;

Jorgensen, pp. 86–100 *et passim*). But neither would suggest that Shakespeare wrote a war play merely to demonstrate his knowledge of the subject or to show how wars ought to be fought; the military handbooks took care of that. And, as Professor Walter has demonstrated, Shakespeare has made his King Harry compact of almost all the kingly qualities required by sixteenth-century writers on that subject (Walter, pp. xvi–xvii). But Shakespeare did not write a regal courtesy-book, although some such thing can be extracted from the play. And Shakespeare has his Prologue promise something like an epic—something really too grand for the stage. A play can't, by definition, be an epic, but the point of the promise is probably to suggest something of the epic hero and the epic range, to imply that King Harry and his adventures should be seen on that scale.

The epic tone of the Prologue suggests that King Harry and his conquest of France will (probably) excite our wonder and admiration, and the Chorus, from Prologue to Epilogue, seems intended to keep these feelings active (so does much of the play's action). *Henry V*, bringing the great tetralogy to a close, certainly makes its patriotic affirmations; but no one, from Hal-haters to idolaters, doubts that it does much more than that.

I have suggested that the tetralogy moves consistently from anarchy to order, from regal irresponsibility to rational government, from injustice to justice, from dubious and dangerous notions of divine right and divine kingship to man-centered kingship—with a king responsible to God but responsible also to his country and his countrymen. I have also suggested that Canterbury's excruciating exposition of the Salic Law (*HV*, I.ii.33–95) not only provides a justification of sorts for the King's French war but also suggests the validity of James VI's claim to the English crown. This is not at all to say that Shakespeare's King Henry "stands for" James Stuart, no doubt an impossible burden on the imagination (some imaginations have borne it, of course); and whatever *Henry V* is, it is not a political allegory. It is the claims that are analogous, not the characters. If Shakespeare's Henry resembles any contemporary figure in any way, it is Essex, who gets a brief and famous compliment from the Chorus before the last act; and Shakespeare is not campaigning for Essex, no matter how much he, like other Englishmen, might have admired him. Some resemblance to Essex would, however, be important if one accepts the proposition that Shakespeare uses King Harry as a model: so we have the dash and flair, the gallantry, the affability, the immense popularity with people of all stations and persuasions, the mercy shown to conquered civilians, and the fine reputation as a military commander (in Essex's case about to go down the drain). But a model, particularly a model monarch, needs to show something more than a general resemblance to Robert Devereux.

I suggest, then, that *Henry V* is designed to provide serious answers to questions that I assume lie in its immediate background. The questions are not about King Harry's morality or about the justness of his war: those are legitimate concerns of the modern reader and audience, but they are not Shakespeare's questions. His, the questions behind the play, are, I believe, what kind of ruler do we Englishmen want, right now, in 1599, what sort of government, what kind of monarchy, what kind of civil polity, what sort of world? And I believe that Shakespeare raises, and answers, these questions with James VI in mind, although the answers can stand on their own if we want them to. The questions, anyhow, are reasonable enough, and there is no doubt whatever that many people were asking them. An era was finally and definitively coming to an end; the last Tudor was after all mortal and would soon endure her eclipse; England had not been at peace for years—English forces were engaged in Ireland and in the Low Countries, and in the past wars with Scotland had been frequent and savage. The succession had become a crucial issue—not merely a pressing one—and the problem of religion was "settled" only by the most brutal definition of that word. Certainly it was time to think about the future (that subject was not a new one); and, in historical and political terms, thinking about the future necessarily requires contemplation of the past.

I suspect that there is nothing ironic about the Chorus's famous phrase describing King Henry as "the mirror of all Christian kings" (II. Chorus.6) although many modern critics want to see it that way. I think that Shakespeare has set about representing on the stage the quintessence of kingship, a mirror not only to be wondered at but also to be emulated. That is, he is the kind of ruler that we Englishmen want, right now, in 1599 (or as soon as possible), and the monarchy and civil polity over which he presides are the sort of monarchy and civil polity we want. It goes almost without saying that we won't get either, but our kingmakers and our potential kings would do well to regard them as models, constituting an Idea.

The nature of the king-model is partly indicated by the epic tone of the Prologue. More is suggested by Canterbury's description of the King, I.i.22-69. He is "full of grace and fair regard," and is, as Ely quickly adds, "a true lover of the holy Church." His body is as a Paradise, containing "celestial spirits." He is a scholar, a master of divinity, an authority on statecraft and "policy," and "his discourse of war" becomes "a fearful battle render'd you in music." When he speaks,

> . . . the mute wonder lurketh in men's ears,
> To steal his sweet and honey'd sentences;
> So that the art and practic part of life
> Must be the mistress to this theoric.

(49–52)

Even ignoring the apparent extravagance, this is all very surprising for the prelates "since his [youthful] addiction was to courses vain." How did this astonishing transformation come about? Ely has an easy and simple-minded answer: "the prince obscur'd his contemplation/Under the veil of wildness" since "wholesome berries thrive and ripen best/Neighbour'd by fruit of baser quality." Canterbury goes along with the homely analogy, although he would apparently prefer to attribute the change in the young king to a miracle; but "miracles are ceas'd;/And therefore we must needs admit the means/How things are perfected." We know that Hal has done what he said he would do in the second scene of *1 Henry IV*, and we have seen him in the process of doing it. But what Canterbury and Ely discuss resembles a miracle (and a late medieval archbishop is well-informed on Protestant doctrine regarding miracles); and, as we shall see, there is some point to that: it is like an act of providence, sending England such a king.

The passage may have been designed for those members of an audience who had somehow missed *Henry IV*, informing them that a once wild and dissolute prince has suddenly become, through some kind of conversion,[5] a wonderfully gifted king. But it is much more likely to have been intended to specify the nature of the new king and to describe those qualities that will not be fully displayed in a play mainly devoted to a military campaign—qualities that will nevertheless have something to do with the success of that campaign. I see no reason not to take seriously what Canterbury says about the King. In another context it could easily have been the most fulsome flattery; but you are not flattering someone if he isn't there to hear your praise. Canterbury believes what he says, and his description establishes King Harry as a master of the "theoric" of kingship; furthermore, the theoretical part is not separated from "the art and practic part of life." If we can believe Canterbury (he may of course be wrong, but he is not a liar), what we have is something like a philosopher-king or, as has been sometimes suggested, an Aristotelian sage—with the additional and essential attributes described earlier: he is full of grace and fair regard, and a true lover of the holy Church; not, for example, the bigoted heretic-hunter described by Tyndale and Foxe. Coming from a bishop, a phrase like "full of grace" is not hollow praise. These particular attributes are important because of the topic that is (strangely) under discussion as the play begins. The praise of King Henry is introduced by that topic, which is briefly revived at the end of the catalogue of his virtues and then dropped altogether except for an exceedingly oblique allusion in the following scene.

It would be hard to miss the striking contrast in tone, subject, and language between the Prologue and the very beginning of the play's opening scene. Criticism has offered nearly every conceivable comment, little of it flattering to the bishops. The issue that they discuss is obviously a serious one, but the play does not specify how, or if, it is resolved. What is clear is that the two clerics are not discussing some question of church politics. The business about the bill in Parliament is not here simply to characterize the clerics, to show us that priests are like that, to demonstrate that while the rest of England is responsibly going about its business, they merely want to protect their turf. What they are discussing is national policy, and it is important that Shakespeare uses this topic to begin his play: it is directly related to the questions posed above. It is an important matter that must ultimately be settled by the King, a fact that makes its disappearance from the play all the more curious. The disappearance is there to be noticed, and members of a contemporary audience probably did notice it; if they did, it reminded them of something. Some of them, at least, did not need to be told how the historical Henry V resolved the issue, and Shakespeare chose not to deal with it more concretely in this play. He makes his point deftly enough. The so-called Lollard Bill was designed to do what Canterbury (and Hall and Holinshed) says it was designed to do: deprive the Church of most of its temporal holdings and hence of its income and wealth. It was an episode in the early history of the Reformation in England. It is not surprising that two ranking churchmen should be concerned, and it is not necessarily discreditable for a bishop or an archbishop to be opposed to such a bill. It is what is to be expected: priests are (sometimes) like that; but the coming of the Reformation to England, even by indirect and crook'd ways under the policies, not directed to that end, of Henry VIII, was something more than a matter of church politics. There is no discernible reason why Canterbury and Ely should not be concerned, no reason why Ely should not ask, "But what prevention?" (I.i.21). No reason unless we assume automatically that all manifestations of popery are by definition bad or that Shakespeare himself made such an assumption—and I find no persuasive evidence for this anywhere in his work. The "prevention" is that the "king is full of grace and fair regard./And a true lover of the holy Church." A king with these attributes is not likely to sanction the kind of bill described by Canterbury in lines 9–19. The implicit contrast with Henry VIII is clear enough, as it is hereafter at every point in the play where we encounter the King's somewhat rigorous views about stealing things from churches (rigorous but scarcely bloodthirsty or unusual for an age in which cutting purses was a hanging offense).

It is only fifty lines later, after the account of the new king's remarkable virtues, that we learn of a large sum of money to encourage the King to prevent passage of the Lollard Bill and, perhaps, to pursue his interests in France. However, after what Canterbury and Ely have been saying about the King, they can hardly have any illusions that *they* are going to busy *his* giddy mind with a foreign quarrel. The King whose intellectual qualities they discuss between themselves is hardly going to succumb to a simple-minded confidence game, nor is he going to be easily susceptible to bribery: it's not money he needs to bring off the French enterprise. If he does not sanction the Lollard Bill, it is because he does not like it. As for the "bribe," the convocations of 1588 and 1593 granted large subsidies to the crown in order, among other things, "to hinder occasions of a *melius inquirendum*, and of racking the clergy" (Strype paraphrasing Whitgift, quoted by Campbell, pp. 269–270). The *"quid pro quo* nature of the Convocations's generous contribution to war in *Henry V* must have seemed familiar to the Elizabethans" (Campbell, p. 270). That was probably the idea, or part of it: Henry V rejected the Lollard Bill, naturally, but the Church that contributed so generously to Elizabeth's government was under different auspices from that which contributed to King Henry's because of the policies of Thomas Cromwell and Henry VIII, Cranmer, and others. The immediate point is that good kings do not encourage the spoliation of the church—not the kind of king described in the opening scene.

Some idea of the significance of Shakespeare's handling of this subject may be gained by looking at how Hall dealt with it (Holinshed's treatment is relatively tame, with only a *pro forma* allusion to Chichele's [Canterbury's] avarice): Hall sums up the provisions of the bill that Shakespeare has Canterbury describe, I.i.7–19, and then observes:

> This before remembred bill was muche noted and feared emõgest the religious sort whom in effect it muche touched, insomuche that the fat Abbotes swet, the proude Priors frouned, the poore Friers curssed the sely Nonnes wept, and al together were nothyng pleased nor yet cõtent. [Hall, p. 49; it is characteristic of his direct approach.]

Some wise prelates, Hall tells us, did not like the idea of offering the King money to encourage him not to sanction the Commons bill and "determined . . . to replenishe the kynges brayne with some pleasante study that he should nether phantasy nor regard the serious peticion of the importunate commons" (Hall, p.49).

The "pleasant study" was of course the war in France, motivated by the King's title, or claim, to the French crown. The difference in tone is obvious. Hall's (and Holinshed's) clerics are Machiavellian politicians who have worked out a way to bring the King over to their side. Shakespeare's clerics have nothing but the greatest respect for the King's intellectual abilities. Their "flattery" of the King is between themselves, and they have no illusions about his intelligence: it is first rate. They understand that the King cannot be hoodwinked, that *their* best hope lies in the fact that he is full of grace and fair regard, and a true lover of the holy Church. Furthermore, both Hall and Holinshed show the bishops taking their bright idea of the French war to the King uninvited, like a pair of clever serpents in the world's best garden. Shakespeare manages it very differently: the King summons Canterbury into his presence and speaks to him with unmistakable seriousness, commanding him to expound the Salic Law truthfully and accurately. (The subject had been broached earlier by Canterbury, we are told [I.i.72-81]; the King has apparently been thinking about it and now wants to know more. We can assume that he would like to own most of France, but not dishonestly or dishonorably.)

Two details are of particular importance here: Shakespeare has ignored the anticlericalism, or anti-Catholicism, of his sources, as he had done in *King John*; and he has made the King seek, and follow, the advice of the Church on a matter of fundamental national policy, morality, and justice—the war with France. And the resounding silence on the fate of the Lollard Bill must mean that it is no longer an issue; the problem with which the play begins is no longer a problem—a change altogether consistent with the two priests' assessment of their young king. We are of course free to assume the worst if we wish to, but the play's whole tone and whole action make such a wish at best gratuitous. Furthermore, it ought to be obvious that this particular king does not need to be bribed to undertake this war (or reject this bill): he wants to go and intends to do so; if he is "spoiling for a fight" (Burckhardt, p. 192), the cause must be more than plausible. Canterbury makes it plausible; the tennis balls turn it into a legitimate duel (see below). It is not just that other concerns supersede the Lollard Bill in importance: Shakespeare does not begin plays with serious discussions of matters trivial and irrelevant. As

soon as we hear the King requesting the Church's judgment on the
French question, we know, or should know, what will happen to the
bill—nothing, under the mirror of all Christian kings. Shakespeare's
sources gave him an opportunity that he could hardly have been expected to ignore. Good kings, the kind described by Canterbury
early in the first scene, love and respect the Church.

The play's opening scene defines some kingly qualities with specific reference to King Henry. It would be churlish to quarrel with
them: surely a king should have those intellectual and spiritual gifts
described by Canterbury. He should even be full of grace and fair
regard and a true lover of some holy church or other. On the question of which church, a popular playwright had to proceed with
some circumspection, but the historical setting of the play and the
business with the Lollard Bill make the question an easy one. For the
Lollard Bill, Shakespeare went right to his familiar sources, but Hall
would have been annoyed, and Holinshed surprised, by the particular interpretations he put on the issue: a true lover of the holy Church
is soon to be described as the mirror of all Christian kings (which is
also how Hall described him), and Shakespeare obviously has in mind
a specifically Catholic Christian king, not an Erastian king, and certainly not the Supreme Head of the Church of England. Henry VIII
(fetchingly called "Prince Hal" in his youth) was selective in his efforts to imitate Henry V.

Now, about the extravagant praise that Canterbury heaps on the
King: it *is* extravagant—he sounds almost too good to be true. That,
I think, is deliberate on Shakespeare's part. If Harry the fifth is to be
our model, we will clean up an already well-laundered product.
When we see the King in action, beginning with the play's second
scene, it is obvious that he likes his work and that he is good at it; and,
as Canterbury has said, he certainly talks well. But would it really be
possible to write a play about a great king and show him demonstrating convincingly *all* the gifts that Canterbury ascribes to him?
Theoretically, I suppose, it would, and Walter has shown that
Shakespeare at least glances at virtually all of the sixteenth-century
kingly qualities. But on purely practical grounds, the way to manage
the problem is to have someone credible describe the virtues; then,
perhaps, an audience will assume that those virtues make it possible

for the King to function so exceedinly well in those actions in which
we see him engaged. Canterbury and Ely are, I should think, talking
about an ideal king who seems, almost miraculously, actually to have
materialized. What we see in the play is a national hero devoting
most of his energies to the great adventure that made him a national
hero.

The first scene defines and describes the model: this is the kind of
king we want. The rest of the play, except for one crucial episode,
shows this kind of king in action, on public display, so to speak.
Shakespeare does not give this king much time to himself; he wants
us to see his paragon in action rather than in meditation; but the one
meditation we get is pure gold. For the purposes of this play, the
King is— as rulers must or should be—a very public sort of figure.
What he is *personally*, Canterbury tells us; and what Canterbury tells
us seems to be confirmed by what follows. But although we get a
clear sense of the King's temperament and person, or personality, as
the play goes on, it is a public personality. More than that, it is a
highly polished and refined image, and polished quite consciously,
we can hardly doubt, by the King himself. The image is the result of
his conception of how kings should go about their business and how
they should act, and speak, while doing it. He knows very well how a
king should talk to an archbishop, to foreign ambassadors, to confessed traitors, to troops and officers before a battle, to an enemy's
herald, to the princess he knows very well he is going to marry. And
he knows how to talk to the people of a besieged city. His truly fero-
cious speech to the citizens of Harfleur (III.iii.1–43) is a masterpiece
of warlike rhetoric, describing in terrifying detail what happens
when cities are sacked. The purpose of the speech, clearly, is to prevent what it so vividly describes; and we ought to remember that
Holinshed's Harry, the historical Harry, *did* have the city sacked
whereas Shakespeare's does not. Instead, when (naturally enough)
the town surrenders, he orders Exeter to "use mercy to them all"
(III.iii.53). The question of what *this* Harry would have done if the
city had not surrendered does not arise: his oration *made* it surrender,
and his soldiers in any case do not appear to be like those of Charles V
sacking Rome in one of warfare's less edifying episodes. The per-

fected image of a conqueror can save a lot of bloodshed, and a proper conqueror should want to do just that.

But what if he gives the order that "every soldier kill his prisoners?" If Shakespeare puts the Harfleur speech to a special use, he does something similar with this famous, or notorious, order, about which, not surprisingly, much has been said. And, not incidentally, he cleans up what he found in Holinshed. Killing prisoners has always been a good deal worse than merely bad military etiquette, and a cold-blooded order to do so deserves more than mild censure. Holinshed gives a just barely digestible account of the killing of the prisoners at Agincourt (Hosley, p. 133), and Shakespeare could hardly have overlooked it even though he does not use it. Can such an order ever be justified? Only, one would think, under the most desperate circumstances: if a sudden turn of battle should threaten the actual destruction of an army by making the prisoners themselves a prime danger. One can easily imagine conditions in which prisoners could rearm themselves with weapons discarded by men in retreat or by men killed or wounded (see Keegan, p. 111).

What happens in the play is that the King hears a "new alarum" and thinks that the "French have reinforc'd their scatter'd men" (IV.vi.35-36). Since the English are greatly outnumbered, it is not only the outcome of the battle that is at stake but, literally, the existence of the English army, the lives of most of its men. This is not necessarily an idle or exaggerated fear: the reader and audience will not have forgotten that the preceding scene (only forty lines earlier) had ended with Bourbon, the Constable, and Orleans preparing to return to battle like berserkers, to "die in arms," "on heaps go offer up our lives," "To smother up the English in our throngs" (IV.v.18,20). Our knowledge must suggest that King Henry's instinct was correct: the French lords will not throw away their lives without taking some Englishmen with them—as many as possible.

It looks, however, as though the new alarum was *not* the French reinforcing their scatter'd men, but the French killing "the poys and the luggage," as Fluellen puts it, and that too is "expressly against the law of arms" (IV.vii.1-2). The French lords achieve none of their aims. When we next see Bourbon, he is a prisoner (IV.vii.56, S.D.), and not the only one ("*Enter* King Henry *and* Bourbon *with prisoners*"). If the other French lords have regrouped, they have done it more prudently than their words in scene v might have led one to expect since they are now apparently "on yon hill," not obviously ready to fight and die.

In the desperate resolution of the French lords, Shakespeare has given the audience objective information about something that King Henry, no amateur general, grasps instinctively. If the order to kill the prisoners still seems unwarranted (to many critics it *is*—they know not "seems"), *ex post facto* warrant arrives, two lines after the King gives his order (a little hard to see how it could have arrived sooner), in Fluellen's outraged explosion. If King Harry did not have a wholly satisfactory reason for ordering the killing of the prisoners, the French gave him one on the instant.

If the slaughter at the baggage park will not satisfy a scrupulous notion of providence (and I do not insist that it should), providence seems nevertheless to have been at work: unless the stage direction "*with prisoners*" and the King's promise to "cut the throats of those we have" (IV.vii.65) refer to prisoners remaining alive after the slaughter, or to new prisoners taken in an almost incredibly brief interim, the order to kill the prisoners was not carried out. (John Keegan [pp. 110-112] arrives, interestingly, at a similar conclusion about the infamous order when he confronts the mystery of how the historical Henry escaped the opprobrium that would normally have followed such an order if it had actually been carried out. Keegan also notes that King Henry took between one and two thousand prisoners home to England and doubts that they were taken after Agincourt, or after the command.) It would seem that Shakespeare, stuck with a famous historical fact about King Harry and the battle of Agincourt, has done everything possible to clean up the fact, to give solid justification to what in other circumstances would have been a cruel and discreditable order, what Holinshed called "this dolorous decree and pitiful proclamation" (Hosley, p. 133), although it is not clear why Holinshed chose to offer an eyewitness account of something that didn't happen. Then, lest the mirror tarnish a bit anyhow, Shakespeare has implied, via a stage direction and a threatening speech, that in fact the order was not carried out. Thus the way is cleared for a brief reprise of the speech before Harfleur, although here it is genuine anger and not high rhetoric that is in control: one can hardly doubt that the King means exactly what he says:

> I was not angry since I came to France
> Until this instant. Take a trumpet, herald;
> Ride thou unto the horsemen on yon hill:
> If they will fight with us, bid them come down,
> Or void the field; they do offend our sight.
> If they do neither, we will come to them,
> And make them skirr away, as swift as stones
> Enforced from the old Assyrian slings.
> Besides, we'll cut the throats of those we have,
> And not a man of them that we shall take
> Shall taste our mercy. Go and tell them so.
>
> (IV.vii.57–67)

Few readers will question the rightness, or righteousness, of King Harry's wrath; the threat clearly works, and you cannot credibly threaten to kill your prisoners if they have been killed already. The King's original order to kill the prisoners may demonstrate that he is not infallible: he thought, wrongly but with good reason, that his army was in danger of destruction. The standard by which he is to be judged is merely human, and Shakespeare has gone out of his way to clean up a serious historical blemish.

King Henry has worked hard to achieve the image of a king (it should be clear enough that he was thinking precisely of that in the famous soliloquy in act I, scene ii. of *1 Henry IV*). It is decidedly worth remembering that "image . . . is a vital, valid concern of anyone who hopes to govern. And image needs cultivation, attention, work."[6] In the speech quoted above, image and substance are inseparable; the image can't be a hollow one, like King Richard's. Harry's is substantial: if you work hard and intelligently at achieving the image of King Harry, you will be King Harry, no trivial achievement. If you are altogether successful, you might become (Shakespeare's) mirror (image) of all (Catholic) Christian kings.

Although we do not hear the King "unloosing" the Gordian knot of policy "as familiar as his garter," the first scene is nevertheless a good indicator of things to come: the dramatic representation on a (reduced) epic scale of a consummately gifted politician and general going about his business, practicing his mystery.

*   *   *   *   *

Now, with respect to James VI and man-centered kingship, by 1599 James was by far the strongest contender for the crown of England; if there was a consensus candidate, he was it. His claim was purely hereditary, and as we have seen, Shakespeare believed strongly, if not absolutely, in the validity of lineal descent and hereditary right—including the hereditary right of James Stuart, figured forth in the curiously stated hereditary right of Henry V to the crown of France. And I have argued that Shakespeare had little use for notions of divine right and divine kingship. Even though all sixteenth- and seventeenth-century theories of divine right specifically include indefeasible hereditary right, Shakespeare neatly split them apart, having seen, one supposes, no *necessary* connection between them; the theoretical connection was that indefeasible hereditary right rules out the possibility of purely human intervention, and Shakespeare remained discreetly skeptical of that kind of theory. Instead, and by implication, he argued for man-centered kingship.

The mirror of all Christian kings is a paragon of man-centered kingship, and 1599 was a good year to write about him because, in addition to the reasons given earlier, in 1599 the likeliest successor to the crown had published the age's most uncompromising statement on the doctrine of divine right, *The Trew Law of Free Monarchies* (first published anonymously, but King James's style is about as anonymous as Henry James's). James espoused an idea of kingship already completely familiar in Tudor England, through the Homilies of 1547 and 1570 and through other official and unofficial pronouncements, an idea that Shakespeare had thoroughly battered about in *Richard II*. I do not suggest that, in 1595, Shakespeare was "showing" James Stuart the fractured face of divine kingship—although he was certainly showing it to *someone*; but in 1599, after the publication of *The Trew Law* and at a time when James's candidacy had been considerably strengthened, Shakespeare was representing on the stage the virtues of man-centered kingship with some reference to the monarch that most Englishmen expected would succeed to the throne and whose candidacy was being quietly but aggressively pushed by both Cecil and Essex and was very likely accepted by the Queen herself. The "message" was as follows: James VI of Scotland has an indefeasible hereditary right to the crown of England, and he is a desirable candidate on other grounds as well (he is a scholar, a theologian, no lover of Presbyterians, an authority on statecraft—although one might disagree with some of his views—a poet and hence in some sense a master of language, possessing, in short, qualities that a king should have, including some of the qualities that Canterbury attributes to Henry V); but he *does* hold some regrettable notions of kingship, and most specifically he believes in the discreditable doctrine of the divine right of kings, on which he is a notable authority. "Our bending author"[7] therefore proposes that he reconsider, that he give some thought to the virtues of man-centered kingship.

The idea of man-centered kingship need not have been offensive to James. We have seen that King Harry enjoys most of the advantages of divine right without its inherent dangers—dangers to the commonwealth as well as to the king himself. Man-centered kingship leaves plenty of room for authority (altogether too much for most modern tastes): it does come from God, after all, but as a form of stewardship, an idea James would probably not have been inclined to reject. And it would certainly appeal, almost as strongly as divine right itself, to James's distrust and dislike of both popery and presbyterianism.[8] And it could do so without any necessary compromising of Shakespeare's own religious principles (and, as we shall see, with good reason). I would not argue that the publication of *The Trew Law* had any decisive influence on the general shape and content of *Henry V*. (I am speculating, if with some private certainty: put to it, I could not *prove* that it had any influence at all or, for that matter, that Shakespeare had even read it by the time he wrote *Henry V*. There is no question that he read it by the time that James VI became also James I of England.) But I think it might well have induced some sense of urgency; look at what has happened: our leading candidate for the crown has just published a book upholding with total clarity those views our players so thoroughly demolished a few years ago in *Richard II*. And now, here we are, writing a play about King Harry the fifth. The fact that King Henry is so precisely antithetical

to King Richard surely suggests that Shakespeare was giving some
thought to the last play in his tetralogy while he was still at work on
the first. The appearance of *The Trew Law* perhaps contributed to the
precision of the antithesis and to the process whereby Shakespeare
went about making King Henry more impressive than he found him
in the chronicles, as well as recognizably and thoroughly human.

*   *   *   *   *

Thus far I have been more or less content to give a brief definition
of man-centered kingship and to treat it, in rather negative terms, as
the opposite of the view of kingship expressed by Gaunt and by the
King and his supporters in *Richard II*. But it is a little more than that,
and it helps explain why Shakespeare does more with King Harry
than represent him as a king who shares the common humanity of
those around him. It adds a dimension of meaning to the catalogue of
virtues supplied by Canterbury in act I, scene i, and it underlines the
point of Canterbury's beautiful speech on the orderly society of the
bees (I.ii.183-220). I have already argued, or asserted, that King
Henry's adoption of Justice as his father in *2 Henry IV* was not a casual gesture and that we are to understand that although the Lord Chief
Justice is not a character in *Henry V*, Justice is nevertheless present
and in command. The administration of justice is not the theme of
Henry V, but I suggest that Canterbury's speech describes something
like the conditions that we are to assume exist in Henry's kingdom,
as I assume that the description of the King's virtues is to be taken as
an account of an ideal king who has, somehow, actually materialized, seemingly like a miracle.

Canterbury's allegorical apiary is like Ulysses' universe when
Degree has not been "shak'd," and it is introduced, and elicited by,
an observation of Exeter about government, an observation that
seems intended to describe England under King Harry, an England
well equipped to manage its affairs at home and abroad:

> While that the armed hand doth fight abroad
> Th'advised head defends itself at home;
> For government, though high and low and lower,
> Put into parts, doth keep in one consent,
> Congreeing in a full and natural close,

Like music.

Canterbury.   Therefore doth heaven divide
The state of man in diverse functions,
Setting endeavor in continual motion;
To which is fixed, as an aim or butt,
Obedience: for so work the honey-bees,
Creatures that by a rule in nature teach
The act of order to a peopled kingdom.

(I.ii.178–189)

(It is, I suppose, at this point unnecessary to call attention to Canterbury's, and hence the Church's, role in providing information and commentary, here supported by Exeter, for the King and the nobility. If we assume that Canterbury is merely venal, well, that's that.) Exeter and Canterbury are describing an ideal state of affairs that seems actually to have materialized—if it had not, then the enterprise of France could hardly be urged and would not be successful if undertaken.

The key word, I am afraid, is obedience. Where there is obedience, in Canterbury's and Shakespeare's sense, there is Justice. It is analogous to Exeter's and Shakespeare's music, and we are asked to accept the existence of the harmony of obedience, and therefore of Justice, in the monarchy over which King Harry presides. It is not a liberal blueprint, and it would be fatuous to expect it to be. Modern readers tend rather to dislike the way the King administers justice to the traitors at Southampton, but it is defective by standards that Shakespeare and his age would have found astonishing. And the fates of Bardolph and the others cause much resentment. But they violate an order based on the general's opposition to looting, which tends to cause resentment among the people with whom one expects one day to be at peace, and on his reverence for the Church. The King *is* willing to pardon an abusive drunk. (In the nether regions of scholarship, there is a circle the inmates of which condemn him for [a] pardoning the drunk and [b] executing the confessed traitors, but here I seem to lose the thread. . . .)

As a principle of Justice, obedience means obeying laws—e.g., laws against conspiring to murder the king, laws against theft, from churches or wherever. It means submission to rule or authority, and

no society has ever been able to forego submission to some form of
legitimate authority and survive. If the source and center of authority is itself corrupt, then of course Justice becomes an obscenity—
endless instances come to mind. But for Shakespeare, at least, there
seems to be some sense that Justice should be rational and not
capricious, that it ought to be just by standards that almost anyone
can comprehend: the authority that lies in government, "Put into
parts, doth keep in one consent,/Congreeing in a full and natural
close,/Like music." We are told in the play that King Harry has
formidable virtues and that he presides over a just society, i.e., one
whose parts are harmonious, like music. And we are *not* told that his
kingship is hedged with divinity. Without *this* King, obviously,
England would be very different; and that is the point on which man-
centered kingship assumes its importance. When the Epilogue tells
us that with his sword King Harry achieved "the world's best garden," we are being told that he achieved something like an earthly
paradise, another Eden, demi-paradise.

The achievement of Justice is reflected in an harmonious body
politic analogous to a natural order like that of the bees. The opening
scenes of the play lead us to believe that the King himself is responsible for this achievement. Justice has already been defined one way,
impressively, by the Lord Chief Justice in *2 Henry IV*. A potent and
concrete principle is reemphasized in Exeter's brief remarks on
government and music and Canterbury's discourse on the bees.
Canterbury's praise of King Henry in act I, scene i describes someone capable of bringing about a kind of earthly paradise. The
Epilogue tells us that this star of England achieved the world's best
garden—with his sword. In connection with a theory of man-
centered kingship, the importance of the achievement is that it has
nothing to do with any kind of political mysticism. It was brought
about by a particular king who assumed the throne legitimately on
the death of his father and immediately committed himself to a
principle of Justice that then permitted, or required, him to go to
war and, with his sword, extend the boundaries of the world's best
garden, the evidence consisting, as far as we can tell, of the double
marriage of Harry and Kate, England and France (which probably
signifies an inherently less unlikely union, between England and

Scotland, and theoretically an end to the terrible succession of wars between the two countries). The marriage, as Burckhardt suggests (pp. 199–205), provides the "model" of permanence against the "combat model," the changes and disasters of history.

"Since miracles are ceas'd," we have to find rational explanations, through homely natural analogies, for the young king's singular gifts: he developed them all quietly, secretly, while no one was looking, as "wholesome berries thrive and ripen best/Neighbour'd by fruit of baser quality" (I.ii.61–62). We know that he had already displayed formidable abilities in the two earlier plays, but they do not prepare us for what Canterbury tells us in the first scene of this play, or even for what we hear and see when the King goes into action, for what we hear in the camp the night before Agincourt. It is too bad, really, that miracles are ceas'd because by any criteria except those of extreme skepticism or resolute Protestantism, a miracle would be the most *reasonable* explanation of King Harry. The kind of adulation we find in Canterbury's remarks, and in the choruses, had ample precedent in Hall and Holinshed and almost everywhere else (it would appear that hardly anyone, even in retrospect, was willing to state the obvious: that defeating the French was impressive but that no *conquest* of France could conceivably have been permanent and the cost of trying to maintain one had been disastrous). Hall's summation of the life and reign of Henry V looks as though he too were describing a miracle, as this sample from the beginning of the summation shows:

> THIS Henry was a kyng whose life was immaculate & his liuyng without spot. This kyng was a prince whom all men loued & of none disdained. This prince was a capitaine against whom fortune neuer frowned nor mischance once spurned. This capitaine was a shepherde whom his flock loued and louyngly obeyed. This shepherd was such a iusticiary that no offēce was vnpunished nor friendship vnrewarded. This iusticiary was so feared, that all rebellion was banished and sedicion suppressed. [Hall, p. 112]

A captain who is also a shepherd is the kind of captain who (apparently) can use his sword as a pruning hook to make the world's best garden, and it is not surprising that Shakespeare stops well short of the worst extravagances of Hall's fulsome fatuity. Hall continues in this scarce credible vein for two enormous pages. Naturally, he is suspect since his somewhat unnerving master Henry VIII did not object to being compared with Henry V. For Hall, perhaps, extravagant praise of Henry V might be taken as implying the same praise for Henry VIII. Hall may in all innocence (on the face of it unlikely) have honestly thought of Henry V as the loving shepherd of his loving and lucky flock, but Hall was quite capable of applying such grotesque hyperbole to a king who was both Defender of the Faith and, later, Supreme Head of the Church in England.

In any case, the praise of King Harry the fifth is too extensive in this play, the garden references, including Burgundy's splendid speech, V.ii.22-67, too specific to be dismissed or seen simply as ironic commentary on a grim reality. The reality is grim enough, but there is something to redeem it. Shakespeare is giving Henry V credit for creating a kind of earthly paradise, and already in act I, scene ii he has indicated that the paradise is to be defined as a kingdom justly governed and harmoniously obedient. He attributes to King Henry what Dante attributed to his ideal emperor, or world monarch, in the *De Monarchia*, the creation of an earthly paradise; in doing so he is writing something like a *Monarchy* of his own.[9]

Shakespeare and Dante

Dante was writing about the Empire and the Papacy; he wanted the temporal and the spiritual worlds to go their separate but (reasonably) equal ways. Monarchy was ordained by God; monarchs (or the emperor) were not to be appointed or deposed by popes. Quite the contrary: unless the electors were blinded by greed, they would choose the monarch, or emperor, that God wanted them to choose. And history shows that some emperors, like Augustus Caesar, when there *was* no Papacy, have been sent by God, miraculously, when they were needed. Book II of the *De Monarchia* seems to provide parallels to many of the political views that Shakespeare advances in *Henry V*; and various parts of Dante's work can, I think, through some happy accidents, provide a sort of gloss on a few of the problems presented to modern readers of a play that is far from modern.

In Book I Dante had argued for the necessity of a world monarchy on the grounds that unity is preferable to diversity and a world monarchy would ensure peace and the fullest possible intellectual growth of its citizens—the realization of the "possible intellect." The thesis of book II is that the "world rule" of the Roman Empire was achieved by "right," through the will of God. This happened because the Roman people were the world's noblest and had an innate, natural capacity to rule, a natural capacity properly used being by definition an instance of divine will.

But Rome's "right" was achieved by conquest. I mentioned earlier the enormous distance between Agincourt and Gaultree Forest. The Battle of Agincourt was fought and won "in plain shock and even play of battle"—no tricks, so that the victorious general's "Take it, God,/For it is none but thine," seems a good deal more appropriate than John of Lancaster's remarks on divine generalship at Gaultree Forest. And Agincourt is light years from Gaultree Forest for another, perhaps less obvious, reason: it asserts the validity, only temporary, to be sure, of what Burckhardt calls the "combat model" (pp. 189-199). Although the French war is justified after a fashion by Canterbury's exposition of the Salic Law and its loopholes, that lecture, as we have seen, probably serves another purpose that has as much to do with James of Scotland and England as it has to do with Harry of England and France. More important, the war originates as a duel, the English King's response to the French Dauphin's insult of the tennis balls; that certainly was what did the trick for a contemporary audience. King Harry's language as he announces his intentions to the French ambassadors, "is entirely that of the duel, of a 'quarrel' between champions" (Burckhardt, p. 192):

> But all this lies within the will of God,
> To whom I do appeal; and in whose name
> Tell you the Dauphin I am coming on,
> To venge me as I may and to put forth
> My rightful hand in a well-hallow'd cause.
>
> (I.ii.289-293)

What modern readers often see as a mere imperialist adventure is here given a rather special but clear and familiar justification.

England has already issued a general challenge to France in terms left intentionally cloudy and confused; France does not respond to England; the French King does not respond to the English King; we witness nothing much in the way of diplomatic negotiations and maneuverings. Instead, the Dauphin issues a challenge of his own, and King Harry is more than willing to accept: the tennis balls give him not only a wonderful excuse but also an *obviously* legitimate one (roughly analogous to King Richard's disinheriting Bolingbroke after Bolingbroke had [presumably] set sail from France), with the understanding, proper to the trial by combat (as in the projected trial—duel—between Bolingbroke and Mowbray), that the outcome will demonstrate, and prove, which contestant was right. Each combatant hopes and (presumably) expects to win, but each knows, or is supposed to know, who the judge is: "But all this lies within the will of God,/To whom I do appeal." We are also light years from act I, scene iii of *Richard II*, where the Judge's decision was prevented by His self-appointed deputy.

Now, a war is not exactly the same thing as a duel or trial by combat, as Shakespeare, and King Harry, obviously knew (it is not clear that the Dauphin did). There is in *Henry V* far too much talk about what happens in war (including the sacking of cities) for the illusion of a duel to be sustained or for the Idea of a duel to be more than a metaphor. But in poetry, one hardly need note, metaphor is important. The metaphor is particularly important here because although King and Dauphin do not (like Hal and Hotspur) fight a duel, there is most certainly a trial by combat in another, related sense: a test for King Harry and his army (and hence for England): they pass, and the outcome of that trial must signify a judgment. The odds were so fearful that the overwhelming victory must seem nearly miraculous, as nearly so as possible since miracles ceas'd: "Take it, God,/For it is none but thine!"—"'Tis wonderful!"—a wonder, miraculous.

Henry V is a "war play" largely because history and popular sentiment gave Shakespeare few alternatives—not if he was going to write about Henry V; and it would have been an eccentric playwright indeed who in 1599 asked his audience to see something deplorable in the victory at Agincourt. He uses the figure of the duel in such a way (a fight between champions) as to give it something like epic significance, and he uses epic figures, particularly in the choruses, in such a way as to invoke the ideal of a special kind of grace and grandeur in a great military victory—in epic poems, the fates of nations, even of the world, seem to hang in the balance. *Henry V* is not an antiwar play (it has of course been called one), any more than the *Iliad* is an antiwar poem; and it can be made into one only by rewriting it or by misreading it on a—well—epic scale. The shock and even play of battle really does reveal something about the contestants, as well as about the Judge: it reveals His decision.

But the struggle is more than a test in the familiar sense. The play ends with the fundamental Shakespearean reconciliation, marriage, in a last act that seems almost like an epilogue, and it is a momentous marriage since it involves nations as well as individuals. The reconciliation follows a victory, and the victory represents a supreme judgment analogous to that which was supposed to govern the outcome of a trial by combat, a duel.

Dante's use of the figure of the duel throws further light on Shakespeare's use of the figure here. Dante uses the figure of the contest as a revelation of God's judgment. A contest of this sort may be a duel between fighters (champions) or an athletic contest.[10] Thus various nations competed in a race, with the prize being "Empire," "dominion over all mortals" (II.8). Since Rome "won" this race, the conclusion is inescapable: "thus it triumphed by divine decree, thus it won the crown by divine assent; its victory was based upon right" (II.8). In addition, "whatever is acquired by duel is acquired by right" since by its nature a duel involves recourse to the Supreme Judge (II.9). Rome "secured the Empire by means of a duel" (II.10); and since it secured it that way, it necessarily secured it by right (II.10). Dante further argues, in a famous passage, that Christ himself gave the divine imprimatur to the Empire because He "chose to be born of a Virgin Mother under the edict of Roman authority so that the Son of God, by becoming man, might be enrolled as a man in that unique register of the human race; this meant that He recognized its validity" (II.11; see also I.16 and III.13).

Before we return to King Harry's demi-paradise, we should

recall why Dante made these remarkable claims. The purpose of the *Monarchy* was to establish unequivocally the separation of Empire and Papacy; Papacy and Empire have fundamentally different functions and should be separate but (approximately) equal under God, with man's spiritual life the Church's province, his temporal life the Empire's. Dante argues that the Papacy had no divine mandate to elect or to depose temporal rulers; monarchy (empire) was ordained by God, not the Church, and it would be foolish not to perceive this since the Empire existed before the Church, and Christ himself chose to be born in that Empire (II.2; III.13). The point of Dante's argument was, of course, not simply to cut the Papacy down to size, but to define the differences between Caesar and Peter and to define their separate responsibilities. And Caesar—the monarch—is to be a man, the best of men (*optimus homo*), by whom others can be measured, a man by whose philosophical mind and hand his subjects can be brought to the terrestrial paradise—a paradise after the Fall, to be sure, but as nearly like Eden as possible, another Eden, demi-paradise, the world's best garden. It would not be inappropriate if the monarch who fulfills these rather rigorous requirements had himself to undergo some kind of testing, both spiritual and temporal, before he succeeds. Specifically, and most important, Dante saw the achievement of the earthly paradise as an absolutely valid, purely secular and temporal human concern, to be taken with the same seriousness as the purely spiritual achievement of salvation. The earthly paradise was not to be simply a busy waiting room for passengers on the celestial omnibus: it was an end in itself.

Dante puts man and monarch in an almost impossibly exalted position, so we perhaps need to recall his memorable closing passage (particularly important in this context since the Renaissance generally—Shakespeare's as well as Dante's—tended to put man precariously close to the top of the entire creation): "in a certain fashion our temporal happiness is subordinate to our eternal happiness [but only in "a certain fashion"—*quammodo*]. Caesar, therefore, is obliged to observe that reverence towards Peter which a first-born son owes to his father: so that when he is enlightened by the light of paternal grace he may the more powerfully enlighten the whole world, at the head of which he has been placed by the One who alone is ruler of all things spiritual and temporal" (III.16). This has some Shakespearean application too (see note 11), but not to *Henry V* where (and when) it would have been intolerably dangerous.

*   *   *   *   *

Shakespeare had in mind nothing so grand as Dante's world monarchy. The Holy Roman Empire itself was suffering from attrition both political and religious; the Reformation and Counter Reformation were historical facts; nationalism was a much stronger force at the end of the sixteenth century than it had been at the beginning of the fourteenth. Dante's Pope had become, in England, only the Bishop of Rome; and even though Shakespeare's Harry displays some reverence to Canterbury and a good deal to the Church, he could not, on a London stage, display proper reverence for Peter.[11]

Although Shakespeare could not possibly have been thinking of a world monarchy under an English king and although he knew that a united kingdom of England and France was most unlikely to be created, even if it might have seemed desirable, he could easily have had in mind, in 1599, a United Kingdom of England, Scotland, and Ireland, under an admittedly imperfect but far from contemptible philosopher-king. He certainly had in mind an idea of something like an earthly paradise since he refers to it so emphatically in *Richard II* and *Henry V*, and its seal was to be marriage. It is quite possible that he would have liked to have seen a peaceful and united Christendom, but it is certain that he knew he was not going to see it. A vision of Great Britain was more reasonable; it did, after all, materialize although in a union often fractious enough to ruin any marriage. Bacon, contemplating what he thought was going to be the union of England and Scotland, suggested, in 1603, the name Great Britain and described the "perfect union of bodies, politic as well as natural" (quoted by Kantorowicz, p. 24). I think that is what Shakespeare had in mind a few years earlier, and if I am right, there is an added point, political and spiritual, in the marriage figure (used also by Jonson in his epigram on the union): Bacon's (and Shakespeare's) body politic is the united kingdom—England-Scotland, England-France; the body natural is King James VI and I-Henry V. The King's Two Bodies have been reduced to manageable and reasonable proportions.

Dante's monarch is something like the King Body Natural, his world monarchy something like the King Body Politic, the Idea of government; a similar rough analogy can be drawn with Shakespeare's King Harry and the Idea of government that he represents. It is supremely important to recognize that Dante's monarch and Shakespeare's king have each one body—there is nothing mystical about either. And for that reason, a little touch of Harry in the night, wooing a princess, and marriage are also of supreme importance. The night scene before Agincourt magnificently establishes King Harry's membership in that unique natural body, the human race (Dante's figure); wooing a wife is the pleasure of a man (as it is certainly King Harry's pleasure); and marriage is the seal of permanence and of mutual obedience, the mutual commitment to the Idea of a shared spiritual authority.

If a man, without divine pretensions, working at full capacity and realizing his highest potential makes for Dante an ideal monarch, it does pretty much the same for Shakespeare, a point established externally, through description, in act I, scene i and *in propria persona* for most of the play following. It is the point of Canterbury's list of virtues in act I, scene i and Exeter's and Canterbury's observations on government in act I, scene ii. When King Harry, with his sword, achieves the world's best garden, he is achieving something like Dante's terrestrial paradise, and he is achieving it by means similar to those attributed by Dante to Rome, the prototype of his world monarchy.

The idea of man-centered kingship gets its most concentrated treatment in Act IV, scene i, and I don't doubt that the Chorus speaks the playwright's sentiments:

> O, now, who will behold
> The royal captain of this ruin'd band
> Walking from watch to watch, from tent to tent,
> Let him cry, "Praise and glory on his head!"
>
> (IV.Chorus.28-31)

To old Sir Thomas Erpingham, King Harry is a fellow soldier, of a higher rank but still, for now, part of a band of brothers. He prefers having no good soft pillow for his good white head because he can say, "Now lie I like a king." It is to a fellow officer, exalted but familar, that he can say without offense, "The Lord in heaven bless thee, noble Harry!" (IV.i.15-17, 33)—worth comparing, for the tone, with Falstaff's "God save thee, my sweet boy!" (*2HIV*, V.v.43). Most important, with the remarkable Bates, Court, and Williams, those radically atypical soldiers, he is a soldier among soldiers. His famous remark, "Every subject's duty is the king's; but every subject's soul is his own" (182-184), sometimes thought of as an evasion of responsibility, in fact reaffirms a basic distinction between the temporal and the spiritual worlds. War may be God's beadle (174), but the King cannot absolve his subjects of their sins because he is not God's substitute or, in spite of Hall, the shepherd of his flock, except in a very remote sort of way. Quite the contrary: the King is but a man; the violet smells to him as it does to anyone else. "All his senses have but human conditions: his ceremonies laid by, in his nakedness he appears but a man" (101-106): King Richard's opposite; King Harry has nothing to do with the King's Two Bodies.

A little too pleased with himself for the natural ease with which he plays the soldier, he permits himself a rather fatuous jest ("If I live to see it [the King allowing himself to be ransomed], I will never trust him after"); and when the highly intelligent Williams takes him up on it, he even allows himself a man's indulgence in anger. A major point of the whole episode in the camp is to underline the separateness between the temporal and the spiritual and to insist on the King's strictly secular and human identity. That is the point of the so-called practical joke on Williams. The King was angry, but he did not reveal his identity until after the battle. Then he can say, in effect, you couldn't recognize a king when you saw one and for good reason. To have gotten into a fight, however, while still in disguise, to have been struck by Williams, is probably something that even this king could not allow—and it would certainly have demoralized Williams.

The point of the great soliloquy (236-290) is, again, to place the strongest possible emphasis on the King as a man. If one believes that the King protests too much, the reply, I think, is that—even setting aside the impending battle—kings have fearful responsibilities that they must meet with purely human capacities, although capacities in this case of a very high order. They may and must pray, but they must also do the work. They won't know until the event whether or not they did the right work and did it well. King Harry cannot count on a descent of Lancastrian angels; but, as the great speech before the battle indicates (IV.iii.19-67), he does have confidence in himself and in his men; and as his words to Westmoreland and Montjoy indicate, he loves his work.

He enjoys playing, too, but not all the year. His wooing of Kate is a marvelous bit of gallant relaxation and fun, but it is more than that. It may be that nothing tells us more about King Harry than the manner of his wooing. He is jolly well going to marry Kate; she is part of his price for peace; there is very little she or her parents can do about it; no marriage, no peace, and some French cities will be sacked. Not only must there be a marriage but the French king must, and finally does, agree to address the English King as "Our very dear son Henry, King of England, heir of France." Yet Shakespeare has devoted almost two hundred lines just before the end of the play to a scene in which King Harry plays the ardent wooer, amusingly, masterfully, in prose as befits a hearty fellow, producing the rather attractive image of a king turned simple soldier and unskilled lover. The whole performance has aroused some resentment among students of the play: since Kate is part of the package, an article of the spoils of war, why bother to woo when he can wed without going to all that trouble? With a clear implication of hypocrisy—since she is part of Henry's price, he can't really love her, and it won't do to attempt to disguise the stern conqueror's face behind the lover's mask. But Harry the King *is* a man, and he *is* going to marry her; she *is* going to be his wife as well as his queen, and she does not seem to dislike the idea at all. The question should not be "Why bother, since he is going to marry her anyhow?" Why *not* bother? We know how noble and royal marriages were arranged, long before and long after the time of Henry V. But here is, shall we say an *inevitable* husband who actually shows some regard for the lady's wishes and feelings, who seems to have some regard for the lady herself. He knows she will have to marry him, that she really has no choice unless he gives her a choice to make. He has some confidence that he can elicit the right choice, and the English lesson has told us that she is eager to marry the English King. This is the time to show some consideration for the lady's feelings, to be agreeable: since he is naturally agreeable, that is easy enough. And he presents himself as what he is in fact now becoming, a man who loves her and wants to know, "Canst thou love me?" If there are large political considerations, all the more reason to achieve them through love. This love might even extend to love between England and France; it is the French Queen's hope.

In wooing Kate as he does, King Harry is presenting himself, not for the first time, as a man, not a demigod. Perhaps Shakespeare had in mind Erasmus's injuction that kings should marry, but not merely for the sake of alliances—that might breed strife (Walter, p. xviii). But King Harry is well beyond the textbook stage; he is also about as far as it is possible to get from mystical notions of kingship. The standard by which he is to be judged is both reasonable and familiar: it is human, and he knows it. In perfecting the image of a king, he has enhanced the image of a man and therefore stands well in the unique register of the human race. This seems to be what Shakespeare intended to show.

NOTES

NOTES TO PREFACE

1. Sigurd Burckhardt, *Shakespearean Meanings*, Princeton: Princeton University Press, 1968, p. vii. My agreement with Sigurd Burckhardt is partly abstract, a matter of principle. No one would be so naive as to expect that everyone would agree on the precise nature of the message, no matter how strongly one believes that there is one. See note 2.

2. E. D. Hirsch, Jr., in *The New York Review of Books*, XXVI (22 November 1979): 50. Mr. Hirsch, in arguing for the importance of attempting to determine an author's meaning, notes that "absolute certainty is not demanded in even the most rigorous of empirical disciplines, much less in literary discourse. All that is required to establish a meaning-intention [an unfortunate phrase, I should think] is to show superior probability as based on the available evidence." This comforting view seems not to have been intended as an excuse for flagrant misreading. Probability is my criterion in trying to discover Shakespeare's discoverable messages.

NOTES TO CHAPTER I

1. Unless otherwise noted, all quotations from the plays of the tetralogy are from the New Arden texts: *Richard II*, ed. Peter Ure; *1* and *2 Henry IV*, ed. A. R. Humphreys; *Henry V*, ed. John H. Walter. References to introductory or editorial matter, given in parentheses, are to Ure, Humphreys 1 or 2, and Walter.

2. I use *divine kingship* partly as a term of convenience, rather than exclusively in its technical sense. As used here it applies not only to ideas of divine kingship but more generally to what might be called "King Richard's Syndrome"—a combination of various strains of divine kingship, the King Body Politic as defined by Ernst Kantorowicz (see note 17 below), and aspects of the idea of divine right, a theory of kingship that holds specifically that (*a*) monarchy is ordained by God, (*b*) the monarch is accountable only to God, (*c*) the subject's duty is passive obedience, and (*d*) hereditary right is indefeasible. See John Neville Figgis, *The Divine Right of Kings*, Cambridge: Cambridge University Press, 1896 (New York: Harper and Row Torchbooks, 1965—still a valuable book). Hereafter Figgis in text. Indefeasible hereditary right precludes any merely human intervention in the succession.

Passive obedience is the aspect of divine right most trenchantly examined in *Richard II*. There is no necessary connection between divine right and divine kingship, but Shakespeare made one anyhow, very shrewdly.

The historical Richard developed a fairly consistent idea of divine right, partly no doubt, as a theoretical bulwark against rebellious peasants and difficult uncles, including Gloucester and Gaunt. The historical Gloucester, represented in *Richard II* and the thoroughly subversive, and anonymous, *Woodstock* as having been meek, mild, and innocent, almost a martyr, was no more so than Gaunt. One difference between the two brothers was that Gaunt tended to patronize poets and, just possibly, their wives whereas Gloucester was keen for religious establishments and elegant religious books. For Gloucester see Anthony Goodman, *The Loyal Conspiracy*, London: Routledge & Kegan Paul, 1971, pp. 74–86.

Wycliffe had developed ideas similar to Richard's as part of the general Lollard declaration of independence from Rome. It is not clear that Shakespeare was familiar with Richard's theorizing about divine kingship, but he could easily have drawn some inferences from Holinshed. Divine right and divine kingship are almost necessarily antipapal, and although I see no direct evidence that Shakespeare saw matters that way, the thought is likely to have crossed his mind; he certainly saw grave weaknesses and dangers in the whole idea of divine right and divine kingship. By Shakespeare's time the notion of divine right had pretty much become a matter of political orthodoxy. For Richard and Wycliffe on divine right, see Figgis, pp. 66–80.

3. Tudor absolutism did not entertain notions of temporal chastisement of princes or of rebellion against them or of deposition. By the time of this play (1594–1595) there had been several plots to depose Elizabeth, the best known and potentially the most dangerous having been the rising of the northern earls in 1569–1570 and the so-called Babington Plot of 1585–1586, both on behalf of Mary Queen of Scots, who had fled to England in 1567 and was kept under house arrest in the north until her execution in 1587, after the expert counterespionage work that destroyed the Babington Plot. Elizabeth was being compared to Richard, and she knew it. "Richard II and his immediate successors were inherently dangerous subjects because of their potential for infamous analogy." David Bevington, *Tudor Drama and Politics*, Cambridge: Harvard University Press, 1968, p. 245. Hereafter Bevington in text.

4. For an account (of sorts) of Gloucester's murder and Richard's culpability, see Richard Hosley, *Shakespeare's Holinshed*, New York: Capricorn, 1968, pp. 62–65. Hereafter Hosley in text. I have used this severely truncated edition of Holinshed's *Chronicles of England, Scotland, and Ireland*, 1587, for the reader's convenience. In a few places I have had to quote from the AMS reprint (New York, 1965) of the 1807 printing, which of course gives an uncut text. For Hall's Chronicle (*The Union of the Two Noble and Illustre Famelies of Lancastre and Yorke*), I have used the AMS reprint (New York, 1965) of the edition of 1809. Edward Hall was employed by Henry VII to write a history, the culminating glory of which would be the reign of Henry VII; it is somewhat biased but very readable.

5. Sophisticated Tudor politicians must have felt some slight discomfort in ideas about divine kingship, regal infallibility, and the like. But being sophisti-

cated Tudor politicians, they were able to cope in various ways. Thus Bacon at Essex's censure proceedings in 1600 quoted a letter from Essex to the Lord Keeper written in 1598 and complaining that the Queen seemed "devoid of reason, carried away with passion." Bacon's observation: "Far be it from me to attribute divine faculties to mortal Princes, yet this I must truly say, that by the common law of England, a Prince can do no wrong," quoted by G. B. Harrison, *The Life and Death of Robert Devereux, Earl of Essex*, New York: Henry Holt, 1937, pp. 263–264.

6. The idea had already been officially proclaimed in the Homilies, particularly in the notorious homily of 1571. The "Tudor Homilies" were official collections of ready-to-read sermons published during the reigns of Edward VI and Elizabeth, and they offer a basis, grounded largely in Scripture, for institutionalized—one might say constitutional—tyranny. For an engrossing and wrongheaded study, see Alfred Hart, *Shakespeare and the Homilies*, Melbourne: Melbourne University Press, 1934. The sentiments expressed on obedience in the famous homily of 1571 are to be found also in Sackville and Norton's *Gorboduc* (*c.* 1561). See particularly V.i.42–51; the most bloody-minded lines (42–50) were omitted from the edition of 1570 but were present in the first edition, 1565. They are certainly authentic and are consistent with the general political sentiments of the play, which also contains very stern warnings about the house of Stuart up north.

7. *Shakespeare's Histories: Mirrors of Tudor Policy*, San Marino: Huntington Library, 1947 (1968), pp. 195–197. Hereafter Campbell in text.

8. Lily B. Campbell, ed., *The Mirror for Magistrates*, Cambridge: Cambridge University Press, 1938 (New York: Barnes and Noble, 1960), pp. 111–120.

9. It has long been recognized that Tudor historians' and other propagandists' lurid accounts of the struggle between York and Lancaster were grossly exaggerated in order to enhance the absurd notion of Henry VII as savior and reconciler of the two houses and to enhance Tudor views on the absolute evil of rebellion. See Paul Murray Kendall, *Richard III*, New York: Norton, 1955; also the same scholar's *Warwick the Kingmaker*, New York: Norton, 1957 (New York: Grosset and Dunlap, 1968), and *The Yorkist Age*, New York: Norton, 1962. More recently: Margaret Aston, "Richard II and The Wars of the Roses," in F. R. H. Du Boulay and Caroline M. Barron, eds., *The Reign of Richard II: Essays in Honour of May McKisak*, University of London: Athlone Press, 1971, pp. 280–318. Hereafter Aston in text. In the first tetralogy, Shakespeare sticks generally to the official view of things, possibly because it was the view most readily available, more likely because he had not yet sorted out all of his own thoughts about the history of his country. I agree with Sigurd Burckhardt that it is salutary to "unthink" the first tetralogy while studying the second. See *Shakespearean Meanings*, p. 174. His words are, "Let us suppose the loss of four extant plays—the first tetralogy." Yes, indeed.

10. Angelo, appointed the Duke's deputy (the word *deputy* occurs often enough so that we are not likely to overlook its significance), thinks of himself as the Lord's deputy. Both Richard and Angelo are deputies elected by the Lord, or by a lord; both are tested; both fail their tests. Richard is less offensive than Angelo, Angelo luckier than Richard.

11. For an excellent discussion of this subject, see Moody E. Prior, *The Drama of*

Power, Evanston: Northwestern University Press, 1973, pp. 139 ff. Hereafter Prior in text.

12. Full title, utterly typical of James: *The Trew Law of Free Monarchies: or the Reciprock and Mutuall Duetie Betwixt a Free King, and his Naturall Subjects*. Printed in *The Political Works of James I*, intro. Charles Howard McIlwain, Cambridge: Harvard University Press, 1918. In a free monarchy it is the monarch who is free. It should be said that James almost always meant well and was conscientious.

13. Winston Weathers, "The Games People Play: A Shakespearean Footnote," *Southern Humanities Review*, I (Spring 1967): 87-97. This is an excessively modest essay to which I am much indebted.

14. *Richard II* (The New Shakespeare), Cambridge: Cambridge University Press, 1939 (1968). Hereafter Wilson in text.

15. This is what happens when one says that monarchy is ordained by God and hereditary right is indefeasible. One sees the practical advantages of such claims: rebellion becomes both a political and a religious crime.

16. Richard made considerable effort trying to establish divine right as a constitutional principle. See note 2, above.

17. In the following section I am heavily indebted to Ernst H. Kantorowicz's fine study, *The King's Two Bodies*, Princeton: Princeton University Press, 1957 (hereafter Kantorowicz in text), although my emphasis is different from his. *The King's Two Bodies* has become almost indispensable to students of *Richard II*, not invariably for the best reasons. See also a more recent study, Marie Axton, *The Queen's Two Bodies: Drama and the Elizabethan Succession*, London: Royal Historical Society, 1977. In connection with the idea of the "twinned" nature of the monarch, it is worth remembering how specifically Spenser evokes such a doctrine, in terms that suggest its complete familiarity, in the letter to Sir Walter Raleigh: "*For considering she* [Elizabeth] *beareth two persons, the one of a most royall Queene or Empresse, the other of a most vertuous and beautifull Lady, this latter part in some places I doe express in Belphoebe, fashioning her name according to your owne excellent conceipt of Cynthia (Phoebe and Cynthia being both names of Diana.*)," quoted from *The Works of Edmund Spenser, A Variorum Edition*, ed. Edwin Greenlaw, Charles Grosvenor Osgood, Frederick Morgan Padelford, Baltimore: Johns Hopkins, London: Oxford, 1932 (1966), I: 168.

It seems clear enough that Shakespeare systematically undercuts the Doctrine of the King's Two Bodies in the four great histories. I am indebted to Professor John L. Murphy for demonstrating that Shakespeare's views on this complex subject underwent subtle and profound changes over the years, as Professor Murphy makes clear in his superb forthcoming *Darkness and Devils: Exorcism and King Lear*. It is perhaps worth noting that W. S. Gilbert did what I suppose ought to be called His Own Thing with this mystical legal fiction, in *The Gondoliers*. It will be recalled (Act I) that until it is ascertained which is the real King of Barataria, Don Alhambra has determined that Marco and Giuseppe "will reign jointly, so that no questions can arise hereafter as to the validity of any of your acts." "As one individual," Marco observes. "As one individual," Don Alhambra agrees. This arrangement pleases the two royal gondoliers until a complication developes, early in Act II: the court has appropriated funds for rations for one *King*, not for two *persons*, and the two persons want their tea. Giuseppe points out that "although we act as *one* person, we are, in point of fact, *two* persons." Annibale sagely observes, "Ah, I don't think we can go into that. It is a legal fiction, and legal fictions are solemn things. . . ." Giuseppe objects that "It's all very well to say we act as one person, but when you supply us with only one ration between us, I should describe it as a legal fiction carried a little too far." (*The Complete Plays of Gilbert and Sullivan*. New York: Norton, 1976, pp. 472, 481.) Shakespeare apparently chose not to pursue this particular aspect of an already complex problem.

18. I assume that Shakespeare was a moderate Catholic and see no reason whatever why he shouldn't have been. I assume that he was not a strong papist in the technical sense but sympathetic at least to those Jesuits torn to pieces by the unspeakable Topcliffe and his fellow unrefined sadists. About the Catholicism of the Shakespeares of Stratford I think there is no question; for the famous son there is, as far as I can discover, no hard documentation, nor should one expect to find it. At one or two points in this study I call attention to some apparent connection between Shakespeare and the famous Jesuit devotional writer, historian, and propagandist, Robert Persons. They do not necessarily prove anything about Shakespeare's religion, and the connections themselves may be more apparent than real. On the subject of Shakespeare's religion there is of course an enormous bibliography, from which I would mention just four important books written over a period of almost eighty years. Three books deal with Shakespeare's Catholicism, and they take into account the inseparability of politics and religion in Shakespeare's time: Henry Sebastian Bowden, *The Religion of Shakespeare*, London: Burns and Oates, 1898 (assembled partly from notes left by the historian Richard Simpson); J. H. De Groot, *The Shakespeares and the Old Faith*, New York: Morningside Press (Columbia), 1946; Peter Millward, *Shakespeare's Religious Background*, Bloomington: Indiana University Press, 1973. Millward's book is perhaps the most convincing, and his scholarship is prodigious. In *Shakespeare and Christian Doctrine*, Princeton: Princeton University Press, 1963, Roland Mushat Frye strikes some shrewd blows on the "other side," although he is concerned specifically with doctrine, not with the political connection. It is worth remembering that religion was the most important single European and English issue of the sixteenth century (very likely the seventeenth, too).

19. E. M. W. Tillyard, *Shakespeare's History Plays*, New York and London: Macmillan, 1944 (New York: Collier, 1962, p. 297).

NOTES TO CHAPTER II

1. Norman Rabkin, *Shakespeare and the Common Understanding*, New York: Free Press, and London: Collier-Macmillan, 1967, p. 90.

2. For a discussion of the dying king's statement to Prince Hal, that the projected crusade was merely a political ploy, see below, "The Troublesome Reign of King Henry IV."

3. *Cf.* David Bevington's discussion of Lodge's *The Wounds of Civil War*, in *Tudor Drama and Politics*, pp. 234 ff. For a full discussion of Rome as England on the Elizabethan and Jacobean stage, see B. N. De Luna's splendid *Jonson's Romish Plot*, Oxford: Clarendon Press, 1967, *passim*.

4. The notion that Richard III is a "scourge of God," punishing England for its collective wickedness eighty-four years earlier, or during the cleverly invented Wars of the Roses, was, and remains, flummery; and it did not require modern scholarship to perceive the absurdities, inconsistencies, and contradictions in More's providentially unfinished *Life of King Richard III*, a nasty, if brilliantly written, piece of work accepted almost without question until the end of the nineteenth century, when James Gairdner concluded that although Richard was surely a monster, all the evidence pointed the other way. (*History of the Life and Reign of Richard III*, rev. ed., Cambridge: Cambridge University Press, 1898.) For a full discussion of the whole problem, including historical questionings, see Paul Murray Kendall's *Richard III*.

5. As Bevington puts it, "Richard II and his immediate successors were inherently dangerous subjects because of their potential for infamous analogy" (p. 245).

6. In *Titus Andronicus* Shakespeare had gone out of his way to make the selection of Saturninus as emperor conform to an English principle. Thus for Shakespeare not even fair sequence and succession could always guarantee a good king, or even a tolerable one. The principle was sound but not infallible.

7. If my reading is correct, Shakespeare is pursuing a sensible line of legal argument, similar to that used by "N. D." (Robert Persons?) in *A Conference about the Next Succession to the Crown of England*, Antwerp, 1594—specifically, that laws governing the succession are not determined by nature or by heaven—that is, they are not universal—but are the business of each commonwealth. The laws of succession are made by men and are therefore subject to alteration. See discussion in Campbell, pp. 176-182. See also the unpublished University of Oklahoma master's thesis by Patricia Tobey Thomas, " A Study of the Political Problems in Richard II," 1965. This thesis includes a systematic comparison of the political ideas in the play with those in the *Conference*.

8. For brief but adequate discussions of Richard II-Queen Elizabeth, see Wilson, pp. xxx-xxxiv; and E. K. Chambers, *William Shakespeare*, Oxford: Clarendon Press, 1930 (1966), I: 353-355.

9. By Sir John Davies and Thomas Smith, both of whom perceived the obvious fact that when a small country lays claim to and conquers extensive parts of a much larger country, the investment is likely to pay only very short-term dividends. See Aston, "Richard II and the Wars of the Roses," pp. 314-315.

10. E.g., Rabkin, *Shakespeare and the Common Understanding*, pp. 99-100.

11. Briefly, Philip IV (Philip the Fair) ruled from 1285-1314; the crown then went to his eldest son (who was also his eldest child), Louis X (1314-1316); the next in line by virtue of age was Isabella (1292-1358), but she was passed over in favor of Philip V (Philip the Tall, 1316-1322); it next went to Charles IV (Charles the Fair, 1322-1328); and then on to Philip VI, elder son of Charles of Valois, who was the younger brother of Philip III, progenitor of the French kings and English queen just enumerated. Not every edition of *Henry V* makes clear the basis of Edward III's and Henry V's claims to the French throne (and Canterbury isn't very useful either).

12. Essex's commitment to the Stuart succession is perhaps a little less familiar than Cecil's since it was Cecil who engineered the transition. For a brief and

lucid account of Essex's interest, see G. B. Harrison, *The Life and Death of Robert Devereux, Earl of Essex*, pp. 315-318.

13. A suggestion often made. *Cf.* Campbell, p. 261.

14. See Robert B. Sharpe, *The Real War of the Theatres*, Boston: Heath, and London: Oxford University Press, 1935 (Modern Language Association of America Monograph Series V), *passim*.

15. In 1599 John Hayward published what might be called an innocently tendentious work called *The First Part of the Life and Reign of King Henry IV*. With an imbecility almost beyond imagining, Hayward dedicated his book to Essex and described the Earl as, among other things, *futuri temporis expectatione*. The fact that Hayward almost certainly meant no harm (not to the Queen, not to Essex, certainly not to himself) allows us to concentrate on his folly since the phrase can only suggest the idea of Essex as future king or as kingmaker.

16. "Stuarts had used Henry's Agincourt victory as a precedent for their claim to England; 'No king of England if not king of France' rang with a prophetic note at the turn of the sixteenth century. . . . If Henry's claim to France was valid, then so too is the Stuart claim to England." Axton, *The Queen's Two Bodies*, pp. 111, 112. Dr. Axton argues the parallels very strongly and takes Canterbury's praise of Harry as covert (but not very covert) praise of James, who will shape up as Prince Hal did. She sees Hal moving almost instantaneously from Gad's Hill to the mirror of all Christian kings (not quite what happens, of course) and argues that there is some ambiguity about all this because Shakespeare had ambivalent feelings about Henry V (pp. 113-115).

NOTES TO CHAPTER III

1. As we now know, the Wars of the Roses and the horrid villainy of Richard III were both largely invented. For the former, see particularly Margaret Aston, pp. 280-318; and Kendall, *Yorkist Age*. For Richard III see Kendall's study. Since we learn from the past, we had better see that the past is misrepresented in such a way as to teach the right lessons.

2. Hall's view. For an extreme application to Shakespeare, see Irving Ribner, *The English History Play in the Age of Shakespeare*, New York: Barnes and Noble, 1965, pp. 104-106.

3. *Dr. Johnson on Shakespeare*, ed. W. K. Wimsatt, Jr., New York: Hill and Wang, 1960, p. 89.

4. C. S. Lewis, *The Screwtape Letters*, New York: Macmillan, 1970, pp. 49-52.

5. Princeton: Princeton University Press, 1959 (Meridian, 1967). For a radically different approach to the whole Falstaff question, see Professor Roy Battenhouse's "Falstaff as Parodist and Perhaps Holy Fool," *PMLA*, 90 (January 1975): 32-52. Professor Battenhouse notes that his argument may seem "at first glance preposterous" (p. 33), doubts that Falstaff is ever really drunk (but sack does help him sleep through uncomfortable moments), and finds it hard to believe that a "fat sixty-year-old" can be guilty (or capable) of fornication. On this last point, one is at a loss. . . . I find his study interesting, in places fascinating, but on this subject

I believe that the author's redoubtable scholarship does not convince. His essay is certainly instructive, but I find it hard to *believe*, as I find it hard to believe the argument, offered by many scholars, that Falstaff does no real harm, although of course he fails in his main endeavor. In any case, I have in this study tried to indicate what sort of harm Falstaff does as well as what sort of harm he would like to do.

6. *Shakespeare's Typological Satire: A Study of the Falstaff-Oldcastle Problem*, Athens: Ohio University Press, 1979. Although I have not made much use of it here, I should also mention the extremely important pioneering work of the historian Richard Simpson, who published two very suggestive essays in the *Transactions of the New Shakespeare Society*, Series I, Part II, London: N. Trübner, 1874, pp. 371–508, 396–441. For Henry Sebastian Bowden's continuation of Simpson's work, see chapter I, note 18.

7. See Paul Jorgenson, *Shakespeare's Military World*, Berkeley and Los Angeles: University of California Press, 1956. Also Sharpe, *Real War of the Theatres*, p. 72n., and Campbell, pp. 245–254.

8. The historical Bolingbroke was in his younger days a sort of professional crusader—to Prussia and Lithuania. See F. R. H. Du Boulay, "Henry of Derby's Expeditions to Prussia," in Du Boulay and Caroline M. Barron, *The Reign of Richard II*, pp. 153–172. Holinshed reports that in the last year of his reign Henry IV planned a crusade to the Holy Land "there to recover the city of Jerusalem from the infidels" (Hosley, p. 115). He also records the death in "Jerusalem" (p. 117).

9. *"Stabbing him"* is Malone's somewhat redundant stage direction, justified by "with a new wound in your thigh" but also made unnecessary by those words; one version or another of *"He takes up Hotspur on his back"* (or *"Takes Hotspur on his back"*) appears in F and Qq.

10. Robert B. Pierce, *Shakespeare's History Plays: The Family and the State*, Columbus: Ohio State University Press, 1971, p. 183.

11. See Humphreys 1, pp. xiv–xviii.

12. See S. Schoenbaum, *William Shakespeare: A Documentary Biography*, New York: Oxford University Press, 1975. Schoenbaum suggests that Shakespeare probably took the name from the old play without a second thought while leaving the inference that a second thought might have been advisable—Oldcastle was not an obscure name (p. 142).

13. G. R. Owst, *Literature and Pulpit in Medieval England*, Cambridge: Cambridge University Press, 1933, pp. 83–84.

14. Thomas Wright, ed., *Political Poems and Songs Relating to English History, Composed During the Period from the Accession of Edward III to That of Richard III*, London: Longman, Green, Longman, and Roberts, 1861, 2 vols., II: 243 ff.

15. See Sharpe, *Real War of the Theatres*, passim.

16. Quoted by M. D. H. Parker in *The Slave of Life*, London: Chatto and Windus, 1955, p. 249.

17. Reprinted in C. F. Tucker Brooke, *The Shakespeare Apocrypha*, Oxford: Clarendon Press, 1908.

18. In the works already cited, Richard Simpson, Lily B. Campbell, and Alice-Lyle Scoufos call attention to the parallels between Shakespeare's version of the Percy rebellion and the rising of the northern earls in 1569.

19. See Paul Murray Kendall's fine *Warwick the Kingmaker*.

20. Sir Garnet Wolseley, *The Soldier's Handbook*, 1869, quoted by Anthony Cave Brown in *Bodyguard of Lies*, New York: Harper and Row, 1975, p. 9. Wolseley was apparently the very model for Major-General Stanley, who told a regular terrible story and very nearly lost both life and daughters, all of whom were beauties, as a result.

21. Professor Campbell thought that a contemporary audience would have found the treachery "quite orthodox" (p. 26). Paul Jorgensen offers strong evidence to the contrary: "The 'Dastardly Treachery' of Prince John of Lancaster," *PMLA*, 36 (1961), pp. 488-492.

NOTES TO CHAPTER IV

1. Kantorowicz believed that Henry V's "Twin-born with greatness" speech (*HV*, IV.i.236-290) represents "the meditations of King Henry V on the godhead and manhood of a king" (p. 24); and Marie Axton takes a similar view (p. 115). Both rely on the "Twin-born" phrase and on the rhetorical question, "What kind of god art thou, that suffer'st more/Of mortal griefs than do thy worshippers?" (247-248). But the god addressed is "ceremony," and the answer is, "either no god at all, or a purely figurative one."

2. See Kantorowicz, pp. 451-495. The term *man-centered kingship* I take from Kantorowicz, and I use it in his sense, although it occurs in his discussion of Dante, not of Shakespeare.

3. It retains its interest for modern military historians. See John Keegan, *The Face of Battle*, New York: Viking, 1976, pp. 79-116, for a detailed account. Also Desmond Seward, *The Hundred Years War*, New York: Atheneum, 1978.

4. Burckhardt, *Shakespearean Meanings*, p. 194. The literature on Prince Hal-Henry V, for and against, is extensive and covers the entire range from unqualified praise of his character to total condemnation, the most violent and systematic attack probably being that of H. C. Goddard, in a true-blue liberal polemic of remarkable virulence: *The Meaning of Shakespeare*, Chicago: University of Chicago Press, 1951, 2 vols., 1: 215-268. In recent years critics have attempted to find some middle ground that does justice to the play and the character and is reasonably safe from critical crossfire, although such ground is never wholly safe. Professor Norman Rabkin has produced what is perhaps the shrewdest effort in this connection, "Rabbits, Ducks, and *Henry V*," *Shakespeare Quarterly*, 28 (Summer 1977): 279-296. His ducks and rabbits (like Rorschach blobs, they could be either but are neither) are the two opposed views of King Harry, neither quite right. There is instead a profound ambiguity, arising out of "Shakespeare's habitual recognition of the duality of things." Rabkin plays fair by accurately summarizing the arguments of both sides, without comment; the anti side describes parts of the play very inaccurately. (Revised for *Shakespeare and the Problem of Meaning*, Chicago: University of Chicago Press, 1981.)

5. Walter, pp. xvii–xxi, argues that there has been a genuine religious conversion. Maybe.

6. Meg Greenfield, in *Newsweek*, 14 August 1978, p. 76.

7. The unusual humility assigned by the author to himself through his Chorus may be a result of addressing something, indirectly, to the Scottish king.

8. See, for example, Figgis, pp. 137–138.

9. It is just barely conceivable that Shakespeare could have been familiar with Dante's *Monarchy*, of which there were no English editions. Foxe knew it and referred to it briefly and favorably in his *Ecclesiastical History*, having been most taken, with good reason, with parts of the third book. See Charles Dédéyan, *Dante en Angleterre*, Paris: Didier, 1961, pp. 122–123.

10. Dante, *Monarchy* (*De Monarchia*), trans. Donald Nicholl, New York: Noonday Press, 1952, II.7. (Citations are by book and chapter to facilitate reference to the Latin text, to other translations, and to commentators.) Two translations with very useful commentary are Aurelia Henry (in particular), Boston: Houghton Mifflin (Riverside Press), 1904, and Herbert W. Schneider (title tendentiously translated *On World Government*), Indianapolis: Bobbs-Merrill (Library of Liberal Arts), 1949 (1957). Among the armies of commentators I have found particularly helpful are Etienne Gilson, *Dante the Philosopher*, trans. David Moore, London: Sheed and Ward, 1948, and Kantorowicz, *The King's Two Bodies*. Francis Fergusson, in *Trope and Allegory* (Athens: University of Georgia Press, 1977), pp. 71–103, has an extended discussion of the *Comedy*, *Monarchy*, and the histories. It is considerably weakened, in my judgment, by the fact that he accepts Tillyard's view that the two tetralogies constitute Shakespeare's "English epic" and should be read in reverse order: *Richard II* to *Richard III*. Richard II becomes "The Monarch as 'Figura,' " and this, I think, will not work. Fergusson's discussion is nevertheless very much worth reading, especially that part that deals with the *Purgatorio*.

11. For such a display Shakespeare waited another ten years; at the end of *Cymbeline*, England has made itself politically independent of Rome in a war fought with intensity but courtesy (like a duel) but has voluntarily resumed payment of tribute to Rome. England goes its own way in temporal affairs but acknowledges its allegiance to Rome in purely spiritual matters. I assume this explains the fact that the English defeat the Romans, capture their general, and immediately and willingly resume payment of a tribute (like Peter's pence?), nonpayment of which was the original cause of the war.

Index

20279

822.33X4   Thayer,C.G.(Calvin
             Graham)
THAYER   Shakespearean Politics
             Government & Mis-
             government in the Great
$22.95   Histories

	DATE DUE	
Yorke		
Hilke		
DEC 14 1989		
FEB 22 1990		
Yorke		
Yorke		